AN INTRODUCTION TO
BOOK HISTORY

This second edition of *An Introduction to Book History* provides a comprehensive critical introduction to the development of the book and print culture. Each ully revised and updated chapter contains new material and covers recent evelopments in the field, including:

the post-colonial book
- censorship by states and religions
- social history, and the recognition of under-representation of its value to book history studies
- contemporary publishing.

Each section begins with a summary of the chapter's aims and contents, followed by a detailed discussion of the relevant issues, concluding with a summary of the chapter and points to ponder. Sections include:

- the history of the book
- orality to literacy
- literacy to printing
- authors, authorship, and authority
- printers, booksellers, publishers, agents
- readers and reading
- the future of the book.

An Introduction to Book History is an ideal introduction to this exciting field of study and is designed as a companion text to *The Book History Reader*.

David Finkelstein is Dean of Humanities at the University of Dundee, UK.

Alistair McCleery is Professor of Literature and Culture at Edinburgh Napier University, UK.

AN INTRODUCTION TO BOOK HISTORY

Second edition

David Finkelstein and Alistair McCleery

Routledge
Taylor & Francis Group

LONDON AND NEW YORK

First published 2005
by Routledge

This second edition published 2013
by Routledge
2 Park Square, Milton Park, Abingdon, Oxon OX14 4RN

Simultaneously published in the USA and Canada
by Routledge
711 Third Avenue, New York, NY 10017

Routledge is an imprint of the Taylor & Francis Group, an informa business

British Library Cataloguing in Publication Data
A catalogue record for this book is available from the British Library

Library of Congress Cataloging in Publication Data
Finkelstein, David, 1964-
An introduction to book history / David Finkelstein and Alistair McCleery. – 2nd ed.
p. cm.
Includes bibliographical references and index.
1. Books – Social aspects – History. 2. Printing – Social aspects – History.
3. Authorship – Social aspects – History. 4. Book industries and trade – Social
aspects – History. 5. Books and reading – Social aspects – History. I. McCleery,
Alistair. II. Title.
Z4.F49 2012
002 – dc23
2012017005

ISBN: 978-0-415-68805-5 (hbk)
ISBN: 978-0-415-68806-2 (pbk)
ISBN: 978-0-203-15025-2 (ebk)

Typeset in Sabon
by Taylor & Francis Books

Printed and bound in Great Britain by the MPG Books Group

CONTENTS

PREFACE TO THE
SECOND EDITION

This book offers an introduction to the study of book history. Book history has both consolidated and developed since the first edition of the book. Humanity likes to create individual narratives for its achievements, rather than describe the slow accretion of knowledge through experimentation and dissemination. For example, the invention of paper in China has long been associated with a Han court official named Cai Lun, who reported details of a papermaking process to the emperor around 105 AD. Cai Lun's innovation, which according to a later account drew on raw material such as tree bark, hemp, rags, and fishing nets, ultimately replaced its predecessor, silk, as a cheaper, economical writing surface. However, rags, whether of cotton or linen, became the predominant raw material due to a perpetual and relatively abundant supply, particularly in towns and cities. By 150 AD paper use and manufacture had spread to Turkestan, and subsequently made its way to Korea, Vietnam, and Japan. In the coming centuries, paper use and papermaking skills dispersed via key trade routes into Central Asia; by 1150 it was being manufactured in Spain by Moorish craftsmen, and ultimately from here diffused throughout Europe and into the Western world. Such transnational diffusion of knowledge and skills is part and parcel of recent histories of books and print. Such an emphasis upon social and economic development, rather than the actions of one individual, is also part and parcel of book history itself. Accounts of the development of printing displace Gutenberg from the center to stress economic, social, and technological structures in its spread from Germany throughout Europe. This approach in focusing upon processes also avoids puerile competition over who first 'invented' printing and in which country: China, Germany, or Korea.

The emphasis upon national histories remarked upon in the Introduction has now largely come to a natural end as the multivolume sets covering the countries of North America and Western Europe complete the narratives of local growth. These national histories serve an important purpose in establishing the key dates and movements within particular countries; but they have also underpinned in many cases a narrative that is premised upon national exceptionalism and isolation. By contrast, new book histories are being now written that seek to draw together international perspectives: upon post-colonialism, in the sense of the relationship between the publishing industries of North America and Western Europe and the authors and readership of former countries of Empire; upon trading networks – for example, between the UK, South Africa, and India; and upon the globalization of publishing, in terms both of its structures and its products. These new histories challenge the self-sufficiency of the national narratives and provide, across all periods, a greater sense of book history as communication history.

To view book history in this light is also to give greater emphasis to readers and reading. As Chapter 6 notes, there has been a significant growth in studies of reading, particularly of specific 'interpretive communities,' that contribute greatly to our understanding of the circulation and reception of texts. This emphasis upon readers and reading has also gone hand-in-hand with the notion of 'book history from below' – that is, an examination of the common life of print in terms of both the sort of titles issued (e.g. almanacs rather than novels) and the types of people reading them (shopkeepers rather than novelists). Book history, as it has developed since the first edition, does not reflect either a narrow focus upon literary culture or a narrow technological determinism. It examines the wider economic, social, and cultural aspects of the book and includes all the elements singled out by Robert Darnton in his 'communications circuit', discussed in Chapter 1.

While book historians seek an appropriate balance within what book history does, they are also testing the fluid boundaries between it, on the one hand, and literary and social history, on the other. Book history's institutional base in the UK and USA is typically within English departments and its disciplinary roots, as noted in Chapter 1, are in textual criticism and bibliography and the examination of specific books – unlike, for example, in France where it grew out of history departments and its disciplinary roots emerge from economic and social history and the strong focus on social change. Individual book historians may embody integration rather than disciplinary apartheid; but however resistant they are, or just plain unconscious of it, what they do is to a large extent defined by the institutional context within which they work. This accounts, for example, for the large number of Anglophone studies of the creative, production, and reception histories of canonical literary works. Only slowly have some book historians in the UK and USA moved away from literary history to stress a wider engagement with a range of materials, from school textbooks to cartographic atlases.

The final challenge for book history that has become clearer since the first edition of this book is the need to avoid being perceived as a requiem for the passing of print. The term the 'Gutenberg gap,' used by information scientists to denote the time lag between a discovery and its publication, has been pressed into service to describe the period between Gutenberg's first publication and the contemporary move from print to online and onscreen. The relevance of book history as described in this volume to contemporary technological developments can be seen in the types of arguments used for and against each stage of print and textual innovation. The disruption and ultimate absorption into society that marked shifts from oral to written forms, and then to print-ing, seems today to be replicated in the technological shift of print to online screen-based media. The value of history is that it offers us the opportunity to re-examine at our leisure the principles and values informing and involving technological and social change. Books still have value, and their assimilation into new media environments has created a more complex relationship between reader and text that this particular book has taken the first step in exploring. This relationship entails moving beyond the case study to the expression of general models and principles. Our hope is that this second edi-tion follows the first in just such an expression and, consequently, in the assertion of the value of book history itself.

INTRODUCTION

In 1936 the British publisher Stanley Unwin received a package from an Oxford academic specializing in Anglo-Saxon literature. It contained a painstakingly typed manuscript that had originated from bedtime stories told to the author's children. Unsure what to make of the work, Unwin paid his ten-year-old son Rayner a shilling to read it and give his critical judgment. Rayner liked the book, concluding: 'This book, with the help of maps, does not need any illustrations it is good [sic] and should appeal to children between the ages of 5 and 9' (Gekoski 2004: 13). The text in question was, of course, *The Hobbit*, and Tolkien was to become a very rich academic from the sales of it and its sequel *The Lord of the Rings* trilogy, particularly during the late 1960s when the counter-culture, picking up on its mystic and fantasy elements, made it cult reading. *The Hobbit* and its successors have now transcended the years to become the favorite reading of many, coming first, for example, in a 2003 British national survey of the top 100 'best loved novels.' Each succeeding generation has interpreted and re-evaluated it, drawing out different issues from its pages – at one point raising its theme of countryside versus urban life, at another the battle between good and evil, or finally judging its evocation of good nature versus evil urban life. It has become a wildly successful film trilogy (with a 'prequel' of *The Hobbit* planned in two parts), a vehicle for expansion in visual culture, part of a global media industry. The book, with its richly evoked lands and language, reached one type of audience, but the film, stripping out much of its textual complexity to concentrate on the narrative, has succeeded in reaching another. And the film, rather than drawing audiences away from Tolkien's original vision, actually encouraged readers back to the book – sales of the trilogy and *The Hobbit* rocketed after each filmed episode was released.

The book became a place for Tolkien to explore and meditate on contemporary culture, drawing on Scandinavian mythology and religious symbolism. It was also a rich mix of visual material, with highly detailed maps and drawings harking back to a manuscript culture – thus offering a 'complete' experience on the page, richly illustrated, potentially unique to each reader. As a result of its success, Tolkieniana has become an industry in its own right.

Tolkien's letters, papers, and 'association' material command vast sums at auction. Nothing is excluded – even Tolkien's Oxford college gown, used when he gave lectures or ate in the formal dining hall of his college, has been sold for a seriously high sum.[1] Books about *The Lord of the Rings* sell; dolls, toys, and figurines of characters are collected. Tolkien has become a heritage industry, with pilgrims traveling to Oxford to retrace his steps, drink in his local pub, and stretch to see the view from his house. All this had made what were original words, typed on now-faded paper, a major and tangible asset, ensuring profits for the publishers and Tolkien's estate each time an edition sells out. Each time the film and other rights are sold, another check comes their way.

Tolkien's language in the original text drew on speech patterns of oral literature and culture; it was his awareness of the oral epics of the past – of *Beowulf*, for example – that informed his structuring of the text. Websites dedicated to Tolkien, his work, the films, and the books extend the reach of Tolkien beyond paper and print into hypertext/cyberspace. Readers have now become authors in the sense that the World Wide Web allows readers to create and share their own readings, versions, sequels, and interpretations of *The Lord of the Rings* and *The Hobbit*.

The Hobbit and *The Lord of the Rings* trilogy are not isolated cases – there are many other examples of books whose publication has changed or influenced culture, communities, and communication. Books are important vehicles for ideas that often challenge established norms and authorities. The issues raised by studying examples such as *The Lord of the Rings* are endless – likewise, careers and lives have been spent studying the Bible, tracking the impact of works such as Adolf Hitler's *Mein Kampf*, Harriet Beecher Stowe's *Uncle Tom's Cabin*, and Karl Marx and Friedrich Engels's *The Communist Manifesto*. There are differences, as well, between types of printed material, and book history is a place where different print media coexist as equally worthy of study.

The questions book historians ask include:

- What is a text? A text is a written document which is read. But a text has to have some physical form. That form can be a wide range of media – from print in books, magazines, newspapers, to online web pages. The functions of all such texts can include communicating information, narrating, and entertaining.
- What is a book? A cynic might agree with a former dean of architecture at the Massachusetts Institute of Technology, who declared books to be 'tree flakes encased in dead cow' (Mitchell 1995). More prosaically, they are physical objects, the development of whose form is traced in more detail in Chapters 2 and 3. What you are reading now is a book – unless you are reading it in an online version of our text, in which case it is not a book as traditionally defined. You may be reading part of it in the form of an illegal

photocopy, in which case, although it is a facsimile of the printed original, it is not a book unless the sheets are bound together – it remains a text, but in the material form of sheets of paper.

- What is a medium? Medium, as used here, is a generic term for the material form of a text. A book is a medium; a website is a medium; a screenplay can also be a medium. The word 'medium' contains the strong sense of 'mediation,' a key term we will be exploring later in this book. In the plural, 'media', the term is used to refer generically to organizations, including book publishers, that produce different material forms of texts. In the field of media studies, the term has been used almost exclusively to denote broadcasting and the press; we suggest it should not be confined solely to these areas – rather, it also refers to books and book publishing.

There are other questions, both of definition and of substance, that book historians ask, and we will be exploring some of these in the pages that follow.

One of the first people to raise these questions in the context of book history was Robert Darnton. In 1982 Darnton surveyed the field of book history and declared that it was so scattered in approach it resembled 'interdisciplinarity run riot' (Darnton 1982b: 10). At the same time, he predicted it was an area that 'seems likely to win a place alongside fields like the history of science and the history of art in the canon of scholarly discipline' (Darnton 1982b: 9). A demonstrable surge in activity since then suggests he may be correct: national and academic-based centers dedicated to researching the history of print culture and book history have sprung up in North America, Canada, the UK, Australia, New Zealand, and elsewhere; publishers have profited from issuing academic monographs, handbooks, readers, and journals dedicated to the subject; a thriving professional organization (SHARP, or the Society for the History of Authorship, Reading, and Publishing) works hard to promote the area, and scholars engage in substantial dialog through dedicated international conferences, seminars, and colloquia. Equally, courses are springing up on an annual basis to tap into this exciting new field of study.

Why study books? Book historians would respond by saying that the transmission of texts is not as straightforward a process as people might think. Much can be learned through tracing their progress from creator to consumer, in accounting for production and marketing structures, in studying the effect of print on culture. The cultural and personal effects of books are also not easily accountable: books and print, for example, affect 'readers' and consumers differently at different points in life. How to begin discussing this? Material form affects how we read texts, as Don McKenzie once pointed out. Equally, different material forms can prompt readers to read a text in different ways, as Jerome McGann argues in calling for a study of the 'socialization of texts.' Both these issues will be covered in later chapters.

This book is about a subject and field of enquiry where the value of *The Lord of the Rings* and its nature can be studied from all sorts of angles: from looking at its original state as a manuscript to the finished product; from finding out the nature of those who read it and how they read it; from seeing it from the perspective of media commodity, translated into different forms to reach different audiences and international markets; to comparing it to the communication models suggested by Darnton, and Adams and Barker, as well as others, as discussed in Chapter 1. Our aim is to outline what is book history, how book historians go about the business of studying books, print, and texts, and what you can learn by using book history methods. Book historians try to understand what place books and reading had in the lives of people and society in the past, in the present, and even in the future. Grand projects such as the *Encyclopædia Britannica*, the *Encyclopédie*, and *The Oxford English Dictionary* have all had tremendous social and cultural effects, acting as guardians of accuracy, setters of standards, summarizers of important intellectual material. Equally, there are manuscripts and iconic documents that have become emblematic symbols for entire generations, cultures, and communities – witness the Magna Carta, the Declaration of Independence, or New Zealand's Treaty of Waitangi.

An Introduction to Book History sets out to look at these issues. It takes as its starting point the original extracts and texts published in *The Book History Reader*, and expands the range of commentary and themes originally brought out in the *Reader*. Our aim is to provide a book that explains the contexts in which print culture and book history are studied today. We look at how book history has been thought of in the past. We speculate as to how it might develop in the future. Our goal has also been to provide a critical compass to book history and print culture studies, to act as both a starting point and a guide to current issues preoccupying those who teach and research in this area. While this book refers often to the primary texts found in *The Book History Reader*, our general intention is to extend the range of conversation and coverage of topics so that *An Introduction to Book History* can be read profitably on its own as well.

One of the key themes at the heart of the *Introduction* is our view that what differentiates book history and print culture studies as it is practiced now is its invigorating move to understand textual production as part of human social communication structures. Doing this demands an interdisciplinary approach. *An Introduction to Book History* is structured so as to highlight the social communication issues that students might find as they make their way through the history of books in modern times. It is both a narrative of the history of texts in Western European culture and a synthesis of the latest thinking about understanding and contextualizing that history.

Chapter 1 covers the main theories and critical debates that have informed book history studies over the past 100 years. It discusses some of the initiatives pioneered in bibliographic and book studies by the New Bibliography movement, represented in the work of W. W. Greg and Fredson Bowers, and looks at subsequent reactions to the agenda set by such critics. We ask how influential the work of New Zealand academic Don McKenzie was in reorienting bibliographic studies of the book during the 1960s and 1970s, and cover how his conception of the 'sociology of text' tied into the French-influenced social and cultural history of the book movement developed from the 1950s onwards (the *Histoire du Livre*). This section also outlines the place of Robert Darnton's formulation of the 'communication circuit' as a means of studying the circulation of texts in society, Thomas R. Adams and Nicolas Barker's counter-argument for a more bio-bibliographical oriented approach, and other theoretical models emphasizing the study of the paratexts of books and calling for the study of the 'socialization of texts.' Others are included in this chapter whose work on oral, written, and print communication structures have channeled book history interests into new directions: critics such as Walter Ong, Marshall McLuhan, Elizabeth Eisenstein, Benedict Anderson, and Adrian Johns, among others.

Chapter 2 looks at the history of writing, and how this area integrates with book history studies. It provides a summary of how writing developed and spread into Western European culture. It also looks at how oral traditions were incorporated within early writing and manuscript culture, and how writing changed in structure and style as print technology prevailed. We also cover how writing changed in nature due to the development of a literate reading public, moving from being used as a cultural tool meant to be read by one to many, to a process that often directed its results to individual solitary readers. Finally, the chapter examines briefly how critics have described writing in the service of state and institutional power, used for political and cultural colonization of other parts of the world, and in the context of class structures.

Chapter 3 traces continuities between this manuscript culture and the coming of print. It draws attention not only to the production processes involved, but also to the industry structures that developed as the manuscript book, a collectable commodity, gave way to the printed book, a tradable commodity. The chapter outlines, and introduces debates over, the relationship between the printed book and the defining moments of the Reformation, the Renaissance, the Enlightenment, and the Industrial Revolution. The discussion of the development of copyright here looks forward to the issues of authorship and ownership covered in the following chapter, while an outline of changes in book publishing during the twentieth century anticipates the final chapter's analysis of the future of the book.

Chapter 4 focuses on concepts of authorship and how these have changed and developed over the past 1000 years. It examines medieval definitions of authorship and discusses how the introduction of printing from the 1450s onwards redefined authorship as a more creative activity that could lead to individual fame and some fortune. Other topics covered include the place of patronage, the effect of the introduction of copyright on authorship as a profession, and the role of literary agents and publishers' readers in the publishing process. We briefly survey twentieth-century critical interpretations of authorship that have been central to book history studies, and conclude with comments on what redefinitions of authorship are predicted with the onset of the digital era.

Chapter 5 looks at how book historians characterize and discuss the role of the many agents involved in the process of book and print culture production. It provides a survey history of the changing business models of Western European print production that developed following the Industrial Revolution of the nineteenth century, carrying on from material outlined in Chapters 3 and 4. It examines how print culture was exported to European colonial possessions, initially concentrated on the production of local and regional newspapers, and describes briefly the role of print culture in forging national and regional identities. It also highlights the role that cultural agents have played in supporting and shaping print culture production, from literary agents and publishers' readers to intangibly linked but influential literary networks.

Chapter 6 introduces the less well-developed topic, in terms of book history, of the reader and reading. It proposes that the twin perspectives of reading as a social phenomenon and as an individual experience can be brought together in book history, and that pioneering work has already been carried out in this regard by such authors as Jonathan Rose, Elizabeth McHenry, Janice Radway, and Shafquat Towheed. The chapter provides a survey of reading history from the earliest scribal codes to the growth of public library systems in the nineteenth and twentieth centuries. It concludes with a consideration of the nature of reading, drawing on the insights of Wolfgang Iser into the individual act and of Stanley Fish into its social nature.

Chapter 7 tackles the rumors of the death of the book by examining four factors that may play the greatest part in shaping the future of the book: the relationship between new technologies and the printed word; the nature of media globalization in terms of both the structures of book publishing and the influence of books across cultures; the contemporary profile of reading and readers; and, finally, the role of the state in providing support to books, their publishers, and readers.

We conclude the book with a summary of the key themes and issues discussed, and include a glossary of terms you will encounter as you make your way through the work, as well as a bibliography of sources used in writing this text. The bibliography is deliberately intended not to be exhaustive and comprehensive: given that such a list is already provided in the companion *The Book History Reader*, we felt it would be best not to duplicate work unnecessarily. Other writers have often used metaphors drawn from exploration in their discussion of books and reading. You are entering territory that is new and only partly charted. You will have your own opportunities to explore it. We hope this text will act as a guide.

1

THEORIZING THE HISTORY
OF THE BOOK

Introduction

This chapter covers the main theories and general themes that have developed
in book history studies over the past century. It will briefly outline the influence of New Bibliographers such as W. W. Greg and Fredson Bowers in setting the agenda for bibliography and book studies in the first half of the
twentieth century, and discuss the works of those who came afterwards. We
will look at the work of Don McKenzie in the 1960s and 1970s, and his conception of the 'sociology of text' as a means of broadening traditional bibliographical interests to encompass cultural and sociological contexts. The
chapter will also briefly cover how McKenzie's work linked to the *Histoire du
Livre* movement that developed from the 1950s onwards amongst French historians with an interest in studying the social and cultural effects of books on
society. This section also outlines the place of Robert Darnton's formulation
of the 'communication circuit' as a means of studying the circulation of texts
in society, Thomas R. Adams and Nicolas Barker's counter-argument for a
more bio-bibliographical oriented approach, and other theoretical models
emphasizing the study of the paratexts of books and calling for the study of
the 'socialization of texts.' After a brief summary of the terminology now
commonly used to describe book history at work, the chapter looks at how
book historians have characterized different stages in the history of books in
Western European culture, focusing on the work of Walter Ong, Marshall
McLuhan, Elizabeth Eisenstein, Benedict Anderson, and Adrian Johns, among
others. From there the chapter examines how book historians have interpreted
the function of authors and readers in these contexts, and through that how
books are being studied for their 'mediating' effect in society.

Book history origins

Book history (or the study of the history of the book and texts) has a strong
historical pedigree linked to disciplines such as bibliography, literary studies,
and economic and social history. The urge to study all aspects of the creation

of books, whether as physical artifacts, examples of fine art, products of unique production methods, or unique cultural symbols, stretches back almost to the point at which texts became part of the culture and commerce of civilization. The large and lavish manuscript and book collections amassed by church, state, and wealthy patrons over the centuries, many dating from the Renaissance period, testify to the hold that books have had on individuals both as objects of aesthetic beauty and as carriers of human knowledge. This, in turn, has often fostered an interest in classifying, codifying, and studying print culture objects for what they have to say about the people who made them and for the meaning and intentions of their creators.

This certainly was the case at the beginning of the twentieth century, when academics interested in early printed texts started asking detailed questions about their production. The printing of early editions of Shakespeare's work, for example, was problematic. How, literary scholars asked, could one distinguish 'authentic' from 'corrupted' versions of his plays? By what means could scholars arrive at the true text as originally conceived by Shakespeare in the sixteenth and seventeenth centuries, given the lack of original manuscript sources and unreliable printed versions? The answer lay in methodologies proposed by the 'New Bibliography' school, led by scholars such as R. McKerrow (1927), W. W. Greg (1950) and Fredson Bowers (1950b). Establishing authoritative texts became a matter of examining the materiality of original textual production, of studying texts and books as physical objects (determining differences in type, paper, ink, printing methods and so on) to distinguish between 'good' and 'bad' versions of works.[1] The result would be a more rigorous interrogation of the origins of literary and textual production: bibliography, in the words of W. W. Greg, would become 'the science of the material transmission of literary documents' (Greg 1914: 39). By the 1950s, bibliography, as reconfigured by Greg, Bowers, McKerrow, and others, became a ubiquitous presence in many Anglo-American English departments, part of the required syllabus for budding PhDs, who were taught, as Robert Darnton notes, to interpret the material conditions of print with extreme rigor, including 'how to recognize formats, collate signatures, detect cancels (leaves with errors or potentially offensive passages), distinguish typefaces, trace watermarks, analyze art work, and identify bindings' (Darnton 2003: 43).

Reconstructing texts (and printing practices that led to their printed creation) was the defining aspect of 'descriptive' or 'analytical' bibliography as practiced by such bibliographers and textual critics under the mantle of New Bibliography. Seeking original textual and authorial meaning, scholars examined the recension of manuscripts in order to produce the most complete and least corrupted version of a text possible. The intervention of agents other than the author in the transmission of the text was seen as part of that corrupting process. Bowers, for example, warned fellow bibliographers that 'the uncritical use of the last edition within an author's lifetime is now, or should be, thoroughly discredited, although it is still occasionally found': textual authority lay in the 'printed text closest to the author's manuscript, that is, to the first authoritative edition' (Bowers 1950a: 59). The operation of agents in the printing process, including editors and proofreaders, was meant to be retraced in order to distinguish their interference and establish the text that most accurately reflected the author's final intention. How the author's final intention was itself to be deciphered was the subject at times of a much less rigorous analysis, and the doubt remains whether the author's intention existed only as an editorial concept disguising the editor's own predilections and decisions (Tanselle 1979).

The results of New Bibliography inquiry could often inspire, but equally disappoint, particularly in the wake of theoretical trends such as deconstruction, new historicism, and post-colonialism: 'In their imaginations, PhDs became companions of the workers who first turned Shakespeare's words into books,' one commentator notes. 'It was an intoxicating idea, and it did not last' (Darnton 2003: 43). Others were blunter in their view of where bibliography fitted in the academy: a significant figure warned graduates in the 1980s that publishing history was unlikely to move forward without significant funding or academic support in relevant academic departments (Sutherland 1988). Best stick to general history, was the general suggestion, or study texts through strongly theorized filters.

McKenzie and the sociology of texts

Matters began to shift, slowly at first, then with gathering speed from the late 1960s onwards, in part due to the pioneering work of a Cambridge-educated, New Zealand-based academic. The 'New Bibliography' approach to textual production had assumed (rather idealistically) that texts were produced by compositors and printers through rational, consistent patterns and means: that, in essence, printing and print production were 'fixed' constants that had little effect on output, except inasmuch as printers were liable to make accidental mistakes (dropping or misplacing type, mixing up pages during the printing or binding process, omitting particular portions of text, etc.) that 'corrupted' original authorial intentions. Don McKenzie's work in the 1960s and 1970s called this into question, in particular his controversial, highly original essay 'Printers of the mind', first published in *Studies in Bibliography* in 1969. Peter D. McDonald and Michael F. Suarez (2002) provide important interpretations and summaries of McKenzie's thinking in *Making Meaning: 'Printers of the Mind' and Other Essays*, their edited volume of his work on issues pertaining to bibliography and the history of the book. As they note, 'Printers of the mind' challenged the orthodox views of analytical bibliographers who had dominated textual bibliography throughout the 1940s, 1950s, and 1960s by demonstrating that the physical production of a text was very much dependent upon the conditions in which it was produced. Using primary source material culled from correspondence, printing catalogs, and business ledgers of the London printer William Bowyer and his son, McKenzie proved that printing house operations in seventeenth- and eighteenth-century England were not tidy and ordered, but were dominated by what he called 'concurrent production': work habits varied considerably, texts were often run off concurrently, and the typesetting and physical printing of texts was not the result of efforts of a single printer or editor, but could be, and often was, the result of the interlinked activities of several compositors and pressmen working simultaneously in complex and unpredictable patterns on a whole variety of texts. The matter was something that could be applied beyond the purely literary text, as McDonald and Suarez noted: 'The fundamental principles of concurrent production ... applied to virtually all book manufacture' (McDonald and Suarez 2002: 13).

McKenzie would go on in later work to argue that the study of texts necessarily involved inclusion of issues external to textual meaning: 'Meanings are not therefore inherent,' he argued, 'but are constructed by successive interpretative acts by those who write, design, and print books, and by those who buy and read them.' McKenzie also argued that the effects of print culture in other cultures could vary according to their social and communicative contexts: 'It has also come to be recognized that a distinctively Eurocentric notion of the book and its circulation cannot account for the role of such texts in other societies with different communicative traditions and widely varying standards of literacy' (McKenzie 2002: 268). McKenzie applied such sensitivity to his own work, most notably in his groundbreaking study of the formulation of the Treaty of Waitangi in 1840 between British colonial representatives and Maori chieftains, the printed document that established British sovereignty over Maori land, and whose subsequent, controversial implementation colored New Zealand development and offered a physical example of interpretative clashes based on differences between print- and oral-based cultures (McKenzie 1984).

McKenzie's most significant legacy was his emphasis on broadening the Anglo-American study of textual meaning beyond the artificial boundaries posited by competing academic fields. Literary criticism of texts too often ignored meaning beyond the borders of 'the text'; bibliographers too often ignored the sociological context within which the production of texts operated; historians too often ignored the manner in which the products of printing houses entered into the wider public arena and were received and consumed by reading audiences. McKenzie's classic 1981 essay, 'Typography and meaning: The case of William Congreve,' would draw Anglo-American attention to the revolution in textual interpretation being pioneered by the French *annales* school, whose practitioners since the late 1950s had been applying quantitative social history methods to the study of textual production and reception. At the same time, however, McKenzie proposed that scholars move beyond the interpretation of texts solely as the product of an author's intentions, or even solely through quantitative, macro-historical examinations of book publishing and printing trends, towards a study of texts as mediated products within which one could find traces of economic, social, aesthetic, and literary meaning. 'Current theories of textual criticism, indifferent as they are to the history of the book, its architecture, and the visual language of typography, are quite inadequate to cope with such problems,' he concluded. 'Only a new and comprehensive sociology of the text can embrace them' (McKenzie 1981: 236).

Histoire du Livre

The 'sociology of the text' was McKenzie's acknowledgment that texts were a result of a collaborative process, calling for methods of analysis that incorporated attention to the material object and its production and reception, rather than solely to its contents. It would form part of a directed move, led by Robert Darnton and Roger Chartier, among others, towards the 'new-style *Histoire du Livre* of the 1980s and 1990s emphasizing readers, materiality, and meaning' (McDonald and Suarez 2002: 7). As Roger Chartier would later comment, the value of McKenzie's concept of 'the sociology of the text' was in the lessons to be learned and applied as a result:

> Against the abstraction of the text, it shows that the status and interpretation of a work depend on material considerations; against the 'death of the author', it stresses the author's role, at the side of the bookseller-printer, in defining the form given to the work; against the absence of the reader, it recalls that the meaning of a text is always produced in a historical setting and depends on the differing and plural readings that assign meaning to it.
>
> (Chartier 1997b: 85)

The origins of the *annales* school of methodology highlighted by McKenzie could be found in the quantitative social histories of Robert Escarpit's *Sociologie de la Littérature* (published in 1958), and also in the same year in Febvre and Martin's *L'Apparition du Livre* (*The Coming of the Book* in its English translation). Escarpit's work was notable for his attempt to isolate models of book production, dissemination, and reception from the accumulation of data in a manner taken up by Robert Darnton (1982b) in his signal article 'What is the history of books?' and in Thomas Adams and Nicolas Barker's (1993) response to Darnton: 'A new model for the study of the book'. The *annales* approach differed, moreover, from attempts such as Elizabeth Eisenstein's to relate the development of the printed book to broader social and political movements in what has more recently been criticized as an over-determinist and simplistic approach, itself indicated in the title of her major work *The Printing Press as an Agent of Change* (and discussed later in this section) (Johns 1998). Febvre and Martin are perhaps more accurate in their chapter headed 'The book as a force for change.' For them, the printing press was only one of a number of actors in a social and political drama; Lucien Febvre offered as the alternative title for their study, *The Book in the Service of History*. Where the book was primarily active in the promotion of change was in the language of texts; as they argued in a point subsequently expanded upon by Elizabeth Eisenstein: 'The unified Latin culture of Europe was finally dissolved by the rise of the vernacular languages which was consolidated by the printing press' (Febvre and Martin 1976: 332).

The communication circuit

Robert Darnton's groundbreaking essay 'What is the history of books?' drew attention to the plethora of research methods and avenues facing those engaged in the study of the history of the book in the early 1980s. The intrepid researcher faced a disorienting crisscrossing of disciplines, 'less like a field than a tropical rain forest ... analytical bibliography pointing in this direction, the sociology of knowledge in that, while history, English, and comparative literature stake out overlapping territories ... and bewildered by competing methodologies, which would have him collating editions, compiling statistics, decoding copyright law, wading through reams of manuscript, heaving at the bar of a reconstructed common press, and psychoanalyzing the mental processes of readers' (Darnton 1982a: 10). Darnton's solution was to propose a general model for analyzing the manner in which books made their way into society, a 'communication circuit' running 'from the author to the publisher (if the bookseller does not assume that role), the printer, the shipper, the bookseller, and the reader' (Darnton 1982a: 11). The circuit would work within and between these key players – thus allowing room, for example, for demonstrating the manner in which readers could influence textual production (a point those working with nineteenth-century serialized novels had often drawn attention to), or the influence of booksellers on publishing decisions (as Darnton demonstrated with a case study drawn from eighteenth-century French print culture tracking the contraction and expansion of the French book trade through bookselling orders). Darnton's circuit derived from similar models in communication studies; but his intention was to offer book historians a way of conceiving the production of texts as a multifaceted enterprise encompassing social, economic, political, and intellectual conditions. 'Books belong to circuits of communication that operate in consistent patterns, however complex they may be,' he concluded. 'By unearthing those circuits, historians can show that books do not merely recount history; they make it' (Darnton 1982a: 22).

Darnton's model was by no means perfect, as he himself acknowledged. For a start, it was rooted in an understanding of textual production particular to eighteenth-century European printing and publishing conditions (that included such fascinating and unusual matters as 'colportage' and book-smuggling over national borders in times of revolutionary ferment, underground print networks, and the production of illicit or banned texts). Parts of the model were unsuitable for the study of pre-print manuscript culture, or for explicating the inflection of oral culture within written traditions. But, if anything, it signaled an attempt to establish common ground within disparate and competing book history agendas, and was absorbed, developed, and utilized with increasing frequency over the coming years.

Since Darnton's formulation of the 'communication circuit' as a means of examining the role of texts in society, book history has begun increasingly to focus on what McGann (1991) has described as the 'socialization of texts' – that is, the impact of books as artifacts traveling from private to public spaces. In this formulation, production becomes very much part of a process of, as Paul Duguid notes, 'producing a public artifact and inserting it in a particular social circuit' (Duguid 1996: 81). Or, as a key survey suggested, what has now become increasingly important are conceptions of 'the activity of producing and consuming books that decenter the principal elements and make them interactive and inter-dependent: publishing history, in other words, as hypertext' (Jordan and Patten 1995: 11).

The bio-bibliographical communication circuit

But not all have been satisfied with Darnton's (and his successors') definition of key arenas within this 'communication circuit.' In 1993, two eminent British bibliographers (Thomas R. Adams and Nicolas Barker) set out a model that argued with and proposed an expansion of Darnton's model. For them, the point was to draw attention to the bio-bibliographical dimension that many steeped in bibliographic traditions felt was missing from a post-print (that is, after 1500) perspective on print culture and book history. The answer to the questions 'What did people imagine a book was? What was it for?' involved acknowledging a deeper connection between people and texts in antiquity than might be expected. 'The modern tendency is to assume that a book was what it is now, a tool,' they noted, continuing:

> It is difficult to recognize how recent a concept this is, the creation of mechanical multiplication, five centuries old but still new. In one sense, a real and practical sense, it was not new in the fifteenth century. Multiple copying of texts, by a variety of means, had existed for at least two millennia: what was new was an abrupt change of scale, of volume. Books possess an earlier, greater power, as the vehicle of knowledge or inspiration that outlives the time in which they were first conceived or written.
>
> (Adams and Barker 1993: 8)

While acknowledging that Darnton's 'communication circuit' had its uses from the perspective of social history analysis, Adams and Barker critiqued its approach as too centered on explicating communication processes, thus moving away from the significance of books as artifacts. Their model was one based on processes, whereby the circuit was made up of five events in the life of a text (publishing, manufacturing, distribution, reception, and survival), surrounded and affected by four 'zones' of influence (intellectual influences; political, legal, and religious influences; commercial pressures; social behavior and taste). The result was a reversal of emphasis: 'The text is the reason for the cycle of the book: its transmission depends on its ability to set off new cycles.' This is a circuit that does not follow how people interact with texts, but rather one that follows texts 'whose sequence constitutes a system of communication' (Adams and Barker 1993: 15).

Theoretical incursions

Similar issues have been raised by Gerard Genette in his influential work *Seuils*, published in France in 1987 but first translated in English in 1997 as *Paratexts: Thresholds of Interpretation*. Genette's work has dovetailed with Adams and Barker's through his focus on the study of the 'paratext' of a printed work (the liminal devices that control how a reader perceives the text, such as front and back covers, jacket blurbs, indexes, footnotes, tables of contents, etc.). What traditional bibliographers had often sought amongst these areas, though (clues as to printing techniques or variations in textual production), was not of great interest to Genette. Instead, he has focused on how these paratexts become zones of transaction, 'a privileged place of pragmatics and a strategy of an influence on the public, an influence that – whether well or poorly understood and achieved – is at the service of a better reception of the text and a more pertinent reading' (Genette 1997: 2). In other words, an insight into the production devices that are utilized to ensure 'for the text a destiny consistent with the author's purpose' (Genette 1997: 407). Scholars have followed through on this by writing on such liminal issues as footnotes and marginalia (Norton and Norton 1996; Grafton 1997; Jackson 2001). This, in a sense, is an attempt to theorize particular hermeneutical values and processes as a means of contesting cultural representations and receptions of finished texts.

Some have suggested that Genette's approach is limited in value to book historians because it does not reach far enough into the 'sociology' of the text. As Juliet Gardiner has noted, a fundamental flaw in Genette's theorizing on paratexts is his 'frequent failure to account for the distinction between the author and the publishers, his tendency to see the publisher as the enabler, indeed the continuation, of the author's intention, and paratexts as the vehicle, signals an untenable, essentialist fixity of meaning for the text' (Gardiner 2000: 258). Jerome McGann (1991) argues similarly against Genette in *The Textual Condition*, at the same time noting that the value of Genette's approach, a response to past literary theorists whose interests in the linguistic nature of texts (the words contained within the borders of books) had pushed such extra-textual apparatuses to the margins (as it were), was in his insistence that such 'paratexts' were of fundamental value to the study of textual meaning. Contrasting text with paratext was a useful exercise in itself, a means of recovering authorial meaning and intention as their words passed through the publishing process filter.

But McGann's concerns are with Genette's specialist, focused approach, for, as even Genette admitted, his paratextual interests stop when it comes to the more material aspects of textual production – ink, typeface, paper, the physical production process itself – as these do not treat the linguistic and go beyond Genette's literary influenced purview. 'But of course all texts, like all other things human,' McGann argued, 'are embodied phenomena, and the body of the text is not exclusively linguistic' (McGann 1991: 13). In the influential argument that followed, McGann sketched out his opposition to the type of analysis he felt had pervaded textual study up to the 1980s – a linguistic approach that wrapped up literary texts in a close-spun web of hermeneutics and textual interpretation. 'Textual studies remains largely under the spell of romantic hermeneutics,' he declared. 'In such a view texts, and in particular imaginative texts, are not imagined as certain kinds of social acts, and to the degree that they are so imagined, the action of the text has been too subjectively (and too abstractly) conceived in its linguistic conditions.' His solution was to propose grounding the study of texts within contexts that were both social and materialist based: 'One breaks the spell of romantic hermeneutics by socializing the study of texts at the most radical levels' (McGann 1991: 12). McGann's 'socialization of the text' would prove an influential rallying call in the development of book history research, joining Don McKenzie's 'sociology of the text' as a means of underlining how book historians differentiated their areas of investigation from those that worked from a strictly literary or historical base.

Print culture and book history

To be certain, the terminology used to define what one now does in 'book history' is contentious. As we have seen, it has been called variously 'print culture,' 'the sociology of the text,' 'publishing history,' 'textual bibliography,' and so on. In part, the reason has as much to do with the strengths as well as the failings of the label 'book history' – for those whose interests are mainly in the study of manuscripts, or medieval and ancient texts, or who refract texts through culturally inflected analysis of readers and reader responses, the term 'book history' can seem too exclusionary for their purposes.

'Print culture' is one alternative that has been proposed, following the critical influence of work by Lucien Febvre, Henri-Jean Martin, Elizabeth

Eisenstein, and others. Harold Love summarizes 'print culture' as a term used to refer to:

1 a 'noetic world' or consciousness constructed through print;
2 the industrial relationship of book production and distribution;
3 a body of practices arising from the social relationship of reading and information management; and
4 a specialized field of study within the wider discipline of Communication.

(Love 2003: 46)

Love's summary encompasses the type of insights sought by those who drew on Darnton's formulation of the 'communication circuit' for inspiration. But 'print culture,' despite this precise definition, has not satisfied either those whose work on orality and handwritten texts fits outside such a category, or those who have been attracted to Adams and Barker's shift of the 'communication circuit' to inflect and reflect more the physical production and movement of texts within intellectual and social spheres.

In 1998, the editors of a new journal in the area utilized the first issue to establish ambitious parameters for the history of the book that would be broad enough to accommodate all such concerns. *Book History*, they declared, would be about 'the entire history of written communication: the creation, dissemination, and uses of script and print in any medium, including books, newspapers, periodicals, manuscripts, and ephemera. ... The social, cultural, and economic history of authorship, publishing, printing, the book arts, copyright, censorship, bookselling and distribution, libraries, literacy, literary criticism, reading habits, and reader responses' (Greenspan and Rose 1998: ix). Or, as another scholar stated more succinctly, the history of the book 'is centrally about ourselves. It asks how past readers have made meaning (and therefore, by extension, how others have read differently from us); but it also asks where the conditions of possibility for our own reading came from' (Price 2002: 39). Such a broad definition is likely to be the one that finds most favor with those who study book history, given that it covers all aspects of print activity. Let us turn to how it might be seen within the context of the history of communication.

Modeling the rise of the book in Western culture

A simplistic model of the development of the history of the book in Western culture (or, in more generalized terms, the history of human communication), suggested by Walter Ong (1982), Jack Goody (1987), and Marshall McLuhan (1964), proposes that its development can be broken down into three key 'revolutionary phases':

1 the movement from oral to written cultures (subdivided into the development of the alphabet, the acquisition of language, the creation of economic
trading structures, the acquisition of writing tools – ink, paper, codices – and
the fixing of systems of writing);
2 the movement from literacy to printing (the development of manuscript
culture, the development of printing, its gradual insertion into cultural and
social institutions, its provision of materials for mass consumption within
an increasingly industrialized society); and
3 the movement from print to computer-generated content (a transformative
phase we are currently experiencing).

Walter Ong and Marshall McLuhan are frequently cited for their insights into
the social and cultural shifts from oral to written to print cultures. McLuhan's
gnomic utterances about the nature of print in his 1960s bestsellers *The
Gutenberg Galaxy: The Making of Typographic Man* and *Understanding
Media* would prove attention grabbing but later fall from favor (until the
networked electronic world he had predicted appeared to become a reality
from the 1980s onwards). In these works, McLuhan stressed the disruptive
effect of writing and print on oral cultural formations, pointing to the 'breaking
apart of the magical world of the ear and the neutral world of the eye, and to
the emergence of the detribalized individual from this split' (McLuhan
1964: 32). The private nature of reading texts and printed books, he argued,
irrevocably shifted patterns of human interaction. For McLuhan, such splits
were not the result of the evolution of written culture but rather of the
typographical revolution instituted by Gutenberg. As he would pronounce
sententiously: 'It was not until the experience of mass production of exactly
uniform and repeatable type, that the fission of the senses occurred, and the
visual dimensions broke away from the other sense' (McLuhan 1964: 70).
Elizabeth Eisenstein would reformulate and reinterpret this in more restrained
language in her conception of 'typographical fixity' (discussed later in this
section).

Walter Ong revisited the matter in his classic work *Orality and Literacy*,
arguing that the introduction of writing and print imprinted a new kind of
'consciousness' in social communication – writing 'reconstituted the originally
oral, spoken word in visual space,' while print 'embedded the word in space
more definitively' (Ong 1982: 121). The result was an imposition of linearity
on cognitive experiences, a sense of spatial organization that allowed easy
retrieval of material and the encouragement of a sense of closure, 'a sense that
what is found in a text has been finalized, has reached a state of comple-
tion. ... Print encloses thought in thousands of copies of a work of exactly the
same visual and physical consistency' (Ong 1982: 129–130). Later commentators would draw on both McLuhan's and Ong's work in discussing the 'mediating' effect of print and textual culture in social formations, reading
practices, and communication patterns. As one critic would note, McLuhan's

and Ong's insights offered a conception of culture as 'a modality of consciousness, a structure of beliefs and perceptions, a socially constructed subjectivity' (Love 2003: 54).

Tracking shifts in social communication from oral to written to print, however, has led scholars to conclude that demarcations between these communication patterns are remarkably fluid, with a tendency to overlap and coincide. The boundaries between each are not fixed – thus oral culture did not terminate with the invention of writing implements, nor was manuscript culture instantly toppled by the assimilation of printing techniques pioneered by Johannes Gutenberg and his successors from 1450 onwards. As work by Harold Love, Henry Woudhuysen, Margaret Ezell, David McKitterick, and others attests, manuscript transmission remained a vital aspect of many Western European communities through to the late nineteenth century (Woudhuysen 1996; Love 1998; Ezell 1999; Fox 2000; Gómez 2001; Justice and Tinker 2002; McKitterick 2003). The results confound attempts to impose neat chronological finalities to human processes. As David McKitterick (2003: 12) points out: 'Whether one considers scribal texts or illumination and decoration, the boundary between manuscript and print is as untidy chronologically as it is commercially, materially or socially.'

McKitterick's contention is, in part, a response to a view of book history that has prevailed since the publication in the late 1970s of one of the most influential studies on early modern print culture, Elizabeth Eisenstein's (1979) two-volume classic *The Printing Press as an Agent of Change: Communications and Cultural Transformations in Early-Modern Europe*. Eisenstein drew on a wealth of material, utilizing and arguing against a range of unconventional critical sources, including Febvre and Martin, Marshall McLuhan, and Walter Ong, to develop the influential thesis that Western European communication patterns had been ineluctably transformed by the introduction of the printing press: the use of the new technology irrevocably altered methods of data collection, storage, retrieval, and communication amongst learned groupings in Western Europe from the late fifteenth century onwards. The result was what Eisenstein referred to as 'typographic fixity' (Eisenstein 1979: I, 116–120). The term denoted how print culture innovations, by increasing the capacity of society to produce and disperse information, established, as another critic has summarized, 'a series of techniques and practices that allowed the world's stock of recordable knowledge to be put to use with a fearsome new efficiency' (Love 2003: 46–47). Put another way, 'typographical fixity' involved 'the ability of printed books to give to the words and ideas they print a substantial and durable form, and to amplify this objectified verbal reality by the distribution of numerous identical copies of the same organisation of words on the page' (Kernan 1987: 53).

Benedict Anderson (1982) has drawn on Eisenstein's concept of 'fixity' in formulating his influential vision of 'imagined communities' and national identity, arguing that 'print-capitalism,' in particular, has been crucial to establishing the conditions for the creation of national consciousness. For Anderson, the mechanical reproduction of language, 'print-language' as opposed to spoken language, formed the foundation for modern national consciousness and the development of the nation-state in three ways: it 'created unified fields of exchange and communication below Latin and above the spoken vernaculars ... gave a new fixity to language, which in the long run helped to build that image of antiquity so central to the subjective idea of the nation ... [and] created languages-of-power of a kind different from the older administrative vernaculars' (Anderson 1982: 44–45).

Anderson links fixity with human activity, noting that the results of utilizing print technology in the Renaissance period came about due to 'the explosive interaction between capitalism, technology and human linguistic diversity' (Anderson 1982: 45). Anderson, however, is careful to differentiate his stance from Eisenstein's main argument, which he suggests 'comes close to theomorphizing "print" *qua* print as the genius of modern history.' 'It is worth remembering in this context,' he continues, 'that although printing was invented first in China, possibly 500 years before its appearance in Europe, it had no major, let alone revolutionary impact – precisely because of the absence of capitalism there' (Anderson 1982: 44).

Adrian Johns argues similarly that 'fixity' is actually transitive rather than inherent: it 'exists only inasmuch as it is recognized and acted upon by people – and not otherwise' (Johns 1998: 19). Furthermore, Johns argues that the development of print culture during the period covered by Eisenstein was less straightforward, marked by uncertainty and shaky integration. Johns approaches textual production from a position influenced by Darnton, Chartier, and others of the *annales* school: 'a book is the material embodiment of, if not a consensus, then at least a collective consent,' he writes, 'a nexus conjoining a wide range of worlds of work' (Johns 1998: 3). More importantly, he argues against Eisenstein's position that 'typographic fixity' is something that became an inherent quality of print culture – that it was a natural aspect of printing wherever it was transported to. For Johns, the main thrust of Eisenstein's work is that the circumstances of print culture can be characterized by the traits attributed to print – that when books were created, disseminated, and utilized, they were assumed to embody conditions of standardization, dissemination, and fixity. Books could be reproduced exactly, and repeatedly, in any location, utilizing standardized tools and techniques, thus eliminating the corruptive elements inherent in manuscript creation. The result was Eisenstein's influential claim 'that the Renaissance and Reformation were rendered permanent by the very permanence of their canonical texts, that nationalism developed thanks to the stabilization of laws and languages, and that science itself became possible on the basis of phenomena and theories reliably recorded' (Johns 1998: 11).

Such claims have validity within certain contexts. But scholars have countered that this picture is not completely accurate, that circumstances were more complex for the first centuries of book production. The underlying principles that we have inherited from the evolution of book and print culture can be crudely summarized as:

1 knowledge that printed texts will generally be exact duplicates of others printed from the same edition (with minor deviances that analytical bibliographers spend time tracing), thus enabling effective and efficient transmission of knowledge across time and space; and
2 that such fixing of texts enables 'trust' to be invested in the 'author' to whom the words are credited. While 'authorship' as a profession is a relatively recent phenomenon, the authority invested in such figures is an important event ascribed to the early development of print and book production.

Johns counters, drawing on Roger Chartier's work on reading practices, that 'trust' and 'reliability' in a text were less inherent in the reception of printed texts during the first centuries of book production than has previously been suggested. Contemporaries decried the unreliability and textual corruption of early book production, problems that were not resolved for several centuries. As Johns writes: 'The first book reputed to have been printed without any errors appeared only in 1760. Before then, variety was the rule, even within single editions.' Shakespeare's first folio, as many have pointed out, printed over 100 years after the development of printing techniques in Western Europe, could still count over 600 typefaces in its makeup, with erratic and non-uniform spelling, punctuation, divisions, and page arrangements. 'In such a world,' Johns concludes, 'questions of credit took the place of assumptions of fixity.' That is, readers were asked to make judgments of individual texts based on critical appraisals of its identity, credit, reliability, and 'assessments of the people involved in the making, distribution, and reception of books' (Johns 1998: 31–32).

As technology has grown increasingly sophisticated, and society has developed institutional and social filters to control and assess print outputs (publishing houses, editorial staff, periodical and literary reviews and reviewers), we have grown accustomed to placing trust in corporate identities and 'brands.' Our dependency on and trust in the printed text has not diminished in the face of an increasing domination of the personal computer in commercial and social transactions, and the increasing diversity of information and activity now available and utilized via the World Wide Web. And skills in communicating information orally (to which has been added the ability to project a telegenic presence if involved in visual media arenas such as film and television) are still valued within an increasingly globalized world whose media sources intertwine visual, oral, and written communication material in their content and delivery.

On the other hand, commentators such as Roger Chartier have responded to the three-part model of social communication development noted above (oral, written, print) by arguing that it does not fully account for particular innovations that created as fundamental a transformation in society as the writing tool and the printing press (and could, perhaps, be deemed to be more important). It would be more accurate, they argue, to suggest that movements from oral to written to print cultures might be marked off by other additional 'inventions' – namely:

> ... the invention of the codex, which, in the first centuries of the common era, enabled the transition from the book which one unrolls to the one in which one turns pages, thus giving the book the form, structure, and organization it has retained up to the present; the invention of the 'author' in the fourteenth and fifteenth centuries, which endowed certain contemporary authors (above all Petrarch) with the authority of the proper name that had been traditionally reserved for the ancients and Christians of the classical era; the invention of the copyright, which in the eighteenth century established an author's perpetual and imprescriptible control over his work on the basis of the theory of natural law and of a new aesthetic of originality.
>
> (Chartier 1997a: 11)

Authorial intention

One of the legacies of the early nineteenth century that has left its mark particularly in literary criticism has been the tendency to equate authorial activity with creative genius, investing such individuals with value as creative originators, individuals in possession of a creative soul from whom emanate unified texts that resonate through contemporary and future cultures. The rise of the cult of the author is arguably in Western culture a product of the Romantic age, exemplified or typified most dramatically in the figure of Lord Byron, whose tempestuous nature (and even more tempestuous business relationship with his publisher John Murray) epitomized the creative temperament of the period.

How this works its way into book history can be seen in the juxtaposing views of Barthes and Foucault on the issue of authorship and an author's relationship to texts. Roland Barthes's oft-quoted 'The death of the author' in *Image, Music, Text* (1977) set the tone in the 1960s for overturning previous assumptions about the role of the author in the formation of texts. His point, and likewise the point of Michel Foucault's response, 'What is an author?,' was to attempt to shift critical emphasis from author-centered enquiry to reader-based analysis. More on this matter can be found in Chapter 4 when we turn to discussing 'Authors, authorship, and authority.'

Decentering and decoupling the author from texts was not a new concept: elevating the common reader to ultimate creator of textual meaning was. But as Foucault was clear to point out, eliminating the authorial role completely from the textual production equation was not satisfactory. 'Authorship' was a cultural formation inseparable from the commodification of literature: literary reputation could and did shape cultural responses to texts in a manner not accounted for by Barthesian analysis. Subsequent developments in book history studies have expanded and developed critical thinking regarding these matters. Particular attention has been paid to the struggle over authorship as a concept, which can be located in the creation of literary property under copyright legislation in Britain during the eighteenth century, itself a product of national struggle between the Scots and the English (Ross 1992; Rose 1993).

Copyright legislation allowed authors legal rights to be recognized as originators and therefore owners of a specific commodity (in this case, text). It formed the basis for a new profession and industry to develop exponentially in the eighteenth century, one that combined the manufacture and distribution of cultural commodities with an affirmation of the author (rather than as before the printer/bookseller) as the original source of such material. The resulting changes in social and cultural networks of literary production laid the groundwork for the full-fledged emergence of authorship as a respected and lucrative profession in the industrially driven and print-literate world of nineteenth-century Western Europe and North America.

Another French theorist whose work has built on Foucault's reorientation of authorship in commodified terms is Pierre Bourdieu. His articulation of the concept of the 'literary field' has proven fruitful for those concerned particularly with contemporary (nineteenth- to twenty-first-century) print culture and authorship. It has also been used with particular effect in studies linking print culture with the burgeoning field of post-colonial studies (Brouillette 2007; Van der Vlies 2007; Fraser 2008; Fraser and Hammond 2008; Helgesson 2008; McDonald 2009). Bourdieu's 'literary fields' stress the juncture between culture, society, and material production, and are defined as common social, intellectual, and ideological arenas linking producers (publishers, editors, and authors) to products (books, periodical publications, literary works). In particular, Bourdieu is concerned with how 'cultural status' is acquired, lost, or retained by literary elites, with 'literary fields' representing distinctive, relatively autonomous social microcosms within and between which move cultural producers and their products. Crucial to Bourdieu's argument is his contention that such fields are generally self-contained, 'an independent social universe with its own laws of functioning, its specific relations of force, its dominants and its dominated' (Bourdieu 1993: 164). Individuals operate within these fields, struggling to gain cultural capital that can be translated into more material rewards, whether recognition of artistic merit, financial gain, or advance in social status. As Bourdieu (1993: 164) contends:

> This universe is the place of entirely specific struggles, notably concerning the question of knowing who is part of the universe, who is a

22

real writer and who is not. The important fact, for the interpretation of works, is that this autonomous social universe functions somewhat like a prism which refracts every external determination: demographic, economic or political events are always retranslated according to the specific logic of the field, and it is by this intermediary that they act on the logic of the development of works.

It is important to note that Bourdieu's concerns are with general aesthetic and cultural production – his analysis takes in literary texts, as well as art and music. His interest is also less with the material production of texts as with how such cultural production can be manipulated or interpreted within particular social, literary, and artistic structures to enable movements between such 'literary fields.'

Janice Radway has utilized and reinterpreted Bourdieu's concept of literary fields (as literary planes) in her work on US 'middlebrow' culture, and most specifically in her work on the activities of the US Book-of-the-Month Club from the 1920s onwards. As part of its attempt to create a distinctive 'marketing' tool for targeting home-based readers via a mail book service, and, as a consequence, to create a unique identity and role for itself as a mediator, arbiter, and filter of literary production, the Book-of-the-Month Club established an internal panel of 'expert' judges to read texts for subsequent recommendation and sale to Club members. Their procedures, in essence, replicated an internal variation of the Bourdieusian 'literary field,' where texts were evaluated for their cultural capital and then categorized and differentiated for sale to particular audiences. 'The key moves in the evaluative practices of the Book-of-the-Month Club judges,' Radway notes, 'was not judgment at all, but rather the activity of categorization, that of sorting onto different planes' (Radway 1996: 24). The Book-of-the-Month Club established a blueprint for viewing texts within 'a series of discontinuous, discrete, non-congruent worlds.' In doing so, the Club created links between producer (author) and consumer (reader) whereby the disseminator, in this case the Club's organization, with its built-in filters of judges categorizing titles rather than providing aesthetic judgments of books, became less arbiters of worth and more literary managers of textual production (Radway 1996: 24). And in many cases, different arenas or planes of textual production, whether how-to manuals, atlases, science textbooks, biographies, or novels, quite openly operated on differing planes of meaning, meeting differing audience needs with discrete and technically distinct codes, structures, and formats. The Book-of-the-Month Club, begun as a purely commercial proposition, established an overarching identity for itself as a non-judgmental yet trusted provider of quality texts in a variety of subject areas, operating simultaneously on different textual planes and arenas.

Reading and book history

Scholarly enquiry over the past 30 years into the encounter between text and reader has shifted matters to the point where Barthes's stance that the 'death of the author' enabled the 'birth of the reader' can now be read as anachronistic in intent, reflecting the concerns of 1960s post-structuralist revolutions against the literary strictures of New Criticism. More on this can be found in Chapter 6, which covers issues of readers and reading.

The 'reader,' as studies by Roger Chartier, Michel de Certeau, and others have demonstrated, was not as omnipotent and creatively autonomous as Barthes would have us believe (a point Michel Foucault alluded to in his rebuttal of Barthes, 'What is an author?'). Rather, as Chartier reminds us, reading is a historically mediated activity – textual meaning 'depends upon the forms through which they are received and appropriated by their readers (or listeners)' (Chartier 1989b: 48). We must recognize, as Chartier continues, 'that forms produce meaning, and that even a fixed text is invested with new meaning and being (*statut*) when the physical form through which it is presented for interpretation changes' (Chartier 1989b: 48). The result is that any study of reading practices and reader response must necessarily confront the contexts in which such activity takes place: 'A history of modes of reading must identify the specific dispositions that distinguish community of readers and traditions of reading' (Chartier 1989b: 48). To do this appropriately, Chartier argued elsewhere, involved embracing the opportunities offered by book history, whose aims included reconstructing and interpreting 'the conditions of the encounter between the world of the text – which is always a world of forms, supports and objects – and the world of the reader – who is always a reader socially defined by the competency, conventions, expectations and practices of reading that he shares with others' (Chartier 1997a: 10).

Robert Darnton reiterated this call to historicize and contextualize reading studies as part of an expanded, sociologically inflected remit in book history in his 1986 survey piece 'First steps towards a history of reading' (Darnton 1986). Darnton called for further research into a history of reader response that would enable the contextualization of the place of print in ordinary life: 'We need to work through more archives,' he argued, 'comparing readers' accounts of their experience with the protocols of reading in their books and, when possible, with their behaviour' (Darnton 1986: 157). Furthermore, book historians had to be sensitive to the flexible and reciprocal links between readers and producers of text, and the manner in which meanings derived from texts could change over time. Historians of reading were required, in his view, 'to confront the relational element at the heart of the matter: how did changing readerships construe shifting texts?' (Darnton 1986: 187). Having studied reading as a social phenomenon, book historians 'can answer many of the "who," "what," "where," and "when" questions, which can be of great help in attacking the more difficult "whys" and "hows"' (Darnton 1986: 157).

We are now, in Darnton's terms, exploring the 'whys' and 'hows' of the history of reading as much as the 'who,' 'what,' 'where,' and 'when.' The sources for this history remain fertile and problematic: the archival, including booksellers' lists, library records, and state registers, offers generalized data which can be used to ascertain patterns and trends which may or may not be localized; and the personal, including letters, diaries, and autobiographies, offers presentations of the reading self which can provide cautious insights into the individual's reading habits and practices. For example, Richard Altick's (1957) account of reading in Britain from the late fifteenth until the turn of the twentieth century, *The English Common Reader: A Social History of the Mass Reading Public, 1800–1900*, illustrated the richness and density to be derived from this material, as well as alerted us to the need to recreate the *mentalités* of the culture under review – the 'why' and the 'how,' as so rigorously demanded by *annalistes* such as Henri-Jean Martin, Roger Chartier, Robert Escarpit, and others.

Darnton's 'how' included both the paratextual elements of the printed word (a theme already noted in relation to the work of Jerome McGann and Gerard Genette) and the nature of the act of reading itself. The latter theme was the subject of the school of reader-response criticism that emerged from Germany during the 1970s and in which Wolfgang Iser was the predominant figure. Iser restored the reader to the center of the act of reading, a position from which a blinkered focus upon the author's 'intentions' and the structures of the text had dislodged him/her. Within Iser's model of reading, the reader was an active and creative participant in the creation of meaning from the text. This model might seem, then, to underline the importance of the historical, since it follows that different readers at different periods will derive different meanings from their reading. This notion has proved important in allowing the historian of reading to move from data about individuals to conclusions about audiences – to attempt to refute Darnton's assertion that 'the experience of the great mass of readers lies beyond the range of historical research' (Darnton 1986: 177).

Book history and mediation

With such a broad scope of themes and concerns available, book historians have increasingly taken to framing their work in terms of 'mediation' (taking cues from, among other things, Darnton's 'communication circuit'). 'Mediation' is a crucial concept underpinning contemporary interpretations of what is the history of the book and print culture. As Joan Shelley Rubin explains: 'rejecting the view that a printed artifact is simply the embodiment of an author's words, the term denotes the multitude of factors affecting the text's transmission' (Rubin 2003: 562). Michael Winship supports this interpretation, noting: 'Basic to the history of the book is an understanding that literature is a human institution, part of a matrix of social and cultural forces from which it emerges, rather than a pure or abstract ideal, independent of history' (Winship 1993: 95–96). Others have moved outwards in their examination of this matrix from literary works to texts as varied as anthologies, religious catechisms and readers, and children's textbooks (Monaghan 1989; Howsam 1991; Price 2000).

Such diversity also underpins the multifarious national History of the Book initiatives that have emerged since the late 1990s, and from which have come multi-volume publications attempting to map answers to such questions as: what infrastructures and mechanisms underpinned national print culture developments? What cultural values were transmitted and embedded in indigenous settings by texts flowing into and across established and developing territories? And what was transmitted back through 'imperial' circuits and networks? Who manned the machines, what skills and talents were brought into and developed accordingly, and who created the copy and bankrolled the distribution of print and text in all its forms (from written and ephemeral to pamphlet, journal, newspaper, and printed book)? Such discussions feature particularly in Anglophone and English-speaking surveys covering Australia, the UK, Canada, Ireland, New Zealand, Scotland, and the USA, all of whom have heroically dug away and presented us with empirically informed details of the infiltration of print and text across society, and the development of national print infrastructures (Griffith et al 1997; Hellinga and Trapp 1999; Lyons and Arnold 2001; Barnard and McKenzie 2002; Fleming et al 2004; Lamonde et al 2005; Gillespie and Hadfield 2006; Sheahan-Bright and Munro 2006; Amory and Hall 2007; Bell 2007; Casper et al 2007; Finkelstein and McCleery 2007; Gerson and Michon 2007; Morgan and Thompson 2008; Kaestle and Radway 2009; Suarez and Turner 2009; McKitterick 2009; Nord et al 2009; Brown and McDougall 2011; Gameson 2011; Murphy 2011; Walsh and Hutton 2011).

Book history as a field of study marks both an end and a beginning. It is clear that as we move into an era marked by discussions of the 'new' electronic revolution, the 'old' print revolution, begun in the fifteenth century, assumes a clearer focus and a natural closure. Just as manuscript traditions merged with new print technologies, so too we are now seeing similar mergings and complementarities between new and old media. The embedding of visual culture within cultural formations from the twentieth century onwards (the advance of film, television, the World Wide Web) has also meant a reshaping of print culture to accommodate such media of communication. We can see this in the manner in which books now form a part of contemporary Western cultural industries, where creativity, capitalism, and consumption are linked through production of mass media products based on texts (books to films and subsequent film 'novelizations'). It is also evident in the manner in which printed texts (newspapers, journals) are now only one among many media communication systems competing for the attention of mass audiences. One has only to survey the multiple media through which humanity now communicates to see that print culture is slowly being displaced from the center of social communication to the periphery, still necessary but no longer the sole form of information in an electronic age.

But if the book in the future will no longer be the main form of human communication, this does not signify, as some critics would have us believe, the death of the book. In fact, some have argued that new media has the potential to extend the life of the book through individual engagement with written texts, as evidenced by the explosion of online blogs, the creative interaction of image and text through individually tailored and designed web-sites, and the increased consumption of digital versions of print and texts through the iPad, Kindle, and similar devices (Baron 2009). As Dennis Baron points out, new technologies do not obliterate old ones, they merely add new layers of complexity to how we receive and use information; the digital world has opened out readership and authorship in positive ways, radically redefining public and private space and creating new ways to promote the flow of infor-mation across national boundaries (Baron 2009). Furthermore, the history of the book has become enshrined as a subject worthy of study in academic terms, inviting interest from publishers seeking new areas to generate lists and sales: as degrees and courses on the subject have proliferated, so too have the readers, introductions (such as this one), companions, and survey volumes needed to inform students on this subject (Howsam 2006; Finkelstein and McCleery 2007; Eliot and Rose 2009; Bland 2010; Suarez and Woudhuysen 2010). What all share in common is a view that book history is important for what it says about human development. Without the portability and reach of print and texts, social, cultural, legal, humanistic, and religious formations would not have developed, been transmitted, and shaped beliefs and systems around the world.

Conclusion

This chapter has outlined some of the major theories, and briefly surveyed the work of some of the major theorists who have shaped the discipline of print culture and book history studies over the past century. It has shown how book history has moved from past traditions in bibliographic and textual studies that sought to establish stable texts and precise textual intentions, to current preoccupations with understanding books and print within broader and more fluid cultural, sociological, and bibliographical contexts. The chapter has also covered how book history has developed interests in linking book and textual production with studies of authorship and readership. It described how book historians are increasingly framing their work in terms of 'mediation,' shifting the emphasis from recovering exact meanings in text to understanding the place of texts within contemporary society. With new media practices and the World Wide Web challenging the fixity of print and creating new links between visual, oral, and textual communication forms, it is inevitable that we should shift how we view texts (past, present, and future) to acknowledge the wider contexts in which they exist. In order to do this, as this chapter has demonstrated, book history is drawing on and borrowing from a combination of analytical tools and insights derived from various disciplines, ranging from literary studies to history, media, and communication studies. Book history is no longer simply the province of bibliographers or literary critics, but can be seen as an integral part of the history of human communication.

Points to ponder

Here are some key questions to ponder as you reflect on the themes discussed so far. To what extent do the various theories about the history of the book help explain how books can act as a force for change? And what makes the study of texts and books different from other subjects?

2

FROM ORALITY TO LITERACY

Introduction

Society is based on transactions enabled by communication processes. Much of our lives center round this, and our ability to function is often determined by the accuracy and best use of available information and knowledge. From the beginning of time, the skill and ability to process, decode, pass on, and utilize knowledge and information has been highly prized. Oral cultures have had their '*griots*' (storytellers), shamans, witchdoctors, and sages, whose function was to preserve and pass on cultural traditions, who acted as repositories of social and cultural values, and who were called upon to judge, heal, inform, or entertain. Written cultures have called on scribes and philosophers to preserve and interpret human thought and activity. Even today, those who are skilled at gathering, utilizing, and manipulating information in both oral and written form often perform the same functions, and we see this embedded in a variety of work-related practices and traditions, from public relations 'spin doctors' and information officers (information gatekeepers of sorts), to bestselling novelists, journalists, screenwriters, and cultural commentators.

This chapter looks at writing, as it has been integrated within book history studies, as the history of social communication structures. It will outline how writing developed and spread into Western European culture, pointing out links to authority and institutions that will be explored further in Chapter 4. It will look at how oral traditions were incorporated into early writing and manuscript culture, and examine how writing changed in structure and style as print technology prevailed. This chapter also covers how writing changed in nature due to the development of a literate reading public, moving from being used as a cultural tool meant to be read by one to many, to a process that often directed its results to individual solitary readers. Finally, the chapter examines briefly how critics have described writing in the service of state and institutional power, used for political and cultural colonization of other parts of the world, and in the context of class structures.

Social communication through writing

Western European traditions of social communication through writing can be traced back several millennia to the Near East and Mesopotamia. Around 3500 to 3300 BC, it has been argued, Sumerian farming communities started grouping into urban city-states. They invented new irrigation techniques for farming the dry lands, and the complexities of urban life begin to call for laws, rules, and codes for commercial transactions. From this, it has been suggested, writing sprang, not, as one would assume, to record language, but rather as mnemonic devices (memory aids) scratched on hard surfaces such as clay tablets to record economic communications and transactions, and to register ownership and other claims on goods and property (Schmandt-Besserat 1982a, 1982b; Assmann 1994: 18). However, over the 3,000-odd years of Mesopotamian social and political development, its pictographic cuneiform script (cuneiform deriving from the Latin word *cuneus*, or wedge, reflecting the basic shape of the symbols impressed on the clay tablets), along with public reciting, would expand in importance and be linked to sacred acts and rituals, 'the highly protected technological privilege of a select few who were not just scholars but also magicians, physicians and priests' (Noegel 2004: 134).

Mesopotamian writing was one of many scripts developed independently around the world. Among others we can count Egyptian hieroglyphics, developed around 3000 BC; Aegean scripts (the so-called Linear A and Linear B scripts), dated around 1650 to 1200 BC; Indus Valley script, from about 3000 to 2400 BC; Chinese script, circa 1500 BC; the Greek alphabet (precursor of Western alphabets) of circa 800 to 700 BC; Mayan script, occurring about 50 AD; and Aztec script, dating from 1400 AD (Martin 1995: 1–42; Olivier 2001: 197). Egyptian hieroglyphic writing proved a more sophisticated recording system in its initial conception than Sumerian cuneiform: its purpose was 'political rather than economic communication, the recording of acts of special political significance' (Assmann 1994: 18). Egyptian use of iconic signs and symbols, which has led some to view hieroglyphics as a genre of pictorial art, was rooted in offering graphic representations of specific social, sacred, and political moments or acts, carving them in stone and thus securing them for posterity in consecrated spaces. Egyptian hieroglyphic script was complexly layered, simultaneously utilizing phonetic, syllabic, and logographic methods of communication. It featured picture-signs to refer to both names and acts. Like Mesopotamian writing, it too was the province of an elite section of society, a 'priesthood expert in medicine and magic' (Noegel 2004: 135), with hieroglyphics 'reserved for the "writing of divine words," as it is called in Egyptian, for recordings in the sacred space of permanence' (Assmann 1994: 19).

Such reverence for the sacred nature of the word carried through to cultures based in the Sinai and Palestinian regions, as most notably encapsulated in the Hebrew Bible. This, as Scott B. Noegel points out, is not surprising, 'since

Israel became a cultural conduit and receptacle for Egyptian and Mesopotamian influences, and since in Canaan (which eventually would become the land of Israel) writing first appeared in cuneiform script' (Noegel 2004: 135). 'Proto-Sinaitic' inscriptions and hieroglyphically inspired alphabetic signs found in the Sinai Peninsula, dating back to circa 1850 to 1500 BC and often located next to Egyptian hieroglyphics, attest to these cultural links and legacies (Lemaire 2001: 203–204). While there were also obvious differences and deviations between usage and development of writing systems, what united Mesopotamian, Egyptian, and Sinaitic cultures was a belief in the weight of words, both written and spoken, 'a conception of words as vehicles of power, of creation by fiat, and of the oracular use of written and spoken words' (Noegel 2004: 134). What this meant, in practice, was a careful attention to the representation of words, a practice of transcription that believed inaccuracies would violate sacred tenets and have unforeseen, dire consequences. Within such contexts, 'an accurate memory is everything, copying is sacred, and knowledge of the associative subtleties embedded in a text is tantamount to secret knowledge of the divine' (Livingstone 1986; Noegel 2004: 137).

Truth, authority, and the sacred nature of the written word would also become embedded in the most influential religious movement to emerge from the Sinai Basin during Roman times. Christianity, forged in the context of a Sinaitic culture closely connected to the Hellenistic world, under Roman domination, and in contact through trade and commerce with other Mediterranean and Arabic cultures, at first drew on oral traditions to spread its message, with the apostles charging themselves with the task of preaching the Gospel to large crowds, establishing Christian communities through whom religious narratives and messages were spread orally, then leaving these communities with written summaries and versions of their sermons and main teachings for future use.

Through the reiteration, amplification, and written recording of key messages, the Christian community developed a unified set of doctrines that took advantage of new developments in writing technology (codex formats, parchment surfaces) to make its message more transportable. Christianity conquered the Roman Empire because of its ability to offer a universal message appealing to Greek and Latin culture. 'Pagan' works and philosophers were read with a view to borrowing and re-utilizing ideas culled from key texts to convert the relevant non-believer. At the same time, the evolution of a dominant Catholic Church from the fourth century AD onwards involved the formation of notions of tradition, whereby 'the Fathers of the church ceaselessly asserted that the church was the unique depository of the truth, which the apostles had passed on to it, because only the church was inhabited by the Holy Spirit' (Martin 1995: 113) (religious authority as it pertains to emerging notions of authorship is discussed later in this book). The sacralistic nature of the written word became embedded in church ritual, with the written embodiment of the Bible (particularly the New Testament) prominent in sacred spaces (similar in manner to the reverential display of sacred scrolls – the Torah – in blessed spaces in Jewish synagogues), reproduced in other visual media (paintings, stained glass), and copied for use by its priests to teach the faithful.

Throughout the first millennium of the Christian calendar, writing in Western Europe would remain contained within the ecclesiastical sphere, practiced mainly within the confines of monasteries and abbeys. Various moments of historical confluence and individual state initiatives could occasion the move of writing outwards into the public sphere. One such example was the Carolingian cultural revival spearheaded by Charlemagne and his successors in the Rhine and Meuse valley region during the eighth and ninth centuries AD. Charlemagne drew in men of letters to work in his court, extended the copying of important classical manuscripts and texts, encouraged a revival of writing in diplomatic and administrative activities (Charlemagne republished old legal and ecclesiastical rulings and called for new decrees and laws to be written down), and in 787 AD reinforced written values in Italy by issuing a proclamation asserting the superiority of written laws over oral customs.

Charlemagne and his successors also established educational policies with the aim of bringing order to the preparation of clerics and priests for religious duty. Writing as conceived in such educational settings, as Henri-Jean Martin points out, was thus bound up in ecclesiastical contexts, undertaken for the purpose of using 'a common language – Latin – to gain an acquaintance with and a better comprehension of the Scripture, and to perpetuate correct and uniform performance of rites and sacraments for the glory of God and the unity of the West' (Martin 1995: 126). The copying of manuscripts for such purposes also led to improvements in writing style and form: the Carolingian script, as perfected during this period, incorporated new systems of punctuation that would be adapted by members of the humanist movements of the fifteenth century and reshaped into forms that we are familiar with today (see later in this chapter for more on writing style and form shifts).

Oral traditions

It is important to note, however, that the move from oral to written traditions involved social transformations that copied, incorporated and at the same time reshaped old traditions to fit new forms and contexts. Walter Ong has written extensively and eruditely on oral communication traditions and the effect that the development of writing had on pre-literate societies. 'More than any other single invention,' he declared famously, 'writing has transformed human consciousness' (Ong 1982: 77). In *Orality and Literacy*, Ong compared the disjunctions caused by shifts in communicative consciousness, and argued that the development of writing involved new kinds of cognitive experiences distinct from oral cultural communication. Oral cultures, by their very transitive nature, require particular skills and forms of discourse. Ong used a particularly appropriate metaphor in describing oral patterns of communication when he commented: 'Oral discourse has commonly been thought of even in oral milieus as weaving or stitching' (Ong 1982: 13). A particularly important aspect of orality and oral discourse is its reliance on memory and repetition (its weaving together of information – in particular, recognizable patterns), for in order to retain knowledge, information has to be passed on orally in repetitious manner until the listener has internalized and retained its meaning. As Ong (1982: 23) explains: 'fixed, formulaic thought patterns were essential for wisdom and effective administration.'

Writing and manuscript culture, through to the development of printing, retained many of the traditions of oral discourse – repetitive in nature and conceived with a view to engaging in a dialog where one thought through one's views in spoken terms. Thus, in eleventh-century England we find Eadmer of St. Albans commenting that, for him, composing in writing was akin to dictating to himself, while St. Thomas Aquinas, who dispensed with scribes to write out his own manuscripts, composed and organized his texts in 'quasi-oral format,' with each section including a list of objections an interlocutor might pose against Thomas's planned positions, a summary of Thomas's own stance, and a detailed response to each question and query posed by the imaginary objector.

Such positions reflected the adaptation of oral declamatory styles for written purposes. Manuscript culture 'preserved a feeling for a book as a kind of utterance, an occurrence in the course of conversation, rather than as an object' (Ong 1982: 123). The shift from oral to written traditions was often incremental, with individuals versed in the former robustly contesting the validity of the latter. Some of the most famous examples of such contestations are Socrates's philosophical discourses on writing, dating from the fourth century BC (ironically accessible to modern commentators because they were written down by Plato). In various dialogs recorded by his acolytes, Socrates devoted some attention to the deleterious effect he felt writing was having on contemporary Greek society. Greece stood at the cusp of change, when its society had fully assimilated and incorporated writing into all facets of social, political, and cultural activity. This was a shift resisted by influential proponents arguing for retention of an orally based culture. It was to be a losing battle, for, as Ong notes:

> ... by Plato's day (427?–347 BC) a change had set in: the Greeks had at long last effectively interiorized writing – something which took several centuries after the development of the Greek alphabet around 720–700 BC.... The new way to store knowledge was not in mnemonic formulas but in the written text. This freed the mind for more original, more abstract thought.
>
> (Ong 1982: 23–24)

As Plato records in *The Seventh Letter*, Socrates had little interest and even less belief in the value of writing: in one of his most famous statements on the matter, Socrates concluded that 'A written composition on any subject must be to a large extent the creation of fancy [and, as a result,] ... nothing worth serious attention has ever been written in prose or verse.' In *Phaedrus*, which dealt with the nature of love, wisdom, society, and the craft of letters, Socrates retold the legend of the encounter between the King of Egypt and the Egyptian god Thoth (inventor of, among other things, writing), as an admonitory commentary on writing. Thoth offered the king several inventions to pass on to his people and in the process debated with the king the merits and weaknesses of each offering, until they came to writing. 'Here,' said Thoth, 'is a branch of learning that will improve their memories; my discovery provides a recipe for both memory and wisdom.' The King of Egypt was not impressed. 'If men learn this,' he told the god:

> ... it will implant forgetfulness in their souls; they will cease to exercise memory because they will rely on that which is written, calling things to remembrance no longer from within themselves, but by means of external marks. What you have discovered is a recipe not for memory but for reminder. And it is no true wisdom that you offer your disciples, but only its semblance, for by telling them of many things without teaching them anything, you will make them seem to know much, while for the most part they will know nothing. And as men filled not with wisdom but with the conceit of wisdom, they will be a burden to their fellow-men.

A reader, Socrates admonished Phaedrus, 'must be singularly simple minded to believe that written words can do anything more than remind one of what one already knows' (Manguel 1996: 58). What is evident here is the manner in which Socrates was assuming and utilizing old conventions and frameworks of reference (that is, memory and oral culture traditions) to deal with new realities. Those steeped in the traditions that prized memory naturally would not take well to a social form (writing) that changed such norms and values and required the adoption of different skills.

But the tidal wave of change sweeps away those like Socrates. The very nature of writing demanded new cultural accommodation as more individuals became literate. 'High literacy,' as one commentator notes, 'fosters truly written composition, in which the author composes a text which is precisely a text, puts his or her words together on paper. This gives thought different contours from those of orally sustained thought' (Ong 1982: 94). Further shifts from manuscript to print culture occasion what Ong and others have summarized as the creation of a new 'noetic world,' involving shifts from oral to visual spaces, a move to rational, linear processes of thought in printed communication, 'the imposition upon discourse of a sense of closure,' and more formal, mechanistic, impersonal modes of textual address (Love 2003: 54). But, as noted in Chapter 1, such shifts were not totalistic; rather, they were adaptive, blending and accommodating old communication structures within newly evolving communication forms.

Writing played an important role in the evolution of national languages – not only in terms of fixing spelling, syntax, and formal rules and conventions for written and spoken versions of language, but also in terms of providing the basis for the formal teaching and dissemination of language beyond regional boundaries. The fixing (in writing and print) of language and its norms was aided by common frames of reference that allowed all to share in its use.

At the same time, critics such as Jack Goody and Marshall McLuhan have demonstrated that writing (and later print) played a crucial role in redirecting and reshaping experience throughout human history. They have argued that human encounters with the written and printed page, and in particular with the lineal phonetic alphabet (as opposed to pictograms and hieroglyphics), led to a split between, as McLuhan memorably put it, 'the magical world of the ear and the neutral world of the eye' (McLuhan 1962: 32). Walter Ong spends a great deal of time outlining the many changes he saw in the shift from oral to literate cultures. McLuhan, however, focused in many of his influential works (namely, *The Gutenberg Galaxy* and *Understanding Media*) on the 'Gutenberg revolution,' arguing that the effects of Greek alphabets, Roman script, and even medieval manuscript culture were trifling compared to the even more radical splits in human consciousness resulting from the development of print. 'From the point of view of recent intense awareness of the visual components of experience,' he claimed:

> ... the Greek world looks timid and tentative. But there was nothing in the manuscript phase of alphabetic technology that was intense enough to split the visual from the tactile entirely. Not even Roman script had the power to do that. It was not until the experience of mass production of exactly uniform and repeatable type, that the fission of the senses occurred, and the visual dimension broke away from the other senses.
>
> (McLuhan 1962: 70)

Over 20 years later, Elizabeth Eisenstein, although rejecting McLuhan's general prose style as incomprehensible for academic purposes, nevertheless made use of McLuhan's general sentiments in articulating a similar notion of the effect on Western European society of 'typographical fixity,' a point already covered in Chapter 1 (Eisenstein 1983: 41–90).

Technological shifts

Shifts from oral to written cultures were made easier by technological advances and the development of important writing materials. Initially, adaptation of papyrus for use as a writing material enabled Egyptians, Greeks, and

Romans to create smooth surfaces on which to write. Many also used quills cut from reeds, dipping them into ink to write. Papyrus, manufactured from drying stems of marsh reeds, was flexible enough to roll, but too brittle to be cut and folded into sheaves of pages. The Romans are said to have created techniques for gluing papyrus strips together to create continuous scrolls. Such scroll *volumen* were, as a general rule, about 6 to 8 meters long, and the text written on it 'in parallel columns of between 15 and 30 characters to the line, each column being 25 to 45 lines long, which made "pages" of from 300 to 1,350 signs, as compared with today's typewritten page of somewhat more than 1,500 characters or a printed page ... of some 3,000 characters (including the spaces that do not exist in a manuscript text written in *scriptura continua*)' (Martin 1995: 58–59).

The Roman historian Pliny the Elder claimed that parchment, made from the hides of animals, had been perfected in the second century BC by Eumenes, ruler of Pergamum, as a consequence of the banning of papyrus exports from Egypt by King Ptolemy, who wished to keep the secret of papyrus production confined within Egyptian borders. Parchment booklets have been found dated a century earlier, suggesting this account may be inaccurate.

Whatever the truth of the matter, parchment, more flexible than papyrus, enabled the development of the codex (rectangular, bound or linked pages with writing on both sides) circa 40 to 103 AD. While most Romans preferred to retain the traditional scroll volumen, Christians took to preserving their sacred works and medical treatises in codex form and utilizing the more resistant parchment and vellum made from treated animal hides, not only because the parchment codex was easier to consult, but also because its flexible size and durability made it easier to conceal and transport texts forbidden by the Roman authorities. By 400 AD, parchment codices, and their more expensive alternative vellum versions, had become standard across Europe as the main form for manuscript texts, 'produced as gathered leaves in a rectangular format' (Manguel 1996: 127). An alternative to parchment, paper made from hemp or linen, would only emerge several centuries later – invented in China, adopted by the Arabs in the eighth century AD, spread throughout Muslim states along the Mediterranean (including Spain) between 800 and 1000 AD, and finally taken up by the Italians, who throughout the thirteenth century perfected the production techniques (such as introducing pulping processes, watermarks, and smoother surfaces through use of animal gelatin) that made paper mills in towns and cities such as Fabriano, Bologna, Padua, and Amalfi famous throughout Europe. During the fourteenth century, further competition emerged from French and German mills, while other countries followed in the latter half of the fifteenth century (paper mills were established in Strasbourg in 1445, England in 1490, Austria in 1498, Holland and other northern countries in the 1500s).

The use of parchment, paper, and codex formats affected the manner in which writing was preserved. Initially, written material was conserved in the form of continuous sentences (*scripta continua*) on scrolls or parchment codex, and this worked for those who could read aloud, distinguish between the sounds of words, and subsequently interpret them. Problems arose with subsequent misinterpretations of text because of the lack of significant signals to point to stops, pauses, or breaks (Martin 1995: 54–59).

Punctuation of sorts can be found in the early Greek and Latin texts, but was erratic in usage and style, and Western European usage of forms of punctuation to indicate breaks in speech would remain similarly unreliable and erratic throughout most of the medieval period. Sometime after the seventh century AD methods were developed to indicate emphasis and stops in the flow of texts – in this case through scribal introductions of points, dashes, and commas. By the ninth century, monks, now the main keepers of Western European written traditions, began isolating parts of speech in their manuscript transcriptions, adding more punctuation marks and introducing different colors of writing ink to denote when sections began and ended. Early fifteenth-century Italian innovators such as Poggio Bracciolini and Niccolo de Niccoli, part of the humanist cultural movement sparked by the dynamism, enterprise, and patronage of an increasingly wealthy merchant bourgeoisie class emerging in Italian cities such as Florence and Venice, would, in transcribing classical texts for newly commissioned libraries, perfect and improve script writing by using as standard practice italics, quotation marks, commas, periods, parentheses, and other punctuation symbols to indicate clear separations and shifts in textual meaning. Use of such methods would become increasingly common with the advent of printing several decades later, leading to the standardization of print in the forms we are now accustomed to seeing and interpreting.

Writing, authority, and the individual

Through to and even well past the 1500s (when mechanical printing comes into play), writing and knowledge of it was confined to the elite social groupings of society – the court, the law, the laity, monks, and priests. The rise of regional power bases with formal political structures required individuals who could interpret written codes: the decoder, the scribe, whose role in official circles of recording, deciphering, and disseminating information grew and developed so as to become the ears, eyes, and voices of rulers and the political elite. Such access gave them power much like the *griots* and shamans enjoyed in oral culture-based societies. But writing, while a transformative process, also kept the form of oral culture from which it evolved, often conducted in the form of a written dialog and conversation, with rhetorical flourishes and repetitions usually associated with speech patterns.

In this context, Western European manuscript and textual production was undertaken with the assumption that few could read the results, but that many more would end up hearing them. Writing was conceived to be read aloud (a point that is elaborated upon in another chapter of this book). There was often the view that speaking a text was a way of making it come alive, of providing the spirit of it in a way that was different from reading silently. Texts were not meant to be read to oneself, but to be shared. St. Augustine in 383 AD writes of visiting Ambrose, the Bishop of Milan, and seeing what was for him an unusual sight – St. Ambrose reading in silence:

> When he read, his eyes scanned the page and his heart sought out the meaning, but his voice was silent and his tongue was still. Anyone could approach him freely and guests were not commonly announced, so that often, when we came to visit him, we found him reading like this in silence, for he never read aloud.
>
> (Manguel 1996: 42)

If reading aloud was the norm, here was behavior that broke norms, representing an adaptation to new cultural forms. Well until the Renaissance period, writing was undertaken with the assumption that readers heard rather than saw texts. Public readings were common as few could read, and in any case, there were few handwritten texts available for mass consumption (this issue is covered in more detail in Chapter 6).

Those who read held a sort of power, as exemplified in the rituals of all the major religions. The Catholic Church, for example, as did many other organized religions, had at its center representatives who were there as ultimate arbiters and explicators of the word of God (the Sunday sermon, where texts were read aloud and commented on, was an example of a public forum where the oral reinterpretation of written text occurred for the benefit of a larger audience).

Also central to the exercise of that power was a conception of writing as a permanent action that affected the senses. In a famous treatise on truth and its embodiment in writing (*Philobiblon*, 1345), Richard de Bury (1287 to 1345) opined on the worth of writing and texts in a manner that directly contrasts with Plato's views on written culture. For de Bury, writing was a physical manifestation of truth, with a stronger and longer-lasting effect on the human senses than mere speech. As one critic suggests, de Bury's point was that 'truth that appears ... in thoughts, speech, or writing, is more profitable in books.' As de Bury comments, writing had permanency that outlasted oral presentation:

> For the meaning of the voice [*virtus vocis*] perishes with the sound, truth latent in the mind [*mente latens*] is wisdom that is hid and treasure that is not seen; but truth which shines forth in books desires to manifest itself to every impressionable sense [*omni disciplinabili sensui*]. It commends itself to the sight when it is read, to the hearing when it is heard, and moreover in a manner to the touch,

when it suffers itself to be transcribed, bound, corrected, and preserved.

(Müller 1994: 38)

The written word could prove a beneficent teacher, a companion without human flaws, constantly available for use, and living in the sense of providing conversation to those willing to partake of it. It was also a very material presence: in manuscript culture, in particular, 'the body of the book,' the physical form in which writing existed, also acted as 'a guarantor of the longevity of the word and of the presence of author and meaning' (Müller 1994: 44).

The place and 'authority' of the author within manuscript and print culture is something discussed in a later chapter of this book; but what is clear is that throughout the evolution of Western European manuscript culture, writing exerted power through its presence in material form, part of a legacy stretching back to its insertion into human discourse in pre-millennial Mesopotamian and Egyptian times. Writing served to crystallize and exemplify political and religious authority, keeping pace with the evolution of nation-states. As Western European powers grew in strength from the fifteenth century onwards, they expanded their hold on foreign territories and colonies, in the process imposing cultural norms and political realities that were reinforced by legal statutes and agreements reproduced in written (and eventually printed) form.

Writing and power

Much has been written about the effects that the imposition of writing has had in shaping cultural values and justifying political domination in areas colonized by Western European powers. It is a truism to say that history is often written (and rewritten) by those who are dominant in cultural and historical terms. The conquest by Spain of Central and South America during the fifteenth and sixteenth centuries offers a case in point. With the coming of Spanish conquistadores to Mexico in the fifteenth century, for example (and the subsequent destruction of Mayan culture), there appeared in their wake Christian missionaries intent on bringing salvation to pagan races. One of the side effects of this influx was a marginalization and misunderstanding of Mayan culture and its artifacts. The social records that the Mayans kept in the form of the '*quipu*' (intricately woven and knotted belts certain Mayan scribes were expert at deciphering) were destroyed, and Mayan customs were subsequently recorded by both sympathetic and unsympathetic Spanish commentators in manners reflecting Eurocentric values and understandings. Not until the late nineteenth and early twentieth centuries, when the Mayan ruins were discovered and excavated, and social artifacts were uncovered revealing new insight into Mayan culture, did views of Mayan culture begin to be reshaped differently from those formed by the written records of the Spaniards who had replaced it following their conquest of Central America (Ascher and Ascher 1981; Radicati de Primeglio 1992; Lavallée 2001).

Recent work by cultural historians, book historians, anthropologists, and sociologists offers substantial case study material on the results of the collision between colonial powers and colonized groups in oral, written, and print cultures. Work by Chris Bayly and others on Indian oral and written traditions, for example, has skillfully shown how the history of Indian written and print communication shifted in response to invasion and interaction with external cultures and influences (Bayly 1996; Finkelstein and Peers 2000b; Darnton 2001; Joshi 2002; Ghosh 2003). The Mughals brought Persian manuscript traditions to bear on courtly functions and official bureaucratic dealings; the incursion of European powers from the late sixteenth century onwards was frequently resisted through assimilation and redirection of sophisticated tools of communication – those fighting the British during the 1857 Indian uprising, for example, used written materials and oral communication networks to forge resistance in a manner that confounded British intelligence-gathering efforts and understanding of swiftly changing events.

Don McKenzie's classic essay on New Zealand history, focusing on the conflicting interpretations of the Treaty of Waitangi enacted between Maori chieftains and British officials in 1840 (which ceded land rights to the Crown Colony), similarly demonstrates how oral and print cultural discourses (the 'noetic worlds' noted by Walter Ong) could collide at particularly significant moments in human history. In this case, sovereign and tribal power in New Zealand, and the differing means by which such power was exercised (oral versus print), led to widely contested and radically different interpretations of the meaning invested in written and printed documents produced after the event in question (McKenzie 1984).

A similar illustration of the use of writing to exercise political and tribal power is recorded by the French social anthropologist Claude Lévi-Strauss. Lévi-Strauss spent several years during the late 1930s studying indigenous tribes in the Brazilian rainforests. In the following extract from 'A writing lesson,' part of his groundbreaking study *Tristes Tropiques* first published in 1955, he described an encounter with the Nambikwara, an Indian tribe, which involved the appropriation of writing for political purposes:

> It is unnecessary to point out that the Nambikwara have no written language, but they do not know how to draw either, apart from making a few dotted lines or zigzags on their gourds. Nevertheless, as I had done among the Caduveo, I handed out sheets of paper and pencils. At first they did nothing with them, then one day I saw that they were all busy drawing wavy, horizontal lines. I wondered what they were trying to do, then it was suddenly borne upon me that they were writing or, to be more accurate, were trying to use their pencils in the same way as I did mine, which was the only way they could

conceive of, because I had not yet tried to amuse them with my drawings. The majority did this and no more, but the chief had further ambitions. No doubt he was the only one who had grasped the purpose of writing. So he asked me for a writing pad, and when we both had one, and were working together, if I asked for information on a given point, he did not supply it verbally but drew wavy lines on his paper and presented them to me, as if I could read his reply. He was half taken in by his own make-believe; each time he completed a line, he examined it anxiously as if expecting the meaning to leap from the page, and there was a tacit understanding between us to the effect that his unintelligible scribbling had a meaning which I pretended to decipher; his verbal commentary followed almost at once, relieving me of the need to ask for explanation.

(Munns 1993: 107–108)

The significant issue here is the manner in which the tribal chief grasped the importance of writing as a means of maintaining his status, allowing him to act as chief intermediary between external and indigenous groups. In this instance, Lévi-Strauss documented a moment where writing was used as an agent of power, a method of connecting and controlling access to the outside world. But in this case, it was not writing *per se* that was important, the understanding of symbols for communication purposes, but rather writing as a symbol borrowed for social rather than intellectual purposes. Lévi-Strauss used this incident to speculate about the ultimate role of writing and written culture in society, concluding that the grading and placing of individuals into castes and classes was one of the major ends to which the written language had been put in Western civilization, commenting: 'The only phenomenon with which writing has always been concomitant is the creation of cities and empires, that is the integration of large numbers of individuals into a political system.' He concluded rather provocatively: 'My hypothesis, if correct, would oblige us to recognise the fact that the primary function of written communication is to facilitate slavery' (Munns 1993: 110).

Lévi-Strauss's position, although somewhat extreme, is not unique – Foucault, for one, has drawn critical attention to the transgressive nature of writing ('a gesture fraught with risks'), a discourse inexorably hemmed in by censorship, state control and the exercise of legal ownership over texts (particularly after the development of copyright legislation during the eighteenth and nineteenth centuries). Under such circumstances, writing – 'an act placed in the bipolar field of the sacred and the profane, the licit and the illicit, the religious and the blasphemous' – becomes subject to criminal prosecution where it fails to adhere to contemporary social, political, and religious strictures and codes (Foucault 1984: 108–109).[1] The history of the censoring of writing and textual production is beyond the scope of this chapter, but offers a salutary insight into the role of written communication in supporting, contesting, or resisting contemporary cultural formations.

Studies of Shakespeare's work also offer an interesting insight into the continuing resistance to the political utilization of writing to control society during the fifteenth and sixteenth centuries. Shakespeare's 1594 historical play *Henry VI, Part Two*, for example, as Roger Chartier points out in 'The practical impact of writing,' features moments of collision between oral and written cultures (Chartier 1989b: 111–160). Among the events depicted is the 1449 rebellion of Jack Cade, who storms London with the aim of killing 'all the lawyers,' attacking the clerk of Chatham, and destroying the places where written culture is produced and transmitted (in this case, the courts, the record offices, and the paper mills). The stated purpose of the rebels is to reinstate traditional culture and norms of speech – including laws based on oral proclamation, and the recording of debts and commercial transactions not through books and paper but through alternative traditional systems (such as notches on wood). Shakespeare, although writing his play 150 years after the events portrayed, uses it, as Chartier notes, to highlight the tensions between two cultures:

> ... one increasingly based on recourse to the written word in both the public and private spheres; the other based on nostalgic and utopian esteem for a society without writing, governed by words that everyone could hear and signs that everyone could understand. Whatever his intention in depicting a popular uprising as foolish and bloody and the rebels as dupes manipulated by others, it is clear that the underlying cause of the rebellion is hostility to writing, which is blamed for the upheavals that are transforming the society.
>
> (Chartier 1989b: 123)

Here, the lower classes are depicted as concerned about the power embodied in the act of writing, and the authority imposed upon them by official structures supported by written culture (the law, the state, the church). Such concerns would be replaced, in turn, by literate class concerns about the effects of printing on manuscript culture. The advent of print in the late fifteenth and early sixteenth centuries effected a process of cultural change that threatened privileges and areas under elitist control. A good example of such reactions is the case of the sixteenth-century Venetian monk who argued in the Venetian senate (to their general approval) against the adoption of Gutenberg's printing innovations. Printing needed to be resisted in favor of writing because, he pronounced, it corrupted texts (through circulation in poorly manufactured and incorrect editions for profit); it corrupted minds (making available immoral or dangerous texts to a general public without proper approval or consent by the church); and it corrupted knowledge (by making it freely available to the ignorant) (Chartier 1989b: 123).

What Gutenberg's development in 1450 eventually enabled people to do was to mass produce texts and circulate them widely in a way that had not been achieved before. Previously, the circulation of knowledge was limited to texts produced by hand and circulated privately. Information about international events often circulated through handwritten accounts sent between powerful nations, people, church, or other civil authorities, which were then copied and sent onwards, or passed around self-contained networks. Throughout the Renaissance period, reading and literacy rates improved, but knowledge of writing remained confined to a few, a deliberate policy influenced by Protestant and Lutheran initiatives across Europe during the seventeenth and eighteenth centuries to teach all to read the word of God, to 'see with their own eyes what God ordered and commanded through his sacred word' (Chartier 1989b: 118)[2] (more on the development of reading in the modern period of Western European history is noted in Chapter 6).

Conclusion

The history of human communication has been marked by radical shifts in cultural practices, as well as by processes of resistance, accommodation, and internalization. In this chapter, we have explored how, in Western European history, oral cultures faced challenges from the development of a written or literate culture that adopted and overlaid many of its methods and processes onto new cultural templates. As we have shown, influential critics such as Walter Ong and Marshall McLuhan have argued that these processes reshaped human discourse and consciousness from oral to written modes of discourse. The chapter has also examined how a similar process of adoption, adaptation, and reshaping marked the move from written to print culture. It has shown how critics of the integration of oral culture within written culture had to deal with the notion that the spreading of knowledge equaled 'profanation,' and how they had to face changes in their chosen methods of processing information. Contemporary sources complained that print culture, by triumphing over written culture, made society worse by enabling literate cultures equal access (without control) to previously hidden knowledge. Such issues faded as individuals and institutions capitalized on the opportunities for using writing to reach a wider audience. This chapter also discussed how institutions utilized writing in the service of state power, and how critics have described its use in other social and political circumstances. As other chapters in this book will make clear, the history of writing, reading, and textual production has consistently been marked by such processes of change, evolution, and integration, part of the circuit of human communication that is an increasingly important part of current book history studies.

Points to ponder

Here are some questions to ponder as you review this chapter. Key criticisms attending each introduction of new communication tools often focus on their disruptive and destructive potential. So, writing was going to kill off conversation; print was going to replicate error. Can one say the same thing about the internet and digital media in terms of print and textual culture? Can we see new moves to control access to online writing and textual communication in line with past examples? In what ways might writing continue to flourish in a changing digital multimedia landscape?

3

THE COMING OF PRINT

Introduction

This chapter recounts the development of the book in an age of print, not only the processes involved but also the industry structures that developed in the new manufacture. The relationship between the ability to produce multiple copies of books and pamphlets in a fast, efficient, and cheap manner and wider social and intellectual movements such as the Reformation, the Renaissance, and the Enlightenment can no longer be considered in a simplistic causal manner: the printing press as an agent of change. Indeed, Elizabeth Eisenstein, from whose work the term has gained wide currency, has more recently railed against such facile interpretations of her seminal text and finds more in common with the later study of science and printing by Adrian Johns than reviewers and critics were initially inclined to allow (Eisenstein 1979, 2002a, 2002b; Johns 1998 and 2002). We have already outlined the seeming oppositional nature of Eisenstein and Johns in Chapter 1. However, their respective discussions – for example, of the great astronomer Tycho Brahe – need not be so adversarial. The survey that follows in this chapter attempts to provide a history of the coming of print that might not only set the debates of Chapter 1 in context, but also highlight the possibilities for integration.

The investigations by Darnton of the relationship between the Enlightenment (in its French inhabitation) and printing activities, particularly the production of *L'Encyclopédie*, demonstrate that more complex and multiple factors are involved (Darnton 1982a, 1982b). Here, in fact, is one of the areas where book history can cast new light upon orthodox accounts of these great social and intellectual movements through its combination of wider-scale studies of the production and distribution of books and its detailed micro-histories of particular institutions, such as the Société typographique de Neuchatel (STN), particular books, and particular readers or groups of readers. This chapter proceeds in a relatively straightforward chronological manner from the transition period between manuscript and print to the industrialization of book production. Despite its length, the chapter does not offer a comprehensive history but selects in order to supply the context for internal debates within book history and its definition of print culture.

Books before printing

The title of this chapter is similar to *The Coming of the Book*, the title of Febvre and Martin's groundbreaking study; but it also differs from it in its concern to stress a continuity from literacy and the craft production of books to the introduction of a technology that enabled the first stages of the industrialization of that production (a process completed during the nineteenth century – at one end by the introduction of steam power, and at the other by the development of mechanical composition) (Febvre and Martin 1976). From about the sixth century AD until printing superseded the manuscript in the late fifteenth and early sixteenth centuries, books were reproduced by scribes, according to a range of conventions (Cavallo 2003). These scribes were often monks, working in monastic workshops known as *scriptoria*. Part of their work was the reproduction of the liturgical works needed for the education of novices and for worship, although they did reproduce secular texts that were also written in Latin. The texts were written onto parchment or vellum, which would be prepared by being folded into pages that would be marked, and then ruled with lines. The sheet might then be cut into pages and gathered into quires. If multiple copies were required, the text would be shared out between a number of scribes, who would each make multiple copies of his own section. Work was overseen by an intendant, the *armarius*, who furnished the scribes with parchment, pens, ink, and rulers. Copying could proceed only in daylight because the risk of fire prohibited the use of artificial light. The scribe himself would write only body text, using black ink, leaving titles, headings, and initials to be inserted in red by the *rubricator*. It is a world that has been well reproduced by Umberto Eco in his novel *The Name of the Rose* (1983).

Various styles of writing were evolved to speed up the process, and they can be assigned to a number of groups. The Uncials and half-Uncials were developed in the fourth century and were influenced by Byzantine art forms; they spread through Europe and were in use up to the twelfth century, in various national forms. The most famous example of this script is the Irish *Book of Kells*. During the eighth century, under the patronage of the Emperor Charlemagne, an attempt was made to improve the standards of writing, which led to the development of the Carolingian minuscule script that has formed the basis of most European scripts since that time. By the fourteenth century, new national letter-forms had evolved, in harmony with the Gothic style of art then prevalent in Europe. These varied in style and name, such as black letter in England, '*lettre batarde*' in France, '*fraktur*' in Germany, and '*rotunda*' in Italy. The first types were based on these letter-forms (Parkes 1999).

The great *scriptoria* of the Middle Ages, such as in the Abbey of Cluny, produced books for other cloistered monastic libraries; but, as literacy rates increased and demand for books from universities grew, a 'putting-out' system developed. This saw the emergence of commercial *scriptoria* and the *peciae* system whereby exemplar sections were distributed to a network of copyists who would each produce multiple copies of a section (Hamesse 1999). Monastic *scriptoria* experienced a revival during the fifteenth century in the work of renewed religious orders such as the Carthusians and the Brethren of Common Life; but commercial manuscript production, now also serving a market of luxury book collectors, continued to flourish in workshops like that of Vespasiano da Bisticci in Florence (Eisenstein 1979; Grafton 1999).

Particularly important manuscripts, and manuscripts commissioned by wealthy patrons, were often beautifully decorated or 'illuminated' (Febvre and Martin 1976). Illuminations consisted of three main elements: the initial, the border, and the miniature. Miniatures were not necessarily small in size, but were the pictorial element of the decoration. Initials could be decorated with flourishes or intertwining foliage, but sometimes had tiny pictures within the loops, thus being part also of the miniature. The border might surround the whole of the text on the page, but was sometimes restricted to separating the miniature from the text. The drawings forming these decorations could be colored, or could have gold or silver leaf applied. The text and decoration together formed a whole work of art: the book as collectable commodity.

Continuities and changes

The invention of printing transformed books into a tradable commodity that required, like any other, a system of production, sales, and distribution. The late medieval book trade had centered on the stationers and commercial *scriptoria* that supplied universities or luxury manuscript collectors. As such they served a fairly limited local market. The ideals of Humanism, however, and a general increase in literacy during the fifteenth and sixteenth centuries, raised the importance of literature in European culture (Grafton 1999). In response, printing made a greater variety and quantity of books available. In the long run, most enduring printing firms tended to be in commercial and trading centers rather than the intellectual centers around universities and monasteries. During the incunabula period, all the functions of printed book production were usually combined, with the cutting of punches and types, the operation of the press, and the selling of the finished product all taking place within the same firm. Early books closely resembled manuscripts (what else did the market understand?), particularly in their typography, and the decorated initials continued to be added by hand. Innovations of the sixteenth century included the use of copperplate engravings for illustrations and the change from gothic and black-letter type to roman and italic types throughout most of Europe (Müller 1994).

Early printers combined the roles of printer, publisher, and bookseller but could not do so for long even when serving a small local market. The large capital required upfront to run a print shop soon forced both a separation of responsibilities and the pursuit of wider markets. Master printers began to concentrate on the chief publishing tasks of securing financial backing from nobles, wealthy merchants, or institutions, and establishing sales networks in order to ensure survival in the trade and a sufficient return on investments. Successful printers, then, grew into publishing businesses that encouraged a division between production and selling. Famous publishers such as Manutius (Venice), Koberger (Nuremberg), and Plantin (Antwerp) built themselves into firms that, while they continued to do their own printing, also commissioned smaller printers to produce work (Eisenstein 1979).

They also created international sales structures. Traditionally, tutors had sold books to pupils, or peddlers had touted them at markets; but much higher sales figures were needed than these channels could provide. The successful publishers were those, like Koberger, who began printing stock lists, setting up branch offices in large towns and cities, attending international bookfairs, and acting as agents for other publishers. The major bookfairs in Europe were those at Antwerp, Lyons, Leipzig, and Frankfurt. Commercial privileges made these towns a focal point for all merchants, and Frankfurt, traditionally a center for the sale of manuscripts, soon became the biggest fair for printed works, too. By 1506 Koberger's business there was so good that he established a warehouse in the town to store his stock. Fairs such as Frankfurt allowed printers, publishers, and retailers to converge and take orders, exchange books, purchase equipment, and commission works. Book dealers also came to form part of the trade structure. Agents who originally did the rounds of fairs as middlemen for big publishers developed into wholesale dealers concentrating on the major events such as Lyons and Frankfurt and supplying the booksellers in big cities such as Paris (Febvre and Martin 1976).

From quite early on, printers realized that their survival depended upon efficient distribution. Local stationers had traditionally supplied scholarly Latin texts to the universities to which they were often attached, and popular readers had been served by traveling vendors, or chapmen, offering pamphlets, ballads, almanacs, and romances in the vernacular. Itinerant peddlers carrying small quantities of books continued into the eighteenth century, but they could only reach a limited market. Printers and publishers, functions carried out within the one book trade structure, required much more effective circulation of their products. The middlemen, therefore, soon became more useful as publicity agents promoting catalogs and broadsides that described a publisher's stock. Until the seventeenth century, there was little distinction between publishers and booksellers.

Trade in books increasingly took place at fairs such as that at Frankfurt, and it was here that carters made themselves available for the transportation of publishers' merchandise. Boat and wagon were the only means of moving books, which were both heavy and fragile. Consignments of books would be tied up in canvas and stashed in large wooden crates for shipment. Major publishers established warehouses at Frankfurt to keep stock between one fair and the next, while branch offices in Europe's main cities also served as distribution points. In France, Paris and Lyons could take advantage of major rivers, the Seine and the Loire, to aid distribution, while the Rhine and the Elbe carried stock through Germany (Febvre and Martin 1976). Venice was able to become the pre-eminent publishing city in Europe because its established commercial network provided such an effective distribution of stock (Lowry 1979).

The spread of printing in Europe

The innovations for which the Venetian Aldus Manutius is best known in publishing are the introduction of italic type and the use of the octavo format for the publication of pocket-sized editions of classical Greek and Latin texts (Lowry 1979). These two innovations were related: apart from any aesthetic considerations, italic type had the advantages of being narrow and condensed, which allowed the printer to make economical use of the printed area – particularly important for such small pages. The texts that Aldus issued in this format upheld the highest contemporary scholarly standards but were published in a form that made them compact and portable – as well as cheap. The edition size was a further innovation: the print run was 1,000 copies instead of the range of 100 to 250 copies (up to an absolute maximum of 500 copies) usual at that time. These small books were intended to be personal possessions and to popularize classical Greek and Latin authors and Italian poets as part of the Humanist movement. They achieved a wide circulation and had a good reputation, with the result that others soon copied them. The main center of counterfeiting was in Lyons, although the printers in France did not maintain the same high scholarly and typographical standards, in spite of obtaining some types from Aldus's type-designer, Francesco Griffo. Aldus also publicized his work through printed lists of his publications. At least three were printed, in 1498, 1503, and again in 1513. They not only listed the publications available, but also stated the minimum prices to be paid for each title. These were the first publishers' catalogs.

Yet, as Chartier notes in 'The practical impact of writing,' such advances did not come without a resistance similar to that shown to literacy itself, noted in the previous chapter (Chartier 1989b). Where some of the lower classes in society had previously been suspicious of writing because of its links to privilege and power, now some of those who enjoyed that privilege and power were antagonistic to the democratization of knowledge (and power) that printing seemed to entail. A Dominican monk, Filippo di Strata, initially persuaded the Venetian senate to restrict printing on the grounds that it multiplied corrupt texts in editions produced speedily purely for profit; it corrupted minds by making available immoral or dangerous texts to a general public without proper control by ecclesiastical authorities; and it corrupted knowledge by making it freely available to the ignorant. Chartier quotes the Venetian judgment that: 'The pen is a virgin, the printing press a whore' (Chartier 1989b: 124). The two ideas that print (and writing) had to overcome and did overcome were, on the one hand, that it represented a further means of domination and, on the other, that knowledge moving from exclusive to inclusive spheres of society was in itself a threat to the established social order.

However, the dynamic growth of printing in its first hundred years was due, in part, to the absence of the trade structures into which other professions were organized and that might have hindered its development. In the early days the novelty of printing and the fact that it employed men of such diverse skills meant that it was able to evolve outside the restraints of the medieval guild system. The guilds monopolized their particular trade within a town or region and dictated how, when, and where a man might be employed in that trade. Without this matrix, the air of free enterprise brought a rapid development of printing and allowed a proliferation of entrepreneurs to set up shop. Printing guilds only began to appear during the latter half of the sixteenth century once the trade itself had reached the stage where master printers were assuming more of a publishing and selling role – that removed them somewhat from hands-on involvement in the actual printing – and once governments began seeking control of the press. The earliest associations to include printers and publishers were the Guild of Venice, not established until 1548, and the Stationers' Company of London. The latter had represented the interests of English copyists, illuminators, and bookbinders since 1403 but did not incorporate printers and booksellers until 1556 (Feather 1988). Once established, the guilds came to represent the attempts of master printers to control a difficult workforce (Febvre and Martin 1976).

The printing workforce divided into a hierarchy: apprentices, journeymen, and master printers (Darnton 1996). As in most trades, young apprentices were indentured for two to five years into the service of a master who would provide training, food and board, clothing, and occasional payment. The apprentice would clean the workshop, run errands, prepare ink, pull the press, and ultimately learn the more skilled jobs from journeymen. A journeyman was a specialist – an apprentice who had graduated to the role of compositor, corrector, type designer, or press operator. He would move from town to town honing his skills and establishing contacts. Compositors were frequently the most skilled journeymen since they needed a good level of literacy to do their job. A journeying compositor would hope to rise to a position of head compositor in a large firm before establishing himself as a printer in his own right.

By 1500 every significant urban center in Europe could boast of at least one printing workshop (Eisenstein 1979; Müller 1994). They varied in size from the small business, comprising simply the master printer and an apprentice, to the larger ventures that could employ upward of 12 men. The businesses run by Koberger in Nuremberg and Plantin in Antwerp, each running up to 24 presses employing more than 100 men, were exceptional cases of large-scale production. The average print shop supported half-a-dozen workmen, some permanent and some journeymen. The master printer/publisher, or in larger operations a head compositor, would oversee the printing process. One or two compositors would set lines of type by selecting letters from a case and placing them in a composing stick. A finished line was then positioned in a galley tray and separated from the next by narrow strips of lead. A whole page was eventually built up as a forme that was locked into a metal frame called a chase. Compositors needed to be literate and to know Latin in order to compose well. Two men, a printer and an inker, would operate the press itself, supplied with paper by a warehouseman. Another workman might also be employed to hang wet sheets with a long stick called a 'peel' onto a drying rack suspended from the ceiling. Printers did not have huge supplies of type, so a forme would be distributed (broken up) almost immediately after printing so that its letters could be used in the next forme. Thus, a working rhythm of composition, printing, and distributing was maintained throughout a work session. If the business could afford one, a corrector or proof-reader, perhaps a local writer or student, would check copy. With workshops producing about 3,000 sheets per day, work was hard and continuous and depended upon committed teamwork.

The teamwork required to run a press created solidarity between workers that soon manifested itself in brotherhoods and committees which served to protect their interests. Master printers protected their own interests by joining or establishing guilds that sought to impose strict trade practices. Tension between workers and masters centered on disputes over pay, meals, long hours, and the overuse of unskilled apprentices by masters trying to reduce costs. Strikes were not uncommon (Darnton 1996).

Gutenberg and Germany

The application of moveable metal type to printing by Gutenberg was, in some ways, no more than the adaptation and novel application of old materials and practices (Müller 1994). Printing workshops represented a coming together of various established skills. Yet, and in spite of Darnton's early admonitions, there continues to be a residual tension between the social perspective, characteristic of book history, and the celebrity approach, typical of popular history (Darnton 1982b). Along with the screw-press, used in grape and olive pressing, the expertise of the goldsmith, the writing-master, and the woodcutter all converged to create the new technology. However, a contestant on *Jeopardy* given 'Gutenberg' is most likely to answer 'the inventor of printing.' Johannes Gensfleich zum Gutenberg had been born in the 1390s in Mainz into a bourgeois family, and his first trade was that of goldsmith. Between 1428 and 1444 he was in Strasbourg, apparently as a fugitive from disputes between patrician families and craftsmen's guilds in Mainz. While there, he experimented with the development of type: he possessed a press, and purchased a large amount of lead while working on a 'secret project' with partners. By 1448 he had returned to Mainz where he borrowed money from a lawyer, Johann Fust, to complete the work of developing a printing press. The 42-line Mainz Bible, usually attributed to Gutenberg, appeared not later than 1456; but Fust foreclosed on the printer before he could benefit financially from its publication and took possession of Gutenberg's printing equipment. Fust then went into partnership with Gutenberg's foreman, Peter Schöffer. Although it is uncertain what Gutenberg did next, it is thought that he continued to work as a printer for a while, although there are no extant printed works that bear his name. As well as the 42-line Bible, other works attributed to him include another Bible ('36-line'), some grammatical works, a papal indulgence, at least one broadside astrological calendar, and possibly the *Catholicon* of Joannes Balbus de Jannua. He seems to have stopped printing after 1460 and it is thought that he may have become blind. In 1465 he became a pensioner of the Archbishop of Mainz. He died on 3 February 1468 (Eisenstein 1979; Müller 1994).

Within a few years of its first use in Mainz, the new process for reproducing text ascribed to Gutenberg had spread throughout Europe. In Mainz itself, Fust and Schöffer had acquired the bulk of Gutenberg's materials and the business was later carried on by Schöffer's son, Johann. Johann Mentelin established a press in Strasbourg and printed a Bible in 1460 to 1461, competing with Gutenberg. Gunther Zainer was probably trained by Mentelin in Strasbourg, and was summoned to Augsburg by the Abbot of SS Ulric and Afra that was already famous for its *scriptorium*, and the first publication came from his press in 1472. During the same year, the first press to be established in Ulm was that of Johann Zainer; he may have been the brother of Gunther Zainer of Strasbourg (Febvre and Martin 1976).

Presses were soon established in other German towns. Ulrich Zell established a press in Cologne in 1464: this town was an important center of printing in north-west Germany for some years, and it was here that Caxton trained. Anton Koberger's press was active in Nuremberg from 1470. Johann Amerbach was printing in Basel from 1477, although later Zurich printers became pre-eminent in Protestant areas from 1521. Stephen Arndes of Hamburg settled in Lübeck in 1486, a town prominent in the Hanseatic League: from there printers moved on and introduced the craft to towns around the Baltic Sea (Febvre and Martin 1976). Germany possessed an efficient publication system; now it required the material and motive to issue it.

The Reformation

The Protestant Reformation of the sixteenth and early seventeenth centuries amounted to a metamorphosis in the religious imagination of Europe. It was a battle of doctrines, holy books, and modes of worship fought out in a realm of public debate that was opened up by print (Gilmont 1999). As the ideas and methods of Humanism entered Northern Europe from Italy, they provided a new body of German scholars, including Johannes Reuchlin, Sebastian Brandt, and Ulrich von Hutten, with the means to push forward the expression of widespread anti-clerical and nationalist feeling. These men used the rhetorical armory of humanist training to compose social satire and political comment that already tilted at papal authority.

When Martin Luther (1483–1546) took the stage in 1517, proclaiming the results of a humanistic re-reading of the Bible, his embryonic theology was swept into an established arena of popular unrest that was being voiced in pamphlets, books, broadsides, and woodcuts. Luther's personal rebellion was but one expression of a late medieval impulse for reform that, in trying to awaken the spirituality of the laity and revive the Gospel spirit of Christianity, criticized the hierarchy, worldly corruption, and ultimately the theology of the Roman Catholic Church. That Luther became the central personality around which a religious, social, and political revolution turned was due, in part, to the printing press.

In the past, religious innovation had either been absorbed into the church or, like Hussitism in what is now the Czech Republic, classified as heresy and all but extinguished. The mass production of books allowed the new genera-tion of reforming ideas to reach a much wider audience with much greater speed than ever before, and forced issues of reform to be debated in public. In October 1517, Luther is supposed to have followed the medieval tradition of disputation by nailing his arguments against papal indulgences to the church door in Wittenberg. From then on, however, the dispute was trans-ferred to public fora. From 1517 to 1520, printing centers such as Cologne, Nuremberg, Strasbourg, and Basel churned out over 300,000 copies of tracts by Luther, including the famous pamphlets of 1520: the *Address to the German Nobility*, the *Babylonian Captivity*, and the *Freedom of a Christian* (Febvre and Martin 1976).

Many German printers of this period were preachers or former priests with humanist educations who saw the opportunity that the new technology gave to evangelism. Through their editorial role, print became an interface between the scholarship of learned reformers and the different forms of a pre-dominantly oral and visual popular culture. In some ways this prefigured the impact of print at later dates upon oral and literate societies – for example, on the Indian sub-continent (Bayly 1996). In Bible prefaces, and in pamphlets and treatises illustrated with cartoons, sophisticated doctrinal ideas were conveyed clothed in the language, imagery, rhymes, and slogans of common people. From the pulpit, traveling evangelists armed with uniform texts could transmit reforming ideas into the ears of the people and into the taverns, town halls, homesteads, and marketplaces of Europe. At the same time, the thinking of the educated elite was reshaped and redirected by involvement in popular polemics.

The pamphlet war that raged in Germany from 1520 to 1525 made Luther famous; but in demonstrating the kind of support his ideas could inspire, it also encouraged the formerly diffident monk to think through his radical theology and to begin writing a new German translation of the Bible. Luther's notion of the 'priesthood of all believers' encouraged laypeople to bypass the clergy and interpret scripture for themselves (Gilmont 1999). Richard Baxter wrote two centuries later (1673):

> The writing of divines are nothing else but a preaching the gospel to the eye as the voice preacheth to the ear. Vocal preaching hath the pre-eminence in moving the affections, and being diversified according to the state of the congregations which attend it. This way the milk cometh warmest from the breast. But books have the advantage in many other respects. You may be able to read an able preacher when you have but a mean one to hear. Preachers may be silenced or banished, when books may be at hand. Books may be kept at a smaller charge than preachers. Books are, if well chosen, domestic, present, constant, judicious, pertinent, yea and powerful sermons, and always of very great use to your salvation.
>
> (Chartier 1989b: 124)

This viewpoint naturally led to the increased production of Bibles and devotional literature in the vernacular, as well as religious, social, and political satire. The 1520s witnessed a tenfold increase in the production of books in German. Printing, then, enabled reformers both to sustain a wide-scale attack on the abuses of the church and at the same time to supply the material with which to shape alternative forms of piety and build a new church (Eisenstein 1979).

The book played a similarly important role in the distribution of reforming ideas in the rest of Europe. Geneva and Strasbourg became significant points for the publication of Jean Calvin's ideas, while the pamphlets and Bibles of various sects were smuggled into England to propagate change (Febvre and Martin 1976). The reformers themselves were conscious of the importance of printing to their aims. Luther described the press as 'God's highest and extremest act of grace, whereby the business of the Gospel is driven forward.' The Reformation divided Europe into Catholic and Protestant branches of Christianity that were underpinned by distinct literary cultures that informed their religious practice (Gilmont 1999). The Counter-Reformation, too, came to be driven forward by the printing press as new Catholic manuals of faith became available after the Council of Trent redefined orthodoxy.

The Renaissance

During the Renaissance, those engaged in the 'study of humanity' came to be known as *umanisti* (humanists). Many early humanists were either clergy or were attached to the papal court, but the beliefs underlying humanist study embraced more than a clerical elite. On the whole, *umanisti* tended to be educated laymen – lecturers, teachers, notaries, lawyers, secretaries, and chancellors. Theirs was a civic humanism that aimed to revive ancient ideas and apply them in a contemporary setting for the moral regeneration of society. They pursued this aim through literary and rhetorical endeavor: on the one hand, translating classical texts and creating new standards of historiography and philology with which to assess the works of antiquity, and, on the other, composing poetry, ethical treatises, histories, and letters – all in both Latin and Italian (Grafton 1999).

Petrarch (1304–1374) is seen as the pivotal figure in advancing this new intellectual program, the *studia humanitatis*, that sought to improve the human condition through the study of wisdom, as found in classical authors such as Cicero, Seneca, Virgil, and Livy. In the same way that Cicero's studies had helped to transfer Greek philosophy into Roman culture, Petrarch and his followers saw their task as the recovery of ancient learning from its Gothic curfew and its infusion into Italian culture. The *studia humanitatis* championed the idea of knowledge as a virtue that bonded people in society, nurtured compassion, and civilized through education.

The reconstruction of the classical past initially involved the collation, emendation, and reinterpretation of Latin works long familiar to scholars, a process then fortified by the rediscovery of 'lost' texts in university and monastery libraries by bibliophiles such as Niccolo de Niccoli (1364–1437) and Poggio Bracciolini (1380–1459). As Greek texts became available during the Renaissance, due as much to the efforts of Aldus Manutius as any, humanist thought took on a more neo-Platonic character. In the hands of the peripatetic Dutchman Desiderius Erasmus, this new learning developed into Christian Humanism. Erasmus took the key idea of Italian Humanism – a belief in the power of reason to bring about moral reform – and combined it with the '*philosophia Christi*' that he derived from his biblical scholarship to produce a vision of simple Christian piety that had a cosmopolitan appeal. As Italian humanists had tried to restore the texts and wisdom of antiquity, Christian humanists sought to restore the texts and spirit of early Christianity. In this new guise, Humanism was more overtly critical of the abuses of the clergy, and it is in this way that the satires of men such as Erasmus paved the way for the Reformation (Grafton 1999).

Christian Humanism was transmitted through a circle of scholarly companions and trickled into the curricula of Northern European universities, inspiring Thomas More to defend the new learning as a means to 'train the soul in virtue.' The ability of Christian humanists to address and reach all Christendom depended chiefly upon a degree of intimacy with the printing press that no Italian humanist had enjoyed. During the first decade of the sixteenth century, Erasmus worked with Aldus Manutius, producing a revised edition of his *Adages* (1508), and then with the Basel printer Johannes Froben who first published his Greek New Testament (1516). As literary advisor to such publishers, Erasmus was able to influence the nature of books printed during this period. The monastic idea of the 'apostolate of the pen' was fundamental to Erasmus; but by this stage it had become an 'apostolate of the press' (Lowry 1979).

Later in the century, as the ideal of humanity united in Christian wisdom collapsed under the sundering pressures of the Reformation, Christian humanists fragmented. Some firmly joined the Protestant camp, some withdrew into radical sects, and others were recruited into the religious offensive of the Counter-Reformation. In reaction to Protestantism, evangelical Catholic reform became more organized and disciplined and in doing so acknowledged the importance of the printing press as a means of transmission. A new range of devotional literature that promoted the redefined doctrines and practices of Catholicism was produced and used by the Confraternities and new Orders to conduct campaigns that would bolster the role of the traditional church in everyday life. The most renowned of these Orders, the Society of Jesus, the Jesuits, founded colleges throughout Europe that frequently had printing houses attached to them. During the sixteenth and seventeenth centuries, politics and religion were inseparable and during this period the printing industry developed almost as a function of political and religious interests. Under Spanish rule, Antwerp became a center of Catholic publishing (the Plantin dynasty), while Jesuit protection brought Catholic domination of printing in Lyons and Paris (Febvre and Martin 1976).

Knowledge and power

Printing spread through Eastern European countries during the 1470s, reaching Buda in Hungary in 1473, Cracow in Poland, and Prague in Bohemia within the next two or three years. The year 1473 saw the first books printed in Valencia in Spain, although it was some time before the first press was established in Madrid (1499) or in Lisbon (1489).The first press in Scandinavia was that in Stockholm in 1483. Printing soon reached beyond Europe, with a press established in Constantinople in 1488, and one in the Greek town of Salonika in 1515. The earliest Greek types had been cut by Aldus Manutius in Venice during the 1490s. Printing did not reach areas that used the Cyrillic script until much later, with the first printed books not appearing in Moscow and Belgrade until the 1550s (Febvre and Martin 1976). In England, the book trade, linked with Caxton and his establishment of a press at Westminster Abbey in 1476, was initially centered on London. The concern of the Tudors to suppress seditious and heretical literature during the sixteenth century led to a compact between booksellers and the Crown. Mary granted a monopoly on printing to the London Stationers' Company in 1557 that gave them control of book production in the capital, but also prohibited printing anywhere else except at the universities of Oxford and Cambridge (Feather 1988).

Political paranoia continued to restrict printing and bookselling during the English Civil War in the seventeenth century and the Jacobite years in the early eighteenth, but underground printers were always at work in the provinces and were ready to expand once legitimate opportunities arose. The lapse of the Licensing Act in 1695 was one such opportunity that enabled jobbing printers in the provinces to establish workshops and produce local newspapers. Early provincial presses could not afford to compete in the field of book publishing, but the local distribution and advertising networks that they created were attractive to the London booksellers. During the eighteenth century a decentralized book trade infrastructure spread throughout England based on commercial contacts between London and regional centers in the Midlands and the North. The early eighteenth century also saw the Union of the Scottish and English Crowns, and with it a fresh stimulus to the relatively underdeveloped Scottish book trade. Publishers such as James Watson of Edinburgh established links with the continent; but it was the Foulis brothers who in the mid-eighteenth century made Glasgow the center of Scotland's book trade. The threat to London dominance led to the development of statutory copyright (see Chapter 4) (Feather 1988; Rose 1993).

It was not all books and pamphlets. During the early modern period, New World discoveries, new learning and new technology combined to establish a new age of map-making (Eisenstein 1979). As overseas expansion by European maritime states in the fifteenth and sixteenth centuries increased, the arts of map production and reproduction also advanced. The jealousy with which navigational knowledge and geographical discoveries were guarded during the late medieval period meant that if they were to be copied at all, contemporary manuscripts such as the famous Portuguese Cantino map had to be smuggled through channels of diplomatic and commercial espionage. Subterfuge only increased the likelihood of content distortion that was already inherent in hand-copying.

As the New World was opened up, however, the need for new and reliable maps became more apparent and cartographers seeking greater accuracy and consistency in reproduction looked to the emerging print trade. The working relationship that developed between printers and cartographers resulted in more reliable copying and a more open trade in maps, as secrecy was forsaken. Like all artists and scholars influenced by Humanism in the early modern period, cartographers looked back to classical examples and developed an inductive method. The world map of Ptolemy became the model on which fifteenth-century map-makers based their work. As partnership with printing brought maps into the public sphere, however, a more inductive method became possible and the Ptolemaic map, which featured a land-locked Indian Ocean, was gradually improved according to the advice of explorers.

During the sixteenth century the Dutch became the pre-eminent map-makers in Europe (Febvre and Martin 1976; Eisenstein 1979). The works of Gerard Mercator (1512–1594) began to make maps more user-friendly by incorporating typographical developments to make reading easier and by devising the Mercator projection to represent the curved globe on a flat surface. Abraham Ortelius published an atlas of the world, the *Theatrum*, which was continually reprinted with improvements and corrections sent in by explorers and other cartographers.

The process of producing a map was complex since there was such a variety of data to be presented. Hand-copying had allowed the depiction of a broad range of features and the inclusion of different styles and sizes of script, but could not guarantee accuracy of reproduction. On the other hand, the first maps to be printed from woodcuts in the 1470s ensured standardization but could not present fine and precise data. The use of engraved metal plates and rolling presses allowed a sharper and more delicate line, tonal variation, and variety of lettering. Such detail made maps more serviceable not only to travelers, military tacticians, and government administrators, but also to nobles or private scholars for research and flights of the imagination. Allegorical figures, sea monsters, shipwrecks, and armadas, as well as pictorial representations of historical events, decorate and embellish the maps and atlases of this period, making them more than mere reference tools.

The Enlightenment

Maps and books would have been restricted to the wealthy, individuals and institutions, or those passionate for learning. But print emerges into an overlapping private and public sphere. If the wealthy and elite did, as Chartier suggests, end up purchasing texts for consumption at home and in private, the role of print in such 'private spheres' in time began overlapping with what Jürgen Habermas famously termed the 'public sphere' (Chartier 1989b). This concept has its roots specifically in the effect of print culture (books, newspapers, pamphlets) on public debate in the Enlightenment, a period of particularly strong political ferment (Darnton 1982a and 1996). The Enlightenment is the term applied to an intellectual movement in Europe that was at its most influential during the eighteenth century. Enlightenment thinkers were often critical of contemporary society, and especially of religion, which they saw as representing the shackles of superstition that limited the human spirit. It was thought that this spirit could be freed by social progress through the application of reason to human affairs and through advances in scientific knowledge. Although reason was elevated to a greater importance than in earlier intellectual movements, feeling and emotion were not to be completely denied. Thinkers of the Enlightenment were above all critical, neither solely rational nor emotional, and concentrated on the quest for satisfactory rational and scientific explanations of social organization and of the motivations of individuals, summarized by Alexander Pope in the phrase: 'The proper study of mankind is man.'

The writers of the Enlightenment are often referred to collectively as the *philosophes*, reflecting the fact that many of them were French (Darnton 1982a and 1982b). The most prominent of them included Denis Diderot, who was the moving spirit behind *L'Encyclopédie*; Baron de Montesquieu, who wrote *De l'ésprit des lois*, which was published in 1748; Jean-Jacques Rousseau, who wrote *Emile* (1762), which expounded the notion of child-centered education, as well as the political tract *Du Contrat Sociale* (1767), with its famous opening phrase: 'Man is born free but is everywhere in chains'; and Voltaire, author of *Candide* (published in 1759). Contemporary writers of other nationalities included the Britons Jeremy Bentham, David Hume, John Locke, and Adam Smith (*The Wealth of Nations*, 1776), Germans Immanuel Kant and Gotthold Lessing, and the Italian Cesare Beccaria, among many others. The book was the vehicle for Enlightenment thought, a vehicle that crossed international borders (Darnton 1982b).

Many of the *philosophes* contributed to the monumental *L'Encyclopédie, ou Dictionnaire raisonnée des Sciences, des Arts, et des Métiers*, which was originally edited by Diderot and D'Alembert: the latter withdrew after the publication of the first seven volumes. It was published in spite of the difficulties encountered with the religious authorities, of disagreements among the collaborators, and of the expenses of its publication. *L'Encyclopédie* was published between 1751 and 1772 and ran to 35 volumes, including supplements: 12 volumes contained plates, and there were 2 index volumes. Its purposes were to make a summary of all contemporary knowledge and to show that reason was a sufficient basis upon which to rely, thus replacing religion (Darnton 1982b).

Some Enlightenment thinkers, such as Montesquieu, concentrated on political questions, such as the legitimacy of various forms of government and the appropriateness of legislation in the regulation of everyday life. Enlightenment ideas did influence some eighteenth-century sovereigns, known as the 'enlightened despots': this term refers, in particular, to Frederick the Great of Prussia (1712–1786), Joseph II of Austria (1741–1790) and Catherine the Great of Russia (1729–1796), as well as to monarchs of some smaller countries. Although they remained absolute monarchs with despotic powers, they cast themselves in the role of servant of the people, rather than that of master. This made them responsible for improving the lot of their subjects, to be achieved partly through modernization of their states and the 'science' of administration. This involved the establishment or enlargement of a bureaucracy dedicated to the rational and efficient management of government business, and might also cover social matters such as improvements in education and the abolition of restrictions, such as internal tolls, in order to promote trade. The wider development of a literate citizenship itself created a desire for knowledge that stimulated the creation, production, and distribution of new titles that, in turn, promoted the ideals of a literate citizenship and its right to knowledge.

The concept of human natural rights had its origins among the thinkers of the Enlightenment and inspired the thinkers of the French and American Revolutions at the end of the century. The influence of Enlightenment thinkers was blamed by some for the outbreak and excesses of the French Revolution, as is seen, for example, when Catherine of Russia, at one time a patron of Diderot, reversed some of her more enlightened policies. However, the ideas themselves may have been less influential than the critical habits of mind engendered by writers such as Rousseau and Voltaire, whose works were published and read throughout Europe, and from there in its colonies and outposts.

The Industrial Revolution

The Enlightenment created and reflected a spirit of rationalism and scientific enquiry that saw its practical outcomes in the implementation of new processes, particularly the substitution of human by mechanical labor, in the Industrial Revolution. The age of industrialization from the end of the eighteenth century through the nineteenth was a period in which the communication of both materials and information dramatically improved. It was also a period of urbanization in which workers and their families migrated to new industrial centers. These changes affected both the demand for and the supply of print. The improvement in transportation brought by better canals, roads, bridges, and then railways, transformed society and opened up new markets and a new range of products for print. The expanded business community, for example, required a variety of printed products for administration and advertising, while an information network, formed by the postal and telegraph systems and newspapers, created a wider society with shared interests.

With literacy levels always improving, the new urban social conditions produced demand not just for new kinds of printed matter but also for greater quantities of it. In response, the printing industry was able to take advantage of technological developments such as steam power to achieve mechanization and significantly improve manufacturing methods for practically the first time since Gutenberg (Fyfe 2012). For printing, industrialization meant the shift from hand presses to machines. The first step in this process was the replacement, in the first two decades of the nineteenth century, of the traditional wood-screw press by machines made entirely of iron, such as the Stanhope Press and later the Columbian and Albion models. These more powerful instruments were quicker and easier to work, but did not sufficiently increase the number of sheets that could be printed in an hour. The initiative towards full mechanization came from newspapers and periodicals, particularly *The Times* of London (Feather 1988). In the closing decades of the eighteenth and the beginning of the nineteenth centuries, *The Times* was the only newspaper whose circulation figures were large enough to require pursuit of the higher operational speeds that would meet production demands. It was this newspaper that sponsored the development of Koenig's steam-powered machines during the 1810s and their subsequent improvement by Applegath and Cowper during the 1820s (see Chapter 5).

Experimentation by various engineers throughout the nineteenth century meant that innovations such as rotary pressing and inking systems and stereotyping gradually became standard features. As in other industries, steps towards greater mechanization in printing brought opposition from the traditional workforce. The first steam-powered machine at *The Times* was installed in secret for fear of provoking the pressmen. Stereotyping, too, would threaten the position of compositors. Ever since the Reformation, through the Enlightenment, printing had been linked with the dissemination of radical ideas and the raising of political awareness. At the end of the eighteenth century this relationship was manifested in the role of the press in the emergence of a radical culture (Lee 1976). Pamphlets, periodicals, and newssheets championing the cause of reform all contributed to the shaping of public opinion. Tom Paine's *Rights of Man* was published in 1792, and William Cobbett's radical magazine, *Weekly Political Register*, attained a circulation of over 40,000 by 1817. As in the Reformation, the products of the radical press fed into a culture of oral communication from which reading groups, debating societies, and workshop discussions then emerged (this provides a less confrontational view of the oral/literate/print categories provided by Ong, 1982, in his general discussions, or by McKenzie, 1984, in specific relation to the Treaty of Waitangi – as related in the previous chapter).

Because of the greater degree of literacy required by their profession, print-workers were important in the transmission of radical ideas to non-readers within this oral culture. Comradeship had always been strong among print-workers, as noted above, and the brotherhoods found in early print shops had developed in England by the eighteenth century into groups known as Chapels (Feather 1988). These proto-trade unions were organizations of journeymen that controlled working practices, but also acted as a social focus and voiced workers' grievances. Radicalism encouraged the Chapels to become more organized, and the 1790s witnessed the consolidation of related bodies. The Compositors' Association was formed in 1792 and the Friendly Society of Pressmen soon followed. Thanks to the Chapels, and the trade unions that assumed their functions, the print trade was one of the first to successfully negotiate wage agreements.

In a climate of fear roused by the events of the French Revolution, Britain was severe in its suppression of working-class agitation. The Combination Acts of 1799 outlawed trade associations, and many agitators were jailed for political conspiracy. Radical publishers such as Richard Carlile fought for the freedom of the press and often found themselves imprisoned. Statutory and fiscal controls of the press – the latter termed 'taxes on knowledge' – were also introduced at this time. However, as the nineteenth century entered a period of general stability and complacency, after the Napoleonic Wars in Europe and their extensions in North America and India, the will to enforce these controls declined and they were gradually withdrawn (Lee 1976). Policing had become more difficult as communication networks became more sophisticated. Industrialization changed not only practices in the workshops and culture in the towns and cities, but also meant that printing became less centered on London as better transportation of goods and people allowed provincial presses to become established.

The long nineteenth century

The nineteenth century saw a revolution in publishing. Industrialization of most of the book production process meant lowered costs and an increase in output. Inventions such as the steam-powered press, mechanical typecasting and setting, stereotyping, and innovations in the reproduction of illustration ensured that book production was more efficient and much, much faster. Industrialized societies across the world saw the need for a better-educated, certainly literate, workforce to service new processes and occupations. The Education Acts cemented the growth of literacy in Britain so that by the end of the nineteenth century the vast majority of the population constituted the market for books (Feather 1988). Book publishing became a boom industry. Competition grew between the established printers and booksellers, and as they expanded and consolidated, they became the publishing houses that were to dominate the trade until the second half of the twentieth century and beyond.

The book trade benefited from enhanced networks of communication and distribution, improved roads, telephones, and railways: these meant that provincial publishers could manage their businesses on an equal footing with those in London. The increased populations in Europe and the USA (during the nineteenth century, Europe's population doubled and the USA's increased fifteen-fold) provided an eager audience for books and magazines (Fischer 2003). Books were required for reading on train journeys, in the new state schools, in libraries, and for information in new trades brought about by industrialization (this will be discussed further in Chapter 6).

The idealism and the 'love of books' that had characterized a few publishers before the nineteenth century gave way, in part, to a more focused commercialism and viable business aims. More and more titles were published and publishers' niche subjects grew in diversity. In Britain roughly 100 new titles were published each year up to 1750, growing to 600 by 1825, and to 6,000 by the beginning of the twentieth century (at its close, new titles topped the 100,000 mark) (Feather 1988). The professionalization of publishing and of the book trade, in general, was also marked in the formation of the Publishers' Association (PA), the Booksellers' Association, the Society of Authors, and, through the agency of the new PA, in the drawing-up of the Net Book Agreement (Feltes 1986). The role of the author was buttressed by the rise of the literary agent. This is discussed more fully in the next chapter; however, it is perhaps worth stressing at this point that Bourdieu's discussion of the 'field of cultural production' seems most appropriate in a nineteenth- or twentieth-century setting (Bourdieu 1993).

The mid-nineteenth century saw the birth of the popular series, large quantities of books published at low prices and intended for mass consumption: 'Literature for the Millions.' Thirteen hundred titles were published of George Routledge's 'Railway Library' of novels, priced at one shilling each, well within the range of most pockets. Many of these series were reprints, made cheaper by the fact that they had gone out of copyright and no royalties had to be paid. Through the commercial acumen of the publishing houses, print culture reached its apogee (Sutherland 1976).

Intellectual property rights

Yet, as it did so, it also began to move from the physical transport of books to the sale of rights in a text, for reproduction, translation, adaptation – for the theater or for new media such as cinema or radio – and merchandizing – as in the case of the Sherlock Holmes stories that generated a range of products. This transition from the central importance of the book as material object to that of the text as source was based on a secure and enforceable regime of international statutory rights.

By the middle of the sixteenth century, as we have seen, the printing trade in England was effectively controlled by the Stationers' Company. The perpetual right to print a work, and the benefits which followed, were limited to the copy-holder, usually the printer, who bought the work from its author or compiler. Although it was possible to protect a printer's rights to a text by entry in the register of the Stationers' Company, the fact of first publication secured the copyright for many books, even if it was a pirate edition, produced without payment to the originator or the purchaser of copyright. The rights to print some particularly lucrative works, such as the Bible, liturgical books, and some standard schoolbooks, were restricted to a narrow group of printers and were regarded as valuable properties to be traded and inherited.

The first UK Copyright Act of 1709 established that the copyright in a work belonged to its author. The reasons behind this change are discussed in more detail in the following chapter (Foucault 1984; Rose 1993). The effect of the change was to permit some authors to command greater sums when selling their works to publishers – although outright sale of copyright remained a more common arrangement for some time, rather than profit share or royalty agreements. The publication of books on subscription, a popular method of financing publication before 1709, also remained popular. However, while copyright could be enforced within the one country, it did not have any international status. In terms of English-language publishing, this resulted in a lively and largely unchecked piracy of British works in the USA that enraged popular authors such as Dickens. The latter, indeed, lent his name and energy to campaigns for the cross-Atlantic recognition and regulation of copyright on lines already being established within Europe. This lobbying was eventually successful, but not until after Dickens's death in 1870. International copyright protection was established and maintained through treaties such as the Berne Convention of 1886 and the Universal Copyright Convention of 1952. A new UK Copyright Act in 1911 acknowledged the potential of other media than print by extending the protection of copyright to other forms of expression and production. This, in turn, provided a secure basis both for the development of those media and for the adaptation of an author's work for a number of media.

The growth of the paperback

As rights originating in the book began at the beginning of the twentieth century to be exploited across a number of popular media such as the cinema or radio, publishers sought a means of appealing to the mass audiences that the new media had revealed. Allen Lane launched the innovative and pioneering Penguin brand of paperbacks in 1935. Inspired by Albatross paperback reprints that were popular on the European Continent, and dismayed by the lack of reading matter available to him on train journeys, Lane devised the Penguin series (McCleery 2002). Although thought of as 'cheap and cheerful,' Penguins enjoyed high standards of layout and typography for their original cover price of sixpence. Indeed, some first editions of Penguins have become collector's items, prized for their excellence of design. Pundits were skeptical on initial publication. Booksellers feared a reduction in profits compared with hardcover editions, and while Lane gambled on the buyers' tastes, initial print runs were high in order to keep the unit cost of production, and therefore retail price, as low as possible. However, Penguins represented good 'value for money.' Lane's gamble paid off. Penguin became a near-synonym for quality paperback publishing. Penguin, which in the 1930s had represented a risky experiment in the popularization of the book, today constitutes a multi-million-pound business within the Pearson group of companies.

The paperback revolution crossed the Atlantic, where US companies infused book design and marketing with a greater degree of dynamism and brashness. Penguin itself opened an American branch shortly before World War II. The latter conflict was an important moment in the democratization of reading and the book, both fiction and non-fiction. Armies realized the need for a literate soldiery, educated in the principles of what they were fighting for and able to take up the role of active citizens upon the cessation of hostilities. The GI Bill of Rights in the USA and the post-war expansion of the universities in the UK were a continuation of this acknowledgment of the individual's right to, and society's need for, education. Paperbacks provided inexpensive vehicles for knowledge that could inform that education, formal and informal. Many other publishers began to produce paperbacks, and by the 1950s they were an unremarkable sight on bookshelves and in bookshops around the world. Illustrative of every conceivable subject, paperbacks were desirable and affordable to all. Indeed, the proliferation of paperbacks is said to have converted those who would borrow books from libraries into purchasers of books, creating a boom in the publishing and information industries. This new reading public created a market for new writing and rejuvenated many of the industries connected with book buying: retailing, marketing, and design all benefited. Paperback books found their way into all walks of life and were sold in new contexts: drug stores (in the USA), supermarkets, airports, and street vendors among them (West 1985).

Traditionally, paperback books were reprints of hardcover titles, which had been successful and were ready to find a larger audience. However, some publishers, particularly of literary fiction, now publish their first editions in paperback, which keeps down costs and enables the work to be disseminated to the largest possible audience. In academic publishing, it is quite usual for the hardback and paperback editions of a title to be published simultaneously: the hardcover edition for use in public and university libraries, and the paperback edition for the student's own use. The book you are reading now follows this pattern (unless you have the e-book edition).

The late twentieth century and beyond

During the latter half of the twentieth century, publishing houses came together through merger and acquisition to form large, often transnational conglomerates (Greco 1995, 1996). Three factors lay behind this movement: an awareness of the international nature of the publishing industry and the opportunities for transnational marketing of products; the need to exploit products across a number of media, including film and television; and the general under-capitalization of smaller independent houses. Two types of conglomerate emerged: one which was primarily print based and operating in a number of different countries – for example, the German-based Bertelsmann; and the other operating in different media, of which book publishing was only one and not necessarily the most important – for example, News Corporation's ownership of HarperCollins. The formation of such conglomerates was not always regarded as benign. Often the exercise involved little more than asset-stripping of imprints, authors, backlist, and staff. Some authors reacted adversely to a loss of intimacy in their relationship with editors, while others welcomed the more effective exploitation of their work. There was a general perception of tension between the creative aspects of publishing and the need, driven from the central management, to meet common profit targets (Schiffrin 2001). The failure to achieve the latter led to the disappearance of long-established imprints and regionally or nationally important publishers. However, the creative side of publishing continued to thrive through the ongoing

foundation of smaller independent firms, often on the part of former employ-
ees of the conglomerates. Bookselling also saw during this period the growth
of transnational chains, some of which formed part of larger media or publishing conglomerates. The loss of the dominance of print, its institutional
dilution within the multimedia conglomerates, the globalization of information
and culture, itself based on the exploitation of secure intellectual property
rights: all of these factors have led to a questioning of the future of the book, a
topic to be treated in more detail in our final chapter.

Conclusion

This has been a long chapter. Its substance, the production and distribution of
printed books, has, however, been at the core of book history and of defining
debates over the relationship between that production and distribution and its
social context. From a purely internal perspective, that context consisted of
both the adaptation and development of structures already in existence for
manuscripts and the creation of new structures that suited the rapid spread of
printing. From an external perspective, this context consisted of, on the one
hand, the relationship between printing and great social, cultural, and political
movements of ideas such as the Reformation, Renaissance, and Enlightenment
and, on the other, the relationship between printing structures and the institutions of power – state and church. While the nature of those relationships
remains the source of lively controversy, as we saw in Chapter 1, they are
crucial to book history and its ability to provide a cogent analysis of the near
past, as we will see in Chapter 7.

Points to ponder

Here are some key questions to ponder as you reflect on the themes discussed
so far. Analogies are often drawn between print encyclopedias, such as the
original French *L'Encyclopédie* or the *Encyclopaedia Britannica*, and an online
information source such as Wikipedia. What are the major similarities and
differences between the two? If distribution of the physical book moved from
rivers and waterways to rail in the nineteenth century, then how were printed
books distributed in the twentieth century? Are contemporary books purely
functional or can you find examples that would rank alongside the best monastic
manuscripts in terms of their aesthetic appeal?

4

AUTHORS, AUTHORSHIP, AND AUTHORITY

Introduction

This chapter looks at how concepts of authorship have changed and developed over the past 1,000 years. It examines medieval definitions of authorship. Within the context of that period, when the production of manuscripts was based mainly in religious or ecclesiastical settings, 'authors' were often seen as reproducers, compilers, annotators, or commentators. We will examine how the introduction of printing from the 1450s onward redefined authorship as a more creative activity that could lead to individual fame and some fortune. We will also discuss the place of patronage in supporting and shaping textual production. The chapter then moves to consider the question of copyright, and how the introduction of copyright laws from the 1700s onward changed how authors were paid and what they did. We will also briefly cover the effect of nineteenth-century industrialization on authorship, and how new players (such as literary agents) and technological innovations changed the contexts in which authors operated. From this, the chapter progresses to a brief survey of twentieth-century critical interpretations of authorship that have been central to book history studies. It concludes with comments on redefinitions of authorship resulting from the onset of the digital era.

Manuscript culture and the 'author'

Past scholarly thinking has suggested the separation of the evolution of manuscript culture (and its conception of the 'author') in Western Europe into two distinct periods – the 'Monastic Age' and the 'Secular Age' – with the first running from circa 400 AD to the late 1100s AD, and the second evolving from the end of the twelfth century through to the late fifteenth century (and even beyond) (Thomas 1976: 15). From the fall of the Roman Empire in the fifth century AD through to the twelfth century (when the establishment of universities and seats of learning began to challenge such centers of power), monasteries and religious centers held a near monopoly on the production of texts in Western Europe. As noted in earlier chapters, intellectual life was focused on ecclesiastical centers, and manuscripts were produced in line with religious interest in upholding the authority of the church and its teachings. Monastic orders reserved portions of each day for intellectual endeavor and the copying and illuminating of sacred texts. The monastic *scriptoria* or *scriptorium*, in which such work has often been depicted taking place, came to symbolize the essence of medieval culture, 'where copyists, rubricators, and illuminators joined together in pious labor, meticulously copying the word of God' (Taylor 1999: 353).

Such centers could be highly organized in nature, with particular spaces reserved for different aspects of manuscript production, ranging from lettering to calligraphy and illumination work, and specific tasks assigned to individual members of the order. But as Andrew Taylor and others point out, such generalizations can be misleading, for in reality a monastic *scriptorium* often referred to a group of writers, rather than to the space they occupied: some monasteries did not have special rooms set aside for such work, and often monks working on manuscripts were to be found occupying individual spaces scattered round the cloister (Knowles 1950, vol 2: 520–522; Ker 1960: 3–11; Eisenstein 1979, vol 1: 14–15; Taylor 1999: 354).

There is evidence that, from the eleventh century onward, monasteries farmed out work to professional 'scriveners' or scribes hired for the purpose. The German Benedictine monks of Saint Emeric, Tegernsee, and Scheyern, for example, regularly employed professional scribes to transcribe both ecclesiastical and secular texts, ranging from sermons, theological and liturgical works to encyclopedias. This farming-out of piece work accelerated as demand increased for teaching texts in the 'Secular Age' from the universities newly established in places such as Bologna, Paris, Leuven, Basel, Cambridge, and Oxford. The demand soon outstripped monastic capacity to provide texts and spawned a separate commercial book industry, with booksellers providing (among their many services), *peciae*, or original, exemplar texts for students and interested laypeople to rent and copy from.

The foundation of universities from the late twelfth and early thirteenth centuries accelerated the development of a new reading public interested in a wider range of texts than previously produced. Initially, many of these were clerics, attached to their chosen university or college, who along with their professors required texts of classical authors, references, commentaries, and glosses. Universities sought to establish libraries to cater for student demand, and along with this established university-based workshops to cope with the demand for copies of essential works.

At the same time, the rise in the thirteenth century of a reading public drawn from the emerging bourgeois classes – chief among them lawyers, state officials, successful merchants, and doctors – created a demand for the production of texts in areas such as law, politics, science, and medicine, as well as other works of a recreational, popular, and edifying nature (literary works, romances, translations, poetry, and the like). The resulting outpouring of secular 'humanistic' works contrasted with the predominant number of texts reproduced during the 'Monastic Age,' which were religious in nature but also included texts of certain ancient Latin authors, such as Ovid, Virgil, Boethius, and Priscian, who were granted special authority (*auctoritas*) by medieval scholars, and so reproduced accordingly within these ecclesiastical settings.

Authority and the role of the author

With regard to textual production during the thirteenth century, the Franciscan St. Bonaventure argued that the act of writing books (or, in this case, manuscript texts), could be separated into four categories:

> One person writes material composed by other people, adding and changing nothing; and this person is said to be merely the scribe [*scriptor*]. Another one writes material composed by others, joining them together but adding nothing of his own; and this person is said to be the compiler [*compilator*]. Another one writes both materials composed by others and his own, but the materials composed by others are the most important materials, while his own are added for the purpose of clarifying them; and this person is said to be the commentator [*commentator*], not the author. Another one writes both his own materials and those composed by others, but his own are the most important materials and the materials of others are included in order to confirm his own; and this person must be called the author [*auctor*].

> (Wogan-Browne et al 1999: 3)[1]

Bonaventure's arguments proceeded from a very specific scholarly context; he presented scribal authors as individuals working mainly with particular texts in conjunction with others. The act was often difficult (gathering together scarce handwritten manuscript sources to create new interpretations of human activity), and practiced by an elite few. Bonaventure's categories focused on the mechanical reproduction of thought and idea. They did not consider important what our society now finds central to writing – namely, creative, imaginative literature, information provision and intellectual interpretation. It was a reflection of an elite viewpoint that saw textual production as a task carried out within the confines of the Catholic Church and ecclesiastical establishments (Minnis 1988; Brown 1995: 197–206; Kuskin 1999; Taylor 1999: 353–365).

Others had different ideas as to what written and textual production could stand for in the medieval period. Witness Chaucer's famous verse addressed to his 'scribe' Adam Scriveyn, one of the most frequently cited English medieval commentaries on the role of the scribe and the genesis of texts, in which he laments his copyist's tendency to haste and his lack of control in accurately reproducing literary manuscript texts:

> Adam *scriveyn*, if ever it thee bifalle
> *Boece* or Troylus to wryten newe,
> Under thy long lokkes thou most have the scalle,
> But after my makyng thow wryte more trewe;
> So ofte a daye I mot thy werke renewe,
> It to corecte and eke to rubbe and scrape
> And al is thorugh thy neglygence and rape.[2]

Chaucer is the 'authority' here (rather than the church) who tasks his copyist/scribe with maintaining high standards of accuracy, reproducing his words as he originally intended them. On the other hand, Chaucer's verse highlights and adheres to the model of authorship shared amongst medieval contemporaries of a participant in an ongoing intellectual tradition linked to past authorities (Boethius). Authorship in Chaucer's time, as the editors of an anthology on Middle English literary theory argue, 'was more likely to be understood as participation in an intellectually and morally authoritative tradition, within which ... a writer might fill one of several roles, copying, modifying, or translating, as well as composing' (Wogan-Browne et al 1999: 4–5). Authors (or *auctors*) were understood to be individuals who *reshaped* material for their purposes, originating material that glossed on and linked to other material in the same intellectual sphere of activity. They were not 'authors' in the post-Romantic conception of creative artists/geniuses, given that in most cases they did not have ultimate ownership of the texts on which they worked and reshaped.

At the same time, 'authority' was something that could reside in a text independent of its link with an 'author.' Medieval references to material by Ovid, St. Augustine, and others, for example, did not associate or attribute veracity or truth in the work to the creative genius of the individual author, but rather assigned 'authority' to the truth of the text itself. As some commentators have perceptively noted: 'Well into the early modern period it was age, authenticity and conformity with truth, not individual genius, that was thought to confer authority on texts and authors' (Wogan-Browne et al 1999: 6).

Authors in the Renaissance period

Interpretations of what an 'author' did and stood for in Western Europe changed in the Renaissance period. This was due mainly to the reproducibility of printed texts: the shift from circulation of transcribed manuscripts in small numbers to printed reproduction in large quantities from the late fifteenth century onwards. Writing became an individualized activity, a potential source for recognition and social advancement. As Febvre and Martin (1976) point out: 'While in the Middle Ages authors had had little interest attaching their names to a work, printers were led to seek out, or have sought out, the true identity of the authors of the works they printed – where, that is, they didn't invent it.' The result of attaching a name to a text was critical evaluation, recognition, and in some cases an enhanced reputation. It accelerated interest and desire in some to seek fame, if not fortune, from such work. Febvre and Martin (1976: 261) conclude: 'This new kind of stimulus was also the sign of a new age when artists began to sign their works, and authorship takes on an altogether new significance.' It would be a point reiterated by Elizabeth Eisenstein several years later: 'The "drive for fame" itself,' she concurred, 'may have been affected by print-made immortality' (Eisenstein 1979, vol 1: 121).

Printing engaged textual producers in a manner that was different from previous scribal activity, undermining long-established concepts of collective authority. The same principles of individualized authorial activity applied to those whose works were drawn from other media. British playwrights, for example, benefited from the active market in printed plays which coincided with the professionalization of the London stage in the 1500s: the result, as Douglas Brooks argues, was a commodification of playwriting which, in turn, fed and intensified the 'preoccupation with individualized authorial agency' (Brooks 2000: xiv). Printers perceived the commercial possibilities of printed plays displaying the 'presence' of an 'author,' whose authentication of 'authoritative texts' could then be used to enhance their market value. Such actions underscored how printing in the early Modern period shifted the ground to enable authorship to be viewed as an individual activity, completing, as Mark Rose comments, 'the transformation of the medieval *auctor* into the Renaissance *author*' (Rose 1993: 18).

Such transformation realigned authorial interests and activity. It is generally acknowledged that the concept of copyright as a representation of authorial ownership of intellectual property did not prevail until the late eighteenth and nineteenth centuries, when it was aggressively implemented in Britain, France, and Germany, among other places. Scholars, however, have pointed out examples of nascent concepts of literary ownership from the early 1500s onwards, linked to legal recognition of individual rights to patents on inventions (Eisenstein 1979, vol 1: 120; Rose 1993: 16–18; Brown 1995: 1–8). Among the earliest cases recorded in France were two in 1504, the first involving Guillaume Cop, a well-known Parisian doctor responsible for the compilation of an annual almanac, who successfully obtained an injunction against a bookseller in March 1504 to prevent him issuing copies of the almanac without Cop's authorization and authentication. The ruling was significant in its acknowledgment of the value of attaching Cop's signature and name to this textual product. 'In a sense, then,' Mark Rose comments, 'what Cop was securing was as much a right having to do with the use of his name as a right to a text' (Rose 1993: 18–20). Two months later the poet André de la Vigne

71

secured the right to print and sell an anthology of poetic works by him and others as a result of a printer's attempt to reprint an unauthorized version of the book. Such cases, as Cynthia J. Brown notes, signaled a shift in perceptions about the role of creators of texts in a commercial environment. '"Authors" had become marketable commodities outside the courtly circle of wealthy benefactors,' Brown notes, 'and new participants in book production – the printer, the publisher, and eventually a different, more expanded reading public – were crucial determinants in an author's involvement in determining the physical and literary makeup of their books.' She concludes that these and other such legal moves by late medieval writers signaled an important shift in textual production patterns: 'Indeed, the hierarchical triad of patron, poet, and scribe that characterized the manuscript culture evolved into a more balanced sharing of authority in the association of patron, poet, and publisher in the print culture' (Brown 1995: 2).

Such cases also highlighted the fact that, with the advent of legal structures supporting mercantilist exploitation of commodities (and texts), and the subsequent weakening of the ecclesiastical monopoly on 'knowledge,' publishers and booksellers in most Western European capital cities were in a position to capitalize on textual production, and often sought to maintain their legal claim to exploit and market successful printed material. Once authors submitted their work to the production process, though, invariably they lost control over it. But, as Mark Rose points out, an aspect of the literary market was still within the general control of the author: 'Authors may not have owned their texts, but they did of course own their manuscripts, the physical objects they had made with their own hands or caused to be made, and for these objects both the booksellers and the theatrical companies provided a market. The author's claim, however, ceased with the transfer of the manuscript' (Rose 1993: 17–18).

Patronage

Prior to the market changes of the late eighteenth century instigated by authorial use of copyright, the general pattern of exchange for authors was within a highly structured patronage system developed throughout the medieval period as part of the evolution of manuscript culture. 'Authors' operated within particular courtly circles of wealthy benefactors whereby, 'through a complex set of symbolic and material transactions, patrons received honor and status in the form of service from their clients, and in return provided both material and immaterial rewards' (Rose 1993: 16; see also Brown 1995: 2).

Of course, patronage for writers and poets was not original to the medieval period: there is evidence, for example, of elitist literary circles operating under the protection of powerful aristocratic and political figures in Roman times from 250 BC through to 200 AD and afterwards. Literary 'micro-milieus,' as

Henri-Jean Martin denotes them, could be found grouped around figures such as Scipio Africanus (235–183 BC), or Precia and Lesbia (during the first century BC), or the Roman knight Maecenas, patron of Horace (Martin 1995: 99).

Patrons functioned to commission, protect, encourage, and, in many cases, control literary production. Authors without an independent source of income would seek a link with a relevant patron to further their careers and financial position. Throughout the fourteenth and fifteenth centuries, in particular, the patronage system was widely in operation and functioned as a 'gift exchange economy' where authors dedicated or presented works to potential courtly or elite sponsors (kings, knights, princes, noblemen and noblewomen), in the hopes of securing a financial gift in return, and/or securing a sinecure post within the sponsor's household or social and political circles (Mauss 1954; Macherel 1983).

The system also co-existed alongside a 'market economy': securing a dedication to an important sponsor would guarantee a popular success for an author's composition and work, a significant consideration, particularly from the sixteenth century onward, when Western European authorial interaction with publishers and booksellers over the printing and sale of their texts increasingly involved assessments of their financial worth and potential (Febvre and Martin 1976: 25; Davis 1983; Macherel 1983: 151; Brown 1995: 106–107). Yet, as late as the 1740s, in the face of a changing marketplace for textual production, authors were still seeking and gaining benefits from powerful patrons. The English poet James Thomson, for example, worked for several years as a tutor to the children of various obscure English and Scottish aristocrats before securing a pension from Frederick, Prince of Wales, in 1738, and a sinecure post as surveyor-general of the Leeward Islands from Lord Lyttelton in 1744 (the latter position paid UK£300 a year and entailed virtually no exertion on Thomson's part). Or there is the case documented by Robert Darnton of Jean-Baptiste-Antoine Suard, who arrived in Paris during the 1750s in his 20s, intent on making his career in literary circles. Over the next 40 years, Suard carefully cultivated contacts amongst the elite, including the Abbé Raynal, members of the aristocracy and high-placed political ministers, and rose to hold significant sinecure posts (such as royal censor and literary correspondent to the Margrave of Bayreuth). He was duly elected to the Académie Française (an honor which came with a generous annual income). As Darnton concludes, Suard rose through French cultural circles despite producing little prose or verse – living on sinecures and pensions, but not on book sales. 'In fact, he wrote little and had little to say – nothing, it need hardly be added, that would offend the regime. He toed the party line of the philosophes and collected his reward' (Darnton 1982a: 7).

Such cases point to an aspect of patronage that suited the unambitious but could frustrate the energetic author. Patronal links could lead to the subordination of an 'author' and a loss of intellectual independence: often, poets and other sponsored writers were required to compose material reflecting and promoting their patrons' interests, or were specifically commissioned to create and undertake work for particular purposes. In 1369, for example, French King Charles V, who supported numerous translators, set one of them, Nicole Oresme, the task of translating Aristotle's works on politics, economics, and ethics, which he accomplished by 1372. The purpose was to provide reading material to enable Charles V to steer his advisers and state officials into supporting particular political reforms modeled on Aristotelian models. The situation had changed little by the eighteenth century: many notable English authors (individuals such as Joseph Addison, Richard Steele, William Congreve, Edward Gibbon, and Samuel Johnson) pursued independent literary interests through such channels as the burgeoning London periodical press, but frequently found their independence compromised by their holding of government posts and royal pensions because, as John Brewer notes, 'most writers supported by the crown were expected to pen political polemics in favour of the king's ministers' (Brewer 1997: 163).

The results created tensions between authorial interests and practical material considerations: texts had to be framed in a manner likely to attract and retain patronal interest and political approval. As Cynthia Brown concludes, authors often had to compromise morally and creatively to carve out a living. 'In the patronage system, then, the author's writing represented his personal rendition of the patron's desires, needs, or image, inspired either by some form of commission or by the hope of obtaining one' (Brown 1995: 106). Not all critics have viewed patronage in such implied negative terms, though. Raymond Williams, for example, argued that, in contrast to the ruthless workings of a 'literary market' tied to the uncertainties of 'popular taste,' the patronage system often offered a benign, positive environment in which writers (favored ones, it was implicitly understood) could flourish. 'Under patronage,' he comments, 'the writer had at least a direct relationship with an immediate circle of readers, from whom, whether prudentially or willingly, as mark or as matter of respect, he was accustomed to accept and at times to act on criticism. It is possible to argue that this system gave the writer a more relevant freedom than that to which he succeeded' (Williams 1966: 50).

Patrons, publishers, and the public

The role of the patron shifted as the rise of mechanical print production encouraged the development of financially viable printed works during the sixteenth and seventeenth centuries. Booksellers and printers joined nobles and courtly figures as potential 'patrons,' signaling the shift in patronage from that of commissioning and controlling to that of promoting, consuming, and distributing. In the late eighteenth century, the additional development of a vocal periodical press operating with varied degrees of success and levels of censorship in major European capitals offered an additional avenue for textual production. Publishers with established 'houses' of operation frequently adopted the function of literary patron, sponsoring authors to create particular works, setting up literary salons and societies in which professional and social reputations could be established and/or enhanced, and developing newspaper and periodical publications in which anonymous, pseudonymous, or on occasion signed articles and work could feature. Writers vied for the attention of important figures in the printing and publishing world in order to gain interest in their work and entry into these 'literary fields' of activity. Courtly patronage was slowly replaced by more economically driven, market-oriented patronage.

Likewise, throughout the eighteenth and well into the nineteenth centuries, patronage roles were assumed by educational and intellectual societies, as well as informal literary circles and salons. They were part of the social and cultural shifts in the patronage system that grew to encompass 'the support of a writer by a person or institution that protects him but that, in return, expects satisfaction of the cultural need' (Escarpit 1971: 38). Even today we see vestiges of such patronal systems in state-sponsored positions, such as national Poet Laureates. While such social and market-driven patronage functioned as part of an evolving 'professionalization' of authorial activity, contemporaries often complained about the sense of alienation they felt and the fragmented nature of the work they were forced to undertake in eking out a living through writing. In Britain and elsewhere, the 'Grub Street' hack (so called after the London street in which many writers 'for hire' maintained offices and rooms) became an enduring metaphor and image, encapsulating the soulless undertakings of the eighteenth- and nineteenth-century wordsmiths paid piecemeal for the number of words they produced daily. 'Without means and control,' as John Brewer and Iain McCalman comment, the result was that:

> ... writers became manufacturers of components in the factory of literature. Such fragmentation undermined the integrity of writers, who came to bear only a marginal relation to the works they helped to produce. What they wrote was not properly theirs: it was designed by another and had value only as part of a larger whole. They had no vested interest in the completed work, for it was not a thing they could or might wish to acknowledge as their own. Writers were not authors but protean figures whose value lay in their ability to assume a number of authorial roles.
>
> (Brewer and McCalman 1999: 106)

Authors, copyright, and payments

The rise of a reading public during the late eighteenth century (with interests in and ability to pay for printed works) was also a factor in this system change, which created circumstances where authors moved from creating works with a view to soliciting funds and support from a given patron, to seeking publication through subscription and advance payment schemes. Under such schemes, authors or printer/publishers solicited advance payments from interested readers to cover publishing and production costs. This would subsequently give way to general commercial publishing practices associated with current systems of authorial interaction (royalty payments, for example, on copies sold).

Subscription publishing functioned for many years as one of the single most important methods (after patronage) of securing publication for prose and verse works. In Britain, volume subscription rose swiftly during the late 1600s and until the 1730s, maintained a steady level throughout the middle of the century, then rose again during the last 20 years of the eighteenth century. Works subscribed in this fashion ranged from poetry, sermons, histories, medical texts, and advice manuals to biographies, mathematical works, music books, and other non-literary texts.

Other methods of rewarding authors included the half-profits system, where authors agreed to share the risk of publication with a view to receiving 50 per cent of the income generated by book sales (after costs had been deducted). This was commonly used throughout the eighteenth and nineteenth centuries, but sometimes led to abuse by publishers who, through misleading accounting and inflation of distribution and production costs, could emerge with more profit at the expense of the author. A second method that had been in use since the start of printing was that of the publisher or bookseller buying the copyright outright from the author at a fixed price. Under this system the author had no recourse to further sums for reprints should the work prove successful. A third method frequently utilized, following the implementation and defense of authorial copyright interests in the nineteenth century, was the purchase by the publisher of the copyright for an agreed number of years or number of editions, following which the rights reverted to the author. Finally, there was the implementation of the royalty system, which established itself during the nineteenth century in the wake of strong legal action and concerted pressure from interested parties.

Copyright, or the exclusive right to print a particular text, developed mainly as a result of eighteenth-century legal battles in Britain between English and Scottish booksellers. The concept of an 'author' who could control his or her work for financial gain was something which came into its own in the late eighteenth and nineteenth centuries as the resulting legal linkage of copyright to artistic endeavor. But copyright, in the sense of exclusive control over the proceeds and process of the printing of texts, is something that was part of the printing process from the late fifteenth century onward. Febvre and Martin (1976) note some of the first instances of demand for copyright occurring in Italy during the late fifteenth century: there are legal records of Milanese publishers and printers seeking and being granted exclusive copyright privileges as early as 1481 (when Andrea de Bosiis secures publishing rights to Jean

Simoneta's *Sforziade*) and 1483 (when the Duke of Milan issues a five-year privilege to Petrus Justinus of Tolentino for rights to print Francesco Filelfo's *Convivium*). French records show much activity in the sixteenth century, with privileges regularly sought from and bestowed by the king, parliament, and the local courts. Similarly, sixteenth-century printers in Germany received copyright privileges from the Emperor and local authorities. In both Germany and France, such privileges were often used as a means of controlling press production and the type of material emanating from such businesses (Febvre and Martin 1976: 241; Darnton 1982a, 1996).

The renewal of such rights and privileges in profitable titles (some concessions could last up to 30 years) was highly contentious and frequently contested. As Febvre and Martin point out: 'In principle privileges could be given for the reprinting of old books as well as for the printing of new ones, and publishers who enjoyed royal favour therefore sought to renew their monopolies indefinitely, while the government at the same time tended to favour the most orthodox and most tractable publishers' (Febvre and Martin 1976: 241). This often led to powerful monopolies that made it difficult for newcomers to break in and establish credibility in the printing, publishing, or bookselling business.

In Britain, legal skirmishes over similar publishing and printing privileges and monopolies led to the 1710 Statute of Anne, which invested authors and their representatives with ownership rights in printed works for set periods (14, then 21 years, or 28 if the author was still living). Further strengthening of such individual rights was the result of a landmark battle in 1774 between a Scottish bookseller and an English bookseller. The case was argued with the legal help of James Boswell, the literary recorder of Samuel Johnson's life and a Scottish barrister when literary interests were not occupying his time, and settled in the Chancery courts of London. It established the legal precedents and concepts of individual ownership of rights in texts subsequently adopted in international interpretations of copyright.

Donaldson *versus* Becket centered on the right of Alexander Donaldson, an Edinburgh bookseller, to reprint certain texts (at a cheaper price) originally published in London, and in which London booksellers claimed they owned sole and perpetual rights to reprint (thus driving away potential competition). The legal suit threatened the monopoly held by English (mainly London-based) booksellers/publishers to retain sole rights in reprinting authors' works that they had purchased. The monopoly was one that had originated from the structured guild organization of London-based booksellers in the mid-1500s, which became known as the Stationers' Company. A royal charter in 1557 granted the company a monopoly on printing: only those who were entered as members of the Stationers' Company guild or who held particular printing patents had the right to both print books and make copies of them.

While initially the purpose of the royal charter had been to enable more effective government control over what was issued from English presses, ensuing interpretations expanded the matter to involve national exclusivity in reproduction rights – that is, a move to create 'perpetual copyright' in saleable texts. The move involved a shift in interpreting the value of texts – from one where they were seen as actions, valued for what they could represent, their ability to expose injustices or to be used to curry favor for the 'author,' to one where they were seen as things, items of property with a tangible market value. As Mark Rose concludes: 'Thinking of texts as actions, valuing them for what they could do, was commensurate with the regulatory system in which censorship and the privileges of booksellers were conflated, just as later, treating texts as aesthetic objects was commensurate with a system of cultural production and regulation based on property' (Rose 1993: 13).

Donaldson was one of many enterprising booksellers who in the late 1700s began actively challenging the copyright monopoly of London-based businesses. Such challenges from 'provincial' bookselling and publishing centers grew as individuals realized the extent to which careful manipulation and utilization of copyright material could enable the conducting of a profitable business. As a result, more and more bookselling and publishing businesses were started outside London: between 1740 and 1790, for example, the number of such outlets rose from around 400 establishments in 200 towns to 1,000 in over 300 places.

It is within this context that Donaldson's legal challenge was framed. His case argued against members of the Stationers' Company guild having automatic right to perpetual copyright in texts purchased from authors, given that such exclusivity inhibited competition and was inherently unjust to those who had produced the texts in the first place. The courts agreed, and the basic rules regarding an author's right to copyright in their own works was subsequently set in legal terms. Initially, authors, or whoever bought copyright, were granted sole reproduction rights for 14, then 28 years. France followed in 1778 with its own legal implementation of copyright protection (rights that were subsequently strengthened in 1793 with further statutes). Austria followed suit in 1832 and Germany in 1835. Over the next 60 years other nations slowly adopted similar copyright laws (with increasing lengths of time assigned for copyright protection – 50, then 75 years from initial publication), but international copyright regulation was only achieved after much struggle with the ratification of the Berne Convention in 1886.

Authors in an industrial age

Changes in legal rights would be followed by major technological and market innovations and change. Nineteenth-century print culture was transformed by the implementation of new techniques for paper-making and print production, and advances in communication systems (these developments and issues are covered more fully in Chapter 5). The invention of the mechanized Fourdrinier paper-making machine in 1801, for example, replaced hand-prepared paper-making techniques, increasing productivity and driving down paper costs; the implementation of fast typesetting machines and steam-driven rotary presses cut production times; the development of increasingly efficient transport links (steam-powered trains and boats) enabled faster deliveries of books and print across national and international borders; progress in communication networks (postal services, telegraphy, and the laying-down of underwater transatlantic and international communication cables) allowed swift transmission and circulation of information between authors, editors, and publishers that cut down production time.

Industrialized print culture patterns developed in tandem with general industrialization across Western Europe. As Roger Escarpit notes, mechanization enlarged market potential, shifting power in the book trade at the same time. 'Faced with a developing market, printing and bookselling underwent a major change, as nascent capitalist industry took charge of the book. The publisher appeared as the responsible entrepreneur relegating the printer and bookseller to a minor role. As a side effect, the literary profession began to organize' (Escarpit 1966: 22–23). In practice, this resulted in a separation of activity. Major publishing houses emerged who acted as both general and specialist list publishers – these included such heavyweights as John Murray, William Blackwood, Longmans, and Macmillan & Co. in Britain, Hachette in France, Samuel Fischer and Bernhard Tauchnitz in Germany, George Putnam, Houghton Mifflin and Harpers & Co. in the USA, Gyldendals in Denmark, and Norstedts and Albert Bonnier in Sweden. Some had printing operations attached to their editorial and production offices, but, on the whole, firms moving to consolidate reputations as 'publishers' shifted the bulk of their printing onto the shoulders of specialist printing firms, who took advantage of new technologies to produce orders for several publishers simultaneously and at speed.

Britain led the way in industrial production shifts between 1800 and 1850. France saw major changes in the 1830s: with the July revolution in 1830, state censorship was relaxed and liberal trade laws instituted, while general education became compulsory from 1833, thus enabling an increase in the level of literate readers. By 1848, similar industrialized shifts in print production (with accompanying changes in opportunities for authors) had affected Germany, the USA, the Nordic countries, and elsewhere. In tandem with such changes there was a growth in an increasingly active bourgeois class and reading public keen to consume the products of the printing press (Chartier 1981; Gedin 1982: 34–39; Hall 1996: 44).

Such changes in legal statutes, technology, business practices, and social formations created circumstances by which printed texts, manufactured more quickly and at increasingly cheaper costs, could be sold to a widening mass audience, generating larger profits for publishers and allowing individual authors to claim recurring profits from work produced (through already-noted methods such as half-profit contracts, outright sales for a limited period of copyright in their texts, or recuperation of royalties on book sales), thus ensuring some form of stable and continuing income after initial publication.

A profession was born, and particularly during the latter half of the nineteenth century, we see an explosion across Western Europe in the number of people who begin to depend upon writing to generate an adequate annual income. If one could create something seemingly out of nothing and get it published, with an accompanying agreement allowing for annual income from such sources, one could build up enough of a body of work to keep such income flowing in. Star authors began to command high prices for the rights to their works: former British Prime Minister Disraeli was paid UK£10,000 by Longmans for full rights to publish his sensation novel *Endymion* with them in 1881; George Eliot temporarily abandoned her long-serving publisher John Blackwood when London-based George Smith offered her UK£7,000 for *Romola* in 1862; George Smith also persuaded Wilkie Collins to abandon plans to serialize *Armadale* with Charles Dickens and place it instead with Smith's *Cornhill Magazine*, paying him the princely sum of UK£5,000 for serial rights in the process; and across the English Channel, Balzac negotiated an initial payment of 15,000 francs on publication and a second 15,000 francs on sale of two-thirds of the initial edition of his *Comédie Humaine* (Escarpit 1971: 42–43; Laurenson and Swingewood 1972: 120; Sutherland 1976: 105). Such sums were vast, but, as many have pointed out, they were major exceptions in a profession made up, in general, by many who grafted heavily for relatively small rewards.

Not until the late nineteenth and early twentieth centuries, however, do we see full implementation of the royalty system that characterizes most book publications today, where authors receive an agreed sliding-scale percentage of the retail price of every copy of their work sold. This system, adopted from US publishing practices, is said to have become commonplace in Britain from the 1880s onward, most prominently after the publication of the US publisher George Haven's *Putnam's Authors and Publishers: A Manual of Suggestions for Beginners in Literature* (1883) and *The Grievances between Authors and Publishers* (1887), in which he outlined US royalty systems and advocated their adoption in Britain and – by implication – Western Europe (Hepburn 1968: 13–14; Keating 1991: 15–19, 459 footnote 24).

Similarly, it is not until the turn of the twentieth century that we see the development of the marketing and promotions strategies that are now common occurrences today – literary agents to handle fees and sell texts to the highest bidder; organized and concentrated book tours, readings and signings to promote sales in chosen works; use of other media (radio, television, and newspapers) to generate interest in authors' works (Bonham-Carter 1978, 1982; West 1985, Marek 1995; McDonald 1997; Finkelstein 2002). As Juliet Gardiner has commented, the results have led to authors being 'biographized in the drive to get his or her book a front rank space on the front table, in UK parlance, or "on the wall" as US booksellers describe it: in pole position' (Gardiner 2000: 263).

Interpreting the author function

In tandem with the development of authorship as a profession has been the development of critical methods for discussing texts, particularly in post-industrial contexts. For many years, those working in literary academic fields sought to explicate texts through hermeneutical analysis of internal meanings and structures, with little recourse to the external contexts in which works were often produced. Throughout the early part of the twentieth century, a key aspect in academic analyses of textual production was a humanist-led tendency to ascribe creative authority to the author, who was viewed as expressing, intending, creating, and governing all the meanings to be read in the text. For those involved in literary hermeneutics, as Andrew Milner succinctly summarizes, 'the relevant meaning was that intended, either consciously or unconsciously, by the author of the literary text' (Milner 1996: 29). The ultimate task, undertaken, in particular, in Anglophone academic circles, was, as F. D. E. Schleiermacher famously exclaimed: 'To understand the text at first as well as and then even better than its author' (Schleiermacher 1985: 83). An example of such interpretation could be found in the influential works of the early- to mid-twentieth-century British academic F. R. Leavis, who at one point famously declared that there were only six authors in British literature worthy of study – including Joseph Conrad, Henry James, and D. H. Lawrence. Leavis's arguments were based on a view that texts themselves were the ultimate sources of 'truth,' that 'authority' was invested in words produced by creative geniuses standing above human nature. Authors were individuals from whom poured forth undiluted texts of infinite wisdom. (This in bibliographical arenas was then viewed as inevitably corrupted during the process of production. The result has been a veritable industry centered round creating editions seeking to reproduce as faithfully as possible the authorial 'ur-texts.')

Reactions to this have evolved along linguistic, semiological, and socio-logical lines to encompass such critical movements as structuralism, post-structuralism, Marxist-influenced cultural materialism, and deconstruction. A history of such critical movements is outside the remit of this chapter; but there are several insightful summaries already published that offer the reader more details on the matter (Milner 1996).

Coming out of the ferment of 1960s reactions to past authority and critical interests was an important structuralist statement that has relevance for those studying authorship in a book history context – namely, Roland Barthes's short essay 'The death of the author,' published in 1967. Barthes's piece embodied contemporary critical trends that both interpreted and at the same time destroyed conceptions of authorial 'creativity' and 'authority.' An author, he declared, did not exist once his work passed into the public domain. Remove him, and you created room for new meanings, you liberated the text. In an attempt to shift critical emphasis from author-centered enquiry to reader-based analysis, Barthes argued in dramatic fashion that how readers interpreted these texts was now all important to critical reflection. 'The removal of the Author,' Barthes exclaimed, 'is not merely an historical fact or an act of writing; it utterly transforms the modern text (or – which is the same thing – the text is henceforth made and read in such a way that at all its levels the author is absent)' (Barthes 1977: 145). In other words, there was no longer a need to think of texts as a linear procession from the God/Author to the reader, via which were handed down rigid truths needing disentangling. Instead, readers created their own meanings without the aid of this concept of an author – they, in a sense, were authors in their own right. Each time readers read something they would come away with entirely different meanings and significations. Barthes continued:

> The reader is the space on which all the quotations that make up a writing are inscribed without any of them being lost; a text's unity lies not in its origin but in its destination. Yet this destination cannot any longer be personal: the reader is without history, biography, psychology; he is simply that someone who holds together in a single field all the traces by which the written text is constituted.
>
> (Barthes 1977: 148)

The critical position Barthes was jousting against was that which interpreted authorial intention as a guarantor of meaning, 'the historical, concrete individual whom we have already learned not to think of as the expressive subject of her or his text' (Gardiner 2000: 256). Decentering and decoupling the authority of an author from texts was not a new concept. Elevating the common reader to ultimate creator of textual meaning was. But as Michel Foucault pointed out in his famous riposte, published a year later ('What is an author?'), this was not good enough, particularly in the context of material production and capitalist endeavor. To say the author was dead, and thus kill his or her 'authority,' was to ignore the fact that we lived in a world now driven by cultural production and market forces. Authors, and their books, were commodities. And an author's name carried with it all sorts of signification. As Foucault pointed out:

> An author's name is not simply an element in a discourse (capable of being either subject or object, of being replaced by a pronoun, and the like); it performs a certain role with regard to narrative discourse, assuring a classificatory function. Such a name permits one to group together a certain number of texts, define them, differentiate them

from and contrast them to others. In addition, it establishes a relationship among the texts.

(Foucault 1984: 107)

Or, as he succinctly summarized, the author's name 'seems always to be present, marking off the edges of the text, revealing, or at least characterizing, its mode of being' (Foucault 1984: 107).

What Foucault suggested was that the author function could be just as crucial to establishing what texts were, and what we made of them, as anything else. An author could become identified with their 'portfolio' of work, their '*oeuvre*,' a point that has carried over into other media products as well, such as film, where the '*auteur*' function (which assigns creative authority and originality to the film director) holds sway. In Foucault's view, the modern author was to be viewed less as an 'essence' and more as a 'function' emerging from within various technological and social conditions. Foucault's 'author,' in this case, as one critic has succinctly noted, is 'a name that circulates independently of the individual and functions at once as the signatured assertion of a property right, and as a vehicle for whatever significance or reputation that name has come to acquire' (Wernick, 1993; Chartier 1994: 29–59; Gardiner 2000: 256).

One of the results of both Barthes's and Foucault's anti-humanist stances (that is, their rejection of literary humanist critical work that sought to uncover the meaning intended by the author) was a frenetic period of structuralist and post-structuralist semiotic literary theorizing which, as one commentator dryly commented, 'revelled in the theoretical implications of the "death of the author" first announced by Roland Barthes and subsequently endorsed by Michel Foucault' (Milner 1996: 115). This trend was particularly prominent in the Anglophone critical theory battles of the 1970s and 1980s, trenchant disputes that encompassed struggles over the view that 'in literary and cultural theory, retrieving authorial intentions as the central practice in uncovering textual meaning has been long disavowed' (Gardiner 2000: 274).

Recent years have seen a return of the author as a primary factor in textual meaning, reconstituted, however, as part of wider historical and cultural analyses. Promoters of New Historicism, for example (such as Stephen Greenblatt), have demonstrated interest in 'situating the literary work in relation to "ordinary" texts (of a practical, juridical, political, or religious nature) that constitute the raw materials on which writing operates and that make its intelligibility possible' (Chartier 1994: 27). Others have drawn on Pierre Bourdieu's work on the sociology of cultural production to examine the structured relationships of 'literary fields' and the hierarchies of cultural, political, and commercial values within which artists, authors, and other cultural producers operate (McDonald 1997; Radway 1997). Equally, the 'author function' is an important aspect of current print culture and book history work.

What book historians have done particularly well is to demonstrate how far conceptions of the author-figure (and the systems of ownership within which authorial activity is embedded) have come since the medieval period. The 'author' as constituted in manuscript culture is a far cry from current cultural and critical conceptions of authors, who are increasingly seen as part of a complex, commodified, digitally rich public arena. Print and texts increasingly form part of the 'vertical integration' of media commodities by transnational multimedia conglomerates, often sold conjoined to film, television, and other media products (see Chapter 7). Authors participate and jostle for space within public media spaces (appearing on television and radio shows to promote their works, enduring cycles of book festival appearances, signing copies for fans, and responding to email, letters, and general requests). It is part of what Juliet Gardiner has accurately noted as a circulation of the author's name, 'suffused with a Romantic reading of authorship as singular, individual, confessional, allowing the concept of authorial intention to be reinscribed in ways that present the author as the meaning of his/her text beyond the writing of it through a series of specified performative acts in the process of the production of the meaning of his or her book' (Gardiner 2000: 263).

'Authors' can equally find themselves re-inscribed through the burgeoning digital media: digitized, copied, pasted, recombined, and distributed (with or without attribution) online and via the internet. Current attempts to rein in the digital piracy of 'copyright' material illustrate the difficulties inherent in maintaining stable print-culture-defined conceptions of authorship in a fluid, globally linked, shifting medium. Digitized commodities (whether film, music, or print), as Mark Poster argues, 'have a logic that confounds the principles of capitalism at a very basic level,' complicating what had previously been a straightforward process of economic activity and financial return (Poster 2001: 43). We may, indeed, be witnessing a shift from what Poster terms 'analogue authors' (that is, those embedded and bound up within conceptions and physical activities of print technology) to 'digital authors' (those bound up in 'perhaps postmodern, perhaps future, computer-mediated, even networked forms of writing'). Poster argues that digital culture is creating an impact upon cultural production that, while not as apocalyptic in its effect on print culture as some digital technologists (and their critics) would have it, is shifting the grounds on which stands the author figure. '[D]igital writing,' he claims, 'is both a technological inscription of the author and a term to designate a new historical constellation of authorship, one that is emergent, but seemingly more and more predominant' (Poster 2001: 69).

Conclusion

We have looked at the way in which authorship as a concept and an activity in Western European traditions has changed over the past 1,000 years. During the medieval period, authorship was an activity confined mainly to elite ecclesiastical centers, although matters changed as individuals such as Chaucer came forth to challenge the established order. Authors were generally seen as individuals who reshaped past material for contemporary use. With the advent of print from the mid-fifteenth century onward, authorship as a function changed, as did the economic and social structures that supported authorial activity. We have seen how printers, publishers, and patrons played important roles in the lives of authors through to the eighteenth century and beyond. We have also seen how changes in copyright laws and the advent of industrialization in the nineteenth century changed even more the parameters of authorship and book production. We have examined twentieth-century interpretations of the functions of authors for an insight into current debates on the subject, and have noted how new paradigms of authorial activity and redefinitions of what constitutes 'authorship' may result from the onset of digital technology in the twenty-first century. Authorship in the digital era may also be in a process of change. Whether this will require a reinterpretation of the role of authors in society or, as has been the case in past manuscript and print 'revolutions,' will merely involve accommodating overlaps between traditional and new methods of discussing authorship, remains to be seen. Assessing the role of contemporary and future author functions within such evolving terms is therefore a challenge that future print culture and book history scholars will need to face and undertake.

Points to ponder

As you review this chapter, here are some questions to consider. Does contemporary patronage in the form of writers-in-residence programs, teaching on creative writing degrees, and other forms of such support signify a potential regression to the period when authors were unable to make an income solely through their writing? Does the contemporary ability to self-publish online come at the sacrifice of 'quality' and the income to be generated from it? Does online publishing represent something new, or is it a variation of an old theme in print and authorship? In a world where information of all sorts is freely available through digital and online form, can authors maintain their right to copyright and compensation from their readers?

5

PRINTERS, BOOKSELLERS, PUBLISHERS, AGENTS

Introduction

One of the most thoroughly covered areas in recent book history studies is the international history of printing, printers, and the various agents involved in the production, distribution, and reception of books and other texts. Chapter 3 of this book, surveying the coming of print, has taken up most space so far. This has partly to do with the fascination with the book as material object – knowing the history and personalities behind the making of rare, desirable, or unusual books has often been bound up in evaluating the material worth of books – and partly to do with the significant place of books and print in cultural and social development. As previous chapters have suggested, Robert Darnton's 'communication circuit' has been helpful in establishing a shorthand template for mapping out the elaborate networks that supported and influenced the production, dissemination, and consumption of print. Darnton's piece highlights a continuing expansion of the book history field from past bibliographical foci on the materiality of the text to include current interests in the cultural, social, economic, and legal contexts of print culture production. Thomas Adams and Nicolas Barker's response to Darnton, suggesting a 'communication circuit' centered on the book production cycle rather than on forces external to texts, nevertheless still organizes our understanding of books in the context of material concerns, taking into account the economic imperatives governing book and textual production.

This chapter looks at how book historians characterize and discuss the role of the many agents involved in the process of book and print culture production. It provides a survey history of the changing business models of Western European print production that developed following the Industrial Revolution of the nineteenth century, carrying on from material outlined in Chapters 3 and 4. It examines how print culture was exported to European colonial possessions, initially concentrated on the production of local and regional newspapers, and describes briefly the role of print culture in forging national and regional identities. It also highlights the role that cultural agents have played in supporting and shaping print culture production, from publishers' readers and literary agents to intangibly linked but influential literary networks.

Changing business models

As noted in Chapters 3 and 4, the business of printing from Gutenberg's time to the nineteenth century followed fairly simple business models. Early printers combined printing, publishing, and bookselling roles, seeking out likely texts, purchasing rights to print, then attempting through various means to profit from promoting and selling these texts. As trade increased to include international links, these roles began to be separated: by the early nineteenth century, many Western European cities had traders specializing specifically in publishing, subcontracting to printers, illustrators, and other related production specialists to complete material work on books and other printed texts, and subsequently selling the finished products to established specialist book retailers. The British book trade was among the first to transform in its structures, grasping advantages made possible by industrial developments. After 1780 it would begin shifting 'from a series of independent but cooperative bookselling firms into a group of large corporate enterprises' (Hall 1996: 44). Family firms such as Macmillan, Blackwood & Sons, John Murray, Chambers, Smith, Elder & Co., and others, founded at the turn of the nineteenth century, would become pre-eminent in their field by the 1860s, dominating trade in Britain and profiting from exports to Anglophone colonies worldwide. By the late nineteenth century, the economic structure of the book market in Western Europe would be firmly entrenched to include separate but interlocking elements such as printers, publishers and publishing houses, booksellers, newspapers and magazine producers, libraries, literary agents, independent writers, and a growing reading public.

Similarly, we begin to see the movement of print into the public sphere as profitable commodities driven by advances in new technology – the development, for example, of the Koenig steam press (noted in Chapter 4), adopted in Britain in 1814 just as Lord Byron would begin his ascendancy to iconic literary status, revolutionized how authors such as Byron could reach the literary marketplace. 'I am persuaded,' James Brewster commented to Byron, 'that you must write by steam,' recognizing how the poet could become a beneficiary of the cultural powers unleashed by the harnessing of new industrial technology (Mole 2003: 128). Revolutions in industrialized production of texts empowered commentators such as Byron to turn their material rapidly from manuscript to print, while increasingly speedy transportation links ensured their words reached further and more quickly across physical borders than ever before.

Steam power (and the steam engine) would become a major symbol of Western European social and economic restructuring in the period following the French Revolution and the Napoleonic Wars of the 1790s and early 1800s. Steam dominated public debate as a shorthand metaphor for the unprecedented changes occasioned by industrial advances. Information and communication processes grew faster, aided by visible examples of new technology and mass production systems at work, such as national and international postal systems, telegraph lines, fast metal-clad, steam-powered ships and railways, and the steam press producing mass-media newspapers for daily consumption (Fyfe 2012). Karl Marx, commenting during the 1840s on changes in human history wrought by the invention of the steam engine, exclaimed that nature itself was being challenged by human intervention: 'Nature builds no machines, no locomotives, railways, electric telegraphs … These are products of human industry: natural materials transformed into instruments of the human will' (Briggs and Burke 2002: 111).

The unveiling of the Koenig press, a steam-powered rolling-cylinder press secretly installed by the owners of the British daily newspaper *The Times*, capable of producing 1,000 impressions an hour and used for the first time on 29 November 1814, conjoined steam with print activity. With typical hyperbole, the moment was extolled by the paper as 'the practical result of the greatest improvement connected with printing since the discovery of the art itself' (Briggs and Burke 2002: 111). They were not far wrong. Along with advances in paper-making, steam-powered printing proved central in placing print communication at the heart of cultural interaction and interpretation. As James Secord comments, during this period the groundwork was prepared for reading to become a key aspect of mass culture: 'The steam-powered printing machine, machine-made paper, public libraries, cheap woodcuts, stereotyping, religious tracts, secular education, the postal system, telegraphy, and railway distribution played key parts in opening the floodgates to an increased reading public' (Secord 2000: 30). It enabled print culture to mediate more quickly, as well as foster and promote swift circulation of information for an increasingly knowledgeable and literate society. The intellectual ferment occasioned by political revolutions and challenges would become coupled to major economic and industrial revolutions in the mind of the public, thanks to its reporting and representation in books and others forms of print: 'This was the age that saw the invention of the illustrated newspaper, the modern journalist, eye-catching street advertising, the international exhibition, and the paperback book' (Secord 2000: 24). The result was that 'print culture, reporting on itself, occupied a central place in public awareness of industrial revolution' (Secord 2000: 30).

Such success encouraged technological expansion of the printing trade beyond national borders. From the 1830s onward, the British experience would be replicated across the Atlantic and in other European states, and, as David Reed has argued, the 'second half of the nineteenth century saw a complete transformation of the printing trade' (Reed 1997: 44). In the USA, for example, printing formed an important part of the colonial experience, practiced throughout the eighteenth century by significant figures such as Benjamin Franklin, whose long and productive working life began through building a printing and publishing empire in the New England colonies (Brands 2000; Morgan 2002; Isaacson 2003). But, as David D. Hall points out, the 'golden age' of US publishing and printing activity took place after 1830 with the advent of new technology, increasing capacity and communication, and firms such as Harpers in New York, or Carey, Lea in Philadelphia would emerge to become nationally and internationally known (Hall 1996: 44). Their ability to dominate local markets was also due to their size and production rates – typically, American editions were three or four times larger than British printings (which averaged about 750 to 51,000 copies per edition), and prices one third or one quarter less. Inexpensive printings were partially enabled by widespread 'pirating,' a particular concern of British sources from whom such material was 'borrowed.' The problem of copyright infringement, and US protectionist regulations against non-US-manufactured material (justified by the industry as necessary for protecting national printing industry interests), would prove endemic through to the 1890s, when the USA reluctantly adopted some measure of international copyright legislation under the Chace Act.

But such protectionist activity was also part of a move by American print producers to establish a self-sustaining mass market for their products. Thus it is in the USA that we see early experiments in paperback productions, first in the 1840s with paperback 'newspaper supplements' hawked by newsboys and mail-order methods; and then during the 1860s through to the 1890s, when the Boston-based Beadle Brothers pioneered developments in mass-market paperback publishing. Their first paperback, *Malaeska, the Indian Wife of the White Hunter*, published in the summer of 1860, produced profits of over US $13 million. Between 1860 and 1865 alone, the firm's series of titles would sell over 4 million paperback copies, with individual edition sales reaching up to 80,000 copies (Schneirov 1994: 63; Milner 1996: 69).

France witnessed similar seismic shifts in print communication consumption due to technological advances, educational reforms encouraging the expansion of basic literacy rates, and shifts in laws relaxing regulations for the publication and distribution of printed material. The emergence of a mass press catering to an increasingly literate urban French readership dates to the appearance in 1836 of Emile de Girardin's commercial daily *La Presse* and its rival *Le Siècle*. Within a year, general daily newspaper sales across Paris had risen from 70,000 to 235,000 copies a day; by 1870 sales had reached 1 million; by 1880 they had topped 2 million (Escarpit 1966: 28; Motte and Przyblyski 1999: 2). Textual innovations included featuring serialized novels (*roman feuilleton*), a method copied from British sources. Among now-canonical authors of nineteenth-century French literature initially published in this way were Balzac, Dumas, Zola, and Flaubert.

Nineteenth-century French distribution sources also drew inspiration from British models – in the first instance, from the circulating library system begun by C. E. Mudie in London in 1842 (and which for over 50 years monopolized and dictated terms by which Victorian fiction, in particular, was produced and distributed), and also from the newspaper and railway bookstall network developed by W. H. Smith. Guinevere Griest comments on Smith's start: 'In the early part of the nineteenth century Smith's had been the leading newspaper agent of Britain, a position which was not relinquished when the firm started to expand with the railway bookstall business in 1848' (Griest 1970: 31). By 1862, Smith had obtained a monopoly on bookstall operations in almost all of the English railways (another retail competitor, John Menzies, would dominate the Scottish market), a position it would continue to occupy through to the late twentieth century. It would also venture into the publishing market, issuing in conjunction with Chapman and Hall from 1854 onward inexpensive 2 shilling paperback reprints of popular novels for sale specifically at railway stations (they were known as 'yellowbacks' on account of the yellow tint of their paper covers).

French operators would imitate such distribution innovations. The French publisher Louis Hachette, who had begun operations in Paris in 1826, had by the 1860s, through astute engagement with the French government as a major supplier of school textbooks, turned his firm into France's largest publishing house. On his death in 1864, the firm employed 165 people and generated a gross annual turnover of 1 million francs. Visiting Britain in 1851, Hachette observed W. H. Smith's railway bookstall successes. When he returned home he successfully lobbied for rights to establish similar bookstalls at French railway stations. As the railway network expanded (growing 600 per cent between 1850 and 1870), so too did Hachette's railway bookshop empire, extending to several thousand stalls and shops across the nation. Hachette also copied Smith's reprint series with his own 'railway library' editions in the 1850s: he issued 107 titles in the first year of production, and another 60 in the second. Five hundred titles were published during the lifecycle of the series. Successful titles included works by Dickens, who accounted for 28 volumes (of which *David Copperfield* was the most popular, selling 100,000 copies, and *Oliver Twist* a close second at 83,000), Thackeray, George Sand, Victor Hugo, and the Comtesse de Ségur's *Malheurs de Sophie*, which throughout the 1860s sold a steady 40,000 copies a year, eventually totaling 1.7 million sales (Gedin 1982: 39–40). Hachette would grow from strength to strength over the coming decades, opening outlets and selling in overseas book markets such as Algeria and Turkey. On the eve of World War II, its annual turnover would exceed 60 million francs. After the war, however, Hachette ceased functioning as a family-owned firm, and throughout the late twentieth century it would undergo a series of restructuring moves that led to its reformulation as a transnational multimedia conglomerate empire, covering a wide area of entertainment work.

Nineteenth-century publishing successes such as these were also matched by the publishing opportunities available among a cascading cornucopia of pub-lished mass-media sources that included daily, weekly, monthly, and quarterly journals. The rise in the number of journals seeking contributions enabled many authors to earn a living from writing. Literary property proved an increasingly valuable commodity, particularly as individuals gained stronger legal rights in their texts through crucial national and international rulings and trade agreements hammered out over the course of the nineteenth century. Publishers realized that leisure reading material could boost sales of journals and newspapers, as well as serve as useful advertising for their firm's 'brand' of fiction and non-fiction. The use of serialized material from the 1840s onward became ubiquitous in literary periodical and newspaper sources, and a market developed through to the 1880s and beyond whereby texts (either pirated or legally purchased) would be serialized and circulated internationally: 'stories from New York, fashion from France, information from Australia filled the democratic pages of the mid nineteenth-century miscellany' (Johnson-Woods 2000: 355).

New periodical outlets for literary production also encouraged a more systematic organization of the literary and print production professions; in Britain, by the turn of the twentieth century, all major sectors of the publishing and literary professions had founded associations to represent their specific interests (noted briefly in Chapter 4). These included the Society of Authors (founded in 1884), the Publishers' Association (founded in 1896), and the Associated Booksellers of Great Britain and Ireland (founded in 1895). Following the demise of the three-volume format for first-time printings of fiction in Britain in 1894, and the increasingly unprofitable returns perceived from variable cutthroat pricing systems that retailers subsequently experimented with, booksellers and publishers moved toward implementing a consensual fixed-pricing arrangement for new works. The Net Book Agreement would be born after protracted negotiations in 1899 (it would last until 1995). In the USA, the newly established national American Publishers' Association attempted in 1901 to introduce a similar fixed book price agreement; protracted court action led to a Supreme Court ruling 13 years later declaring such price fixing illegal under anti-trust laws.

Exporting print communication practices

Print communication practices as remodeled in the wake of nineteenth-century technological innovations were successfully exported to other countries, drawing on European investment, technology, and skilled labor. Printing networks and activities would flourish or falter according to the specific needs and levels of support by the ruling powers. Initial printing setups were usually part of missionary settlements and official print communication requirements for information purposes. New Zealand print culture and communication history, for example, is one marked by encounter, conflict, accommodation, colonization, and maturation. As many commentators have pointed out, the period between initial and sporadic European encounters with the Maori from the 1770s onward, the missionary settlements from 1814 onward, and the tide

of white settlements from 1840 onward also marked an encounter of conflicting cultural expressions between a Maori culture rooted in oral traditions, on
the one hand, and a European culture with faith in the power of the written
word, and a legal and political tradition and framework upheld and built
on by print culture modes of communication, on the other (McKenzie 1984;
Cave and Coleridge 1985; Belich 1996: 116; Traue 2001).The signing of the
Treaty of Waitangi between Maori and Pakeha notables on 6 February 1840,
which British officials viewed as an official documented ceding of Maori
sovereignty to the British Crown, was just such a moment of collision, interpretation, and reconfiguration between oral and print-based cultures, the
ramifications of which are still contested to this day.

New Zealand's print heritage begins with the tradition of the missionary
book, produced in the indigenous language of the area – in this case, between
1815 and 1845 as part of missionary efforts at producing material in indigenous languages for consumption by those they tried to convert. A second
strand, English-language printing, develops in New Zealand from 1840 with
the publication of a newspaper, *The New Zealand Gazette and Britannia
Spectator*. The newspaper would become the primary expression of printing
activity in New Zealand's colonial development. As J. E. Traue notes, the
growth was rapid: there would be '28 newspapers founded between 1840 and
1848 for a European population of 59,000; 181 newspapers founded between
1860 and 1879; 150 founded between 1880 and 1889' (Traue 1997: 109).

The interposition of print culture traditions in New Zealand, and their
initial expression through the production of newspapers, is one mirrored in
other colonial territories such as the West Indies, Hawaii, Tahiti, Indonesia,
Kenya, and India (Anderson 1982; Cave 1986; Bayly 1996; Finkelstein and
Peers 2000a; Chakava 2001; Traue 2001). India, for example, witnessed the
development of its print communication networks from the mid-1700s
onwards. While the technology and culture of mass media was at least initially
largely borrowed from Europe, its audience was much more fragmented
by language, region, and race. Interestingly enough, the British were among the
last of the European powers active in India to introduce the printing press into
their enclaves. It was not until 1761 that the British in India acquired a press,
and even then it was a press that had been taken from the French. Its role was
primarily the production of official documents and texts. Printing for popular
consumption came much more slowly. The first newspaper in Calcutta
appeared in 1780, followed by one in Madras in 1785 and one in Bombay in
1789. By the mid-nineteenth century, newspapers and magazines were common
elements in 'Anglo-Indian' life. As one commentator noted in 1851, 'The
newspaper is as necessary an adjunct to the breakfast table in Calcutta as it is
in London' (Hobbes 1851: 362).

Australia witnessed a similar arc of printing development. Throughout the
nineteenth century there was little domestic book publishing undertaken in
Australia; indigenous print production developed after the Gold Rush of the

1850s, and focused on the newspaper and magazine market, along with the undertaking of general trade work. Australian wholesale book distributors such as George Robertson of Melbourne circulated titles mainly produced in Britain and North America, albeit with a focus on material of likely colonial interest. Australian writers found outlets for their work through two routes. The first consisted of publication or serialization in diverse local and regional newspapers and literary journals, of which there were many, often short-lived examples. The second was seeking publication (or in the case of initial Australian serialization, republication) with British publishers, particularly after the successful launch in the 1880s of rival inexpensive paper- and cloth-bound 'colonial series' by Bentley, Sampson and Low, Macmillan, and others, geared towards the Canadian, Australasian, and Indian markets. Bestselling Australian titles reprinted or published in such colonial series included Rolf Boldrewood's *Robbery Under Arms*, which sold over half a million copies between its first issue in 1889 in Macmillan's Colonial Library Series and 1937 (Eggert 2003), and Miles Franklin's *My Brilliant Career*, published by the Edinburgh publishers William Blackwood & Sons in 1901 and issued in an Australian-aimed colonial series between 1902 and 1904.

In the last quarter of the nineteenth century, Australian booksellers began to venture into publishing, often through co-publication ventures with British publishers. Thus, Marcus Clarke's *His Natural Life*, a powerful tale of Australian convict life, first published as a serial in an Australian magazine, was brought out by George Robertson in Melbourne in 1874 and reissued under Bentley's imprint in 1875, then followed by a joint Robertson/Bentley issue sold in Australia from 1882 onwards. Similarly, A. B. Paterson's popular *The Man from Snowy River* was co-published to great profit in 1895 by Macmillan in London and Angus and Robertson in Sydney (Johanson 2000: 148–149). From the 1890s through to the 1960s, however, the Australian book market would be dominated to an exclusive extent by British publishers, particularly after the adoption of the Australian Copyright Act of 1912 which 'ensured that overseas publishers could dictate the terms of trade and oblige retailers to obtain their supplies from prescribed sources, thus fixing prices and maintaining them at a higher level' (Kirsop 2001: 326). As late as 1961, exports accounted for 40 per cent of British books manufactured in that year, of which 25 per cent were destined for Australia alone (Johanson 2000: 254–282).

Printing and print culture in Canada developed at a different pace and much earlier, but was equally slow in moving beyond job printing and journalistic work to indigenous literary and prose production. As one survey suggests:

Publishing in Canada began with handwritten manuscripts, circulated privately. This gave way to the newspaper and general publishing output of printing presses using hand-set type, and thence to new technologies as they became available. Distribution of books, in the earliest years, was often by private importation or by purchase from the local printing office, before the population was great enough to support separate bookstores and distribution agents.

(MacDonald 2001: 92)

The development of printing followed progressive settlement across Canadian provinces; the printing press arrived first in Halifax in 1751, then Quebec in 1764, Niagara in 1793, and Toronto in 1798. Work undertaken in this early period was usually 'job printing' (handbills, stationery, account books, and so on); other main sources included state and religious material, as well as newspaper publication. Until the late nineteenth century, the economic structure of print production and distribution in Canada was a combination of pragmatic, individualistic, and regionalized activity, with individuals functioning along older models combining printing, publishing, and distribution roles. As one commentator notes: 'It was not until consolidation began with the arrival of large non-Canadian firms at the beginning of the twentieth century that this changed' (MacDonald 2001: 93).

Print and national cohesion

It is fair to say that throughout the history of post-industrial printing, particularly in its evolution in overseas European-influenced or dominated settlements, print culture initially developed through the production of newspapers, used as a means of informing and binding together local communities. Large-scale newspaper production by mechanical means influenced and facilitated nascent movements toward national cohesion, shaping language and leading, as Roger Escarpit notes, 'to independent national literatures' (Escarpit 1966: 24). Benedict Anderson has persuasively argued that the use of print in this form – print capitalism as he terms it – has been central to the continuing formation of a national identity, the 'imagined communities' explored in his book of the same name. If a book could emotionally and intellectually stimulate and engage individuals, equally the daily newspaper, consumed by thousands if not millions during the same stretch of time, allowed individuals to feel connected in a common language, 'continually reassured that the imagined world is visibly rooted in everyday life' (Anderson 1982: 35–36).

Readers and agents

Such international examples demonstrate the extent to which print production and publishing often evolved along similar lines when successfully exported from Western Europe. At the same time, such international print production and communication systems have also proven susceptible to hierarchies and divisions, part of a 'distinctive, determinate set of interlocking, often contradicting practices' (Feltes 1993: 17). The increasing value ascribed to literary property created space for new intermediaries such as publishers' readers and literary agents to filter and promote the 'raw' material prepared for mass consumption.

The publishers' reader was a role in print culture production that evolved as nineteenth-century outlets for literary activity prompted individuals to submit work to the growing numbers of publishing houses and periodical sources. The publishers' reader was not a new phenomenon: literary advisers to publishers or their predecessors (booksellers) had often been utilized and invoked when judgment was required on particular submissions. Arthur Waugh highlighted the apocryphal figure such informal readers represented in mid-century literary circles when he wrote that 'the literary adviser of the mid-Victorian era was ... a sort of mysterious soothsayer, imprisoned in some secret back room, and referred to cryptically as "our reader"' (Waugh 1930: 139). Late nineteenth-century publishers' readers were drawn from contemporary literary arenas, and with few exceptions were mainstream 'men of letters' such as John Forster, John Morley, Andrew Lang, Edward Garnett, and George Meredith. Women who also played significant roles in assessing material included Margaret Oliphant, Elizabeth Rigby, and Geraldine Jewsbury.

With the relationship between writers and publishers shifting by the end of the nineteenth century to encompass more complex negotiations over publication sources, royalty payments, and serialization rights, the function and position of publishers' readers also shifted. Readers were contracted to undertake particular functions, either serving as individuals who actively sought out, worked with, and encouraged potential additions to particular publishing 'lists,' or as individuals providing assessments based solely on material passed to them by publishers and journal editors. Edward Garnett, who advised Jonathan Cape, was an example of the first type, working, as Linda Marie Fritschner notes, to find new talent for Cape, and offering a comprehensive reader service: 'He revised manuscripts but often the kinds of advising he did went below the surface to touch upon the theme, motivation and structure of a novel' (Fritschner 1980: 93). Geraldine Jewsbury, reader for Bentley, epitomized the second category, an individual who dealt not with authors but with their texts, approving or rejecting material on commercial and aesthetic grounds, with no remit to follow up and develop submissions once assessed. As Fritschner summarizes:

> [Jewsbury's] services were primarily on behalf of the publisher, only secondarily on behalf of the authors, and least of all on behalf of literature. She tried to uphold literary standards within the category of literature as an entertainment or a diversion. Generally her acceptance or rejection of a manuscript depended upon her evaluation of the commercial potential of the manuscript.
>
> (Fritschner 1980: 94)

Such tasks were increasingly required to be performed by 'expert' eva-luators as more individuals sought entry into the literary profession. As one US example demonstrates, the volume of manuscripts received by journal edi-tors did not recede as the century progressed, but increased exponentially: editors of the leading US monthly magazine of the nineteenth century, the *Century* (with a peak circulation in 1897 of 250,000 copies), for example, saw a doubling of submissions, moving from 1,700 manuscripts in 1873, to 2,000 in 1874, 2,400 in 1875, and finally 3,200 by 1876 (Schneirov 1994: 11, 66). The number of titles issued annually in Britain reflected similar exponential growth in the market over much of the 'long nineteenth century' and into the twentieth, rising from an average 580 in the 1820s, to 2,600 in the 1850s, 6,044 in 1901, 12,379 in 1913, and 22,143 in 1958 (Williams 1965: 185, 187, 191–192).

As Fritschner points out, the reader's place in the restructured practices of British publishers, a model exported abroad in subsequent years, involved a powerful mediating role between producer of manuscripts and producer of finished printed product. 'Although the patterns of relationships among read-ers, authors, and publishers differed, the readers, because they advised on the acceptance, rejection, and revision of manuscripts … had substantial power in shaping policy within a publishing firm' (Fritschner 1980: 93–94). The shift exemplified a move away from 'personal' relations, a misty-eyed, genteel pub-lishing approach that favored courtesy and cordial links with authors (at the same time as it disguised a publishing model tilted in favor of publishers' interests), towards a more commercial, profit-driven structure coping with a multiplicity of media outlets for printed products.

It is at this stage that the literary agent made his (and her) entrance. The rise of the professional literary agent from the late nineteenth century onward has been described in detail in several works, including James Hepburn's short ground-breaking study *The Author's Empty Purse and the Rise of the Literary Agent*. Individuals acted informally on behalf of authors throughout much of the nineteenth century. John Forster, for example, described by one commen-tator as a man who 'bridged the gulf between the patron of the eighteenth century and the literary agent of the twentieth,' acted as mediator and coun-selor for, among others, Charles Dickens, Tennyson, Thomas Carlyle, and Robert Browning from the 1830s to the 1860s. Thackeray paid tribute to Forster's negotiating skills when he wrote: 'Whenever anybody is in a scrape we all fly to him for refuge – he is omniscient and works miracles' (Hepburn 1968: 26). Others who performed similar functions for authors included George Henry Lewes for George Eliot from the 1850s to 1870s, and Theodore Watts-Dunton for Algernon Swinburne in the 1880s and 1890s. Thomas Aspinwall, while US consul in London from 1827 to 1854, acted as transat-lantic agent for Washington Irving, James Fenimore Cooper, and the historian William Hickley (author of *Ferdinand and Isabella* and *The History of the Conquest of Mexico and Peru*) (Barnes and Barnes 1984).

By the end of the nineteenth century, literary agency had become professionalized. In Britain, several individuals distinguished themselves in this form. The first to emerge were A. M. Burghes (a shady representative who first advertised his services in 1882, and who was eventually charged in court with defrauding various clients), and the more reliable Scotsman Alexander Pollock Watt, who opened an agency in London in 1875 but only began advertising commercially as a literary agent in 1881. Watt is credited with developing the basis of literary agenting as it is practiced today, establishing a standard commission fee (10 per cent) for successful representation, and acting as 'scout' for material likely to profit both publisher and author. His skill lay in recognizing and perfecting the mediating role of the literary agent as arbiter and evaluator of literary property, or, more precisely, as one commentator noted, in 'participating in, and in fact becoming the source of, the valuation of copyright' (Gillies 1993: 22). His chief rival would be James Brand Pinker, who began his agency in January 1896. While A. P. Watt had made his mark promoting established authors such as Rider Haggard, Rudyard Kipling, Wilkie Collins, and Arthur Conan Doyle, Pinker concentrated on developing the careers of newly emerging authors – in particular, those associated with the modernist movement, including Joseph Conrad, Stephen Crane, Ford Madox Ford, D. H. Lawrence, James Joyce, and H. G. Wells. Until his death in 1922, he served as a prominent and imposing negotiator of literary property, a man of patience who, Conrad wrote, 'has treated not only my moods but even my fancies with the greatest consideration' (Hepburn 1968: 58). Other prominent transatlantic agents included the formidably successful American agent Curtis Brown, who began working in London in 1899, and the Literary Agency, founded and run from 1899 by C. F. Cazenove and George Herbert Perris (Gomme 1998).

These agents soon began negotiating material reproduction rights in a bewildering range of new outlets extending beyond standard print media boundaries. By 1925, for example, there were common cases of agents negotiating over 26 different rights to a book, including rights to playing card and cigarette packet pictures (Joseph 1925: 92–93). But the activities of literary agents were initially resisted by publishers, whose comments on them betrayed anxiety over the shift in power such individuals represented in the 'communication circuit.' William Heinemann, one of the most virulent critics of literary agents of this period, was scathing in his evaluation of their worth:

> My theory is that when once an author gets into the claws of a typical agent, he is lost to decency. He generally adopts the moral outlook of the trickster, which the agent inoculates with all rapidity, and the virus is so poisonous that the publisher had better disinfect himself and avoid contagion.
>
> (Whyte 1928: 124)

By 1917, however, the date of this outburst, literary agents were a significant part of the publishing process, there because of the increasing desire of authors to be saved the personal trouble of negotiating publication rights. In 1894 there were six agents registered in the London Post Office Directory. By 1914 there were more than 30 agencies and syndicates advertising literary services in trade journals.

In the USA, literary agents were usually seen in more benevolent light – American publishers were fond of observing that such agents were a beneficial British invention, attributing their arrival to 'the superior amicability and business wisdom of authors and publishers in this country' (Sheehan 1952: 74). Various agencies, concentrated in New York, were founded during the 1880s, including the Athenaeum Bureau of Literature, the New York Bureau of Literary Revision, and the Writer's Literary Bureau. The foremost US literary agent of this period, however, was Paul Revere Reynolds, who between 1891 and 1916 dominated the field. Others who followed included the accomplished Flora May Holly, who between the late 1890s and early 1940s would, from an office on Fifth Avenue in New York, represent figures such as Theodore Dreiser, Gertrude Atherton, Edna Ferber, and Noël Coward. Similarly Elizabeth Nowell worked tirelessly on behalf of authors such as Thomas Wolfe as a member of Maxim Lieber's literary agency throughout the 1930s (West 1985: 88, 96).

As publishing grew more international in scope, particularly following the creation during the late twentieth century of transnational media conglomerates, as noted in Chapter 4, the role of the literary agent has evolved in scale and importance; agents are now usually the main initial 'filters' of textual material presented for trade publication, replacing publishers and publishers' readers as initial arbiters of literary value (the publisher's reader, usually contracted externally, is still utilized in specialized areas such as academic book and journal publishing). The agent has become a major mediator in print culture, as well as a significant presence in other media, negotiating contracts and valuation of individual talent in sports, film, television, radio, and other entertainment arenas. The expansion signals the continuing enfolding of print culture activity within other communication networks.

Literary fields and networks

Book historians have begun paying attention to the mediating effects of literary networks in negotiating textual value following the publication and dissemination stages. As Jane Tompkins notes: 'The social and economic processes that govern the dissemination of a literary work are no more accidental to its reputation, and indeed to its very nature, as that will be perceived by an audience, than are the cultural conceptions (of the nature of poetry, of morality, of the human soul) within which the work is read' (Tompkins 2001: 201). Pierre Bourdieu, Peter McDonald, and Jane Tompkins, among others, have explored French, British, North American, and other examples of such intangible networks of interconnected individuals, and how they can affect textual publication and reception, whether through steering material to interested publishers (as agents), shaping public perception through reviews and discussions, or through championing particular works in appropriate socio-cultural circles. The American author Nathaniel Hawthorne, for example, was singularly aided from the 1840s onward by a circle of well-connected New England cultural notables (characterized by Lewis Simpson as the 'New England clerisy'), whose judgment on literary matters, disseminated in influential and weighty cultural journals such as the *Christian Examiner*, *The North American Review*, and *The Atlantic Monthly*, was central to the formation of a nineteenth-century US literary canon. Hawthorne's career flourished with help from influential contemporary reviewers such as E. P. Whipple, the publishing support of William Ticknor (half of the publishing firm Ticknor and Fields), and the editorial advice of William Emerson (editor of the *Monthly Anthology* and father of Ralph Waldo Emerson). By contrast, Hawthorne's contemporary Richard Henry Dana Senior, admirer and emulator of English Romantic poets (a movement not supported by the Boston-based cultural elite), would give up on his literary career in the face of rejection and harsh literary appraisal by the same elite of his essays, tales, and collected editions of poetry and prose. Jane Tompkins contrasts Hawthorne's emerging literary reputation with New York-based Sophie Warner's waning cultural significance, illustrating very clearly the manner in which authorial reputation and textual readings can shift as a result of the cultural gatekeeping functions performed by such cultural elite groupings. Both authors emerged into or disappeared from cultural visibility and the literary marketplace as a result of the specific social, literary, and economic circumstances in which they were read and produced.

Intangible arbiters within the distribution process have also functioned in similar gatekeeping fashion. Janice Radway's recent work on the extremely powerful and influential model of book dissemination pioneered in the USA by the Book-of-the-Month Club illustrates how this mail-order-based organization, established in the 1920s, utilized innovative marketing techniques to create a unique identity and role for itself as a mediator, arbiter, and filter of literary production. It did so through utilizing an internal panel of 'expert' judges to read texts for subsequent recommendation and sale to club members, creating a 'filtering process' of textual worth that worked to define appropriate reading material for targeted audiences. As Radway (1996) notes: 'The key moves in the evaluative practices of the Book-of-the-Month Club judges, was not judgment at all, but rather the activity of categorization, that of sorting onto different planes.' Viewing the world of print in this way, as 'a series of discontinuous, discrete, non-congruent worlds,' Radway continues, established a link between producer (author) and consumer (reader) whereby the disseminator, in this case the US-originated Book-of-the-Month Club, with its built-in filters of judges categorizing titles rather than providing aesthetic judgments of books, became less an arbiter of worth and more a literary manager of textual production (Radway 1996: 24). The role of the club in creating, relating to, and reinforcing an 'interpretive community' of middle-class and aspiring middle-class readers is one that has seen subsequent expression in other media, with the development of literary book clubs begun or built round the 'branded image' of television personalities (the US chat-show host Oprah Winfrey with her monthly book recommendations being one significant example).

Conclusion

This chapter has looked at the various players and agents involved in the circulation of print culture. It has briefly surveyed the effect of nineteenth-century industrial and technological advances in changing methods of producing, disseminating, and consuming print and texts, and shown how innovations in Western Europe were exported to, adopted, and adapted in other countries. This chapter also explored how communication circuits that facilitated the circulation and consumption of print involved various cultural agents, whose roles in promoting books and print now form a significant aspect of contemporary book history interests, part of our continuing exploration and study of the central role that print has played in shaping social discourse and national identities over the past 500 years.

Points to ponder

Here are some points to ponder as you review this chapter. Which roles do you think will continue to be involved in the process of book and print culture production in the future? Who do you think functions as gatekeepers of texts in current society, and how do they influence what you read and consume? What type of business models for circulating books and print are likely to be adopted or feature in the future?

6

READERS AND READING

Introduction

This chapter discusses the 'missing link' of book history: the reader. It provides a short history of reading, discusses theories related to readers and reading, and concludes with a brief analysis of the place of reading in the age of new media. Until recently, seminal studies such as Altick and Ginzburg stood out as some of the few willing to examine 'readers and reading' as a vital component within the communication circuit (Altick 1957; Ginzburg 1980). Partly this was due to a comparative lack of empirical evidence available or in use, or that was neither incomplete nor partisan. This has begun to change, as materially and theoretically grounded studies of the history of reading in cultural terms have begun to appear in greater numbers, such those of Martyn Lyons, Elizabeth McHenry, Leah Price, Janice Radway, Jonathan Rose, William St Clair, Towheed, and others (Radway 1997; Rose 2001; McHenry 2002; Price 2004; St Clair 2004; Littau 2006; Lyons 2010; Towheed et al 2010, 2011). Similarly, large-scale research initiatives such as the internationally focused Reading Experience Database (http://www.open.ac.uk/Arts/RED/) the US-based 'What Middletown Read' (http://www.bsu.edu/libraries/wmr/) and the Scottish Readers Remember project (www.sapphire.ac.uk) have gathered valuable empirical data about reading experiences and reading history. What most of these have in common is an approach that considers reading as both a social phenomenon, seen, for example, in Chartier's study of the spread of literacy in both its attributes of reading and writing, and an individual experience, seen in Ginzburg's portrait of Menocchio, the miller (Ginzburg 1980; Chartier 1989b). Studies by Rose, McHenry, Radway, and others attempt to fuse both the social and the individual: Rose in his detailed examination of working-class autobiographies, journals, and letters to create a history of audiences; McHenry in her study of the shaping of African-American reading and reading taste via reading societies, Radway in her detailed studies of groups of readers, whether of romance fiction or through the Book-of-the-Month Club, and Towheed and his collaborators through transnational comparisons of reading experiences across several centuries and seven continents

(Radway 1984, 1997; Rose 2001; McHenry 2002; Crone and Towheed 2011). Radway's discussion of a particular group of women readers provides an empirical representation of what Stanley Fish has termed 'interpretive communities,' itself a development from Iser's views on the nature of reading and interpretation (Fish 1976; Iser 1980; Radway 1997). In considering the latter, book history overlaps once more with literary theory, on this occasion with attempts to explain the individual act of reading.

Such an explanation reflects, in part, the high value given to the act of reading and the ability to read now common in all developed societies (the fact that this was not always so was discussed in Chapter 2). Bernhard Schlink's novel *The Reader* enjoyed widespread success both in its original German and in translation across the rest of Europe and the USA (Schlink 1997). The book reflects upon the responsibility of Germans, particularly of the post-war generation, for their history; but, as the title implies, the story also concerns reading. The younger of the two central characters, Michael, reads to the older illiterate woman, Hanna, with whom he has an affair. Being read to provides her with an important benefit of what otherwise is a relationship built by him on puppy-love and physical intercourse. That benefit echoes her earlier experience as a guard in a work camp where she protected some of the female prisoners so that they, too, could read to her. However, such is the social stigma attached to illiteracy that when she is tried for war crimes, she admits to authorship of an SS report rather than reveal she cannot read or write. Such, too, is the liberating quality, the sense of individual empowerment and self-actualization, reading brings in our conventional view of it that Michael, now older, rejoices when Hanna learns to read and write in prison. 'Illiteracy is dependence. By finding the courage to learn to read and write, Hanna had advanced from dependence to independence, a step towards liberation' (Schlink 1997: 186).

What you have just read is our 'reading' of the novel, where 'reading' clearly means interpretation. Because of the context of this chapter, our interpretation stresses the functionality of reading and its emancipatory role. In a different – perhaps more literary critical – context, our reading might have emphasized the nature of guilt or the specific historic circumstances of the novel. Reading is itself creative, forming meaning from the interaction of reader and text. The material form of the text influences or guides the formation of meaning, while our individuality impresses itself upon it. Yet others would create the same meaning for *The Reader* as we have. In fact, Thomas Docherty does this in an essay (Docherty 2003). We have not colluded nor copied one another. It is a result of two factors: that the range of meanings is bound to the actual words of the text; and that we belong to Stanley Fish's 'interpretive communities,' underlining less our individuality, more our multiple membership of larger groups (Fish 1976). As an individual practice, reading is a form of interpretation. As a social act, reading is part of the history of reception.

For most of you reading this book, the act of reading itself seems natural and unconscious. Yet, as writing developed as a technology from the spoken word, so is reading a skill that has to be learned in order to use the technology of writing (Monaghan 1989; Manguel 1996). The individual act of reading has changed through time. Biologists state that in human evolution, ontogeny recapitulates phylogeny – in other words, the development of the individual repeats the development of the wider group. This is also true of reading. As very small children, we are read to aloud by adults; we first experience reading before we ourselves can read. As we grow older, we are taught at school or at home the relationship between symbols and sounds; we are taught to follow the symbols in one particular direction, perhaps by tracing the correct move-ment with the tip of our finger. We begin by listening to the teacher read and following the text in our own copies; we read aloud as a group in unison. But, when we start to read individual texts, the cacophony that would result in a continuation of reading aloud imposes the need to read silently, inwardly. We may move our lips or vocalize in a whisper as we do so, but this is pedagogi-cally frowned upon and most of us, except when perhaps dealing with a text of particular difficulty or unfamiliarity, learn not to do it. We have moved from reading aloud to reading silently. You are presumably reading these words silently, inwardly.

Proficiency in reading remains more advanced than proficiency in writing, but both are taught simultaneously. We are taught punctuation and paragraphing as mutually recognized means of making clearer the sense of what we are reading. We learn the structure of the book, including its division into chapters and sections and its index, as a means of navigating more effectively around its contents. All that is transmitted to us and that we absorb in our early years of education in order to become literate (in particular, to read with some degree of fluency) is the outcome of many centuries of development.

The history of reading

In the beginning

From the moment that a scribe began to make marks on clay, stone, or wood to record information in a form that at least one other person could under-stand, the history of reading also began. For as long as writing remained the encoding of simple data, such as quantities or commodities or ownership, however, reading was no more than a primitive and instrumental form of decoding (Fischer 2003). All codes imply some form of limited access, and reading remained restricted to the small group of those who, required or wishing to recall the information from its permanent record, had mastered the meaning of the marks. Initially, this group consisted of scribes and bureau-crats, in some cultures drawn from the priestly caste. Tax collecting represents an important spur to the recording, preservation, and verification of such data. The reader simply confirms the tithe due and, as writer, notes its payment.

Not that the role of reader was a passive one in relation to the material form of writing as the messages conveyed developed in complexity. The preference of early Christian readers for the codex over the roll, for example, led to the eventual predominance of the former, as noted in Chapter 2. The parchment codex offered the ability to navigate backwards and forwards, to search, compare and recap, without the inconvenience of unwinding several rolls (Cavallo 1999). As such, it was more suited to the mastery of the finer points of a new religion, Christianity, grown out of and wishing to distinguish itself from an older faith, Judaism, whose sacred texts were in rolls (papyrus rolls had previously held the singular advantage over clay or wax tablets or bark strips that they could hold longer works than tax or mercantile records). The needs of less competent readers led, in addition, to the introduction of spaces between words, paragraphing, and the use of punctuation as additional guidance (Cavallo 2003). In the case of the Christian scriptures, it also led eventually to the splitting of the various books into numbered chapters and verses. After tax collecting, indeed, religion represents the most potent force in the development of reading and literacy. In many Islamic countries and Orthodox Jewish communities, for example, reading is still synonymous with the reading of religious works. As sacred texts attained authority, particularly in monotheistic cultures, through their fixed nature, transcending time and change, so too the ability to read them was seen to grant power and influence – both sacred and secular.

Public inscriptions such as Egyptian hieroglyphs adorning tombs, columns, and mummy cases, or those on the trilingual monument of Darius I from the sixth century BC found at Bisitun in western Iran, may represent a move away from restricted codes to provide wider access (although they also served to impress the gods, presumed literate, and the ignorant, presumed to venerate literacy) (Fischer 2003). Reading of the earliest data records may have been internalized; but as more complex narratives began to be recorded, these were read out loud, partly on the precedent of poets and bards reciting, and partly, as also with recitation, to reach a wider audience than the individual reader, an audience that included the illiterate. In this way, the rarity and expense of the book need not result in its information being unnecessarily limited to that individual at any one time. Rich Romans employed literate slaves to read to them. Pliny the Younger wrote in a letter from the first century AD: 'At dinner, when my wife is present or a few friends, I have a book read aloud' (Fischer 2003: 45). Monastic life in a later period included fixed reading by one brother to his fellows while they worked or ate. In turn, the performance element in reading privileged a rhetorical style of writing. Orality and literacy, in the sense of reading aloud to an audience, need not be mutually exclusive. Silent reading did exist in parallel (evidence for this exists in the plays of

Aristophanes from the late fifth century BC), but it was the exception rather than the norm for most of antiquity (Nagy 2003). It was still exceptional enough for St. Augustine to remark with wonder in the fourth century AD at the sight of St. Ambrose reading silently (Manguel 1996; Parkes 1999).

The movement from communal to individual may also be seen in the increase in private collections of books as well as libraries. The latter performed a key function in making books available to those who could not afford to own them. However, this was in itself a later development of their original role, one of conservation rather than accessibility. The great library of Alexandria seems to have played the part primarily of museum in its stewardship of the largest collection of rolls in the classical world, and secondarily of research center for scholars to undertake the collating, editing, anthologizing, and abridging of texts (Canfora 1989). It did not offer the accessibility characteristic of libraries at a much later period. However, it did classify and order its holdings for the convenience of its scholarly users. At times when books (rolls and, later, codices) were rare and valuable, libraries could be depositories for conquered booty or showrooms for conspicuous wealth. Cicero used the personal library of Faustus Sulla whose father had looted books from Athens in 86 BC; Cicero's own works were copied by the slaves of his 'publisher' Atticus, and no doubt sold to a number of private collections (as well as used in extract in countless 'readers' for students of rhetoric). Cicero's use of the libraries of Faustus Sulla reveals a network of cultivated readers using one another's villas for study. Cicero himself had book collections in his villas at Formia and Tusculum, as well as in his house in Rome (Harris 1989). He divided his collections by language, Latin and Greek, a practice that is also found in the 'Villa of the Papyri' at Herculaneum (Fischer 2003).

This tier of an elite book-owning readership represents only one part, albeit the most prominent in terms of surviving data, of a wider reading public that also included 'professional' readers such as teachers and the functionally literate who had no necessary interest in (or leisure time for) the classics or contemporary literature. The domestic letters found at Vinolanda, or the very graffiti on the walls of Pompeii, demand that we acknowledge the existence of a much wider range of literacy – and where there are writers, there are readers – than evidenced by Cicero, his circle, and their successors, as republic gave place to empire. The first public library in Rome opened as early as 39 BC, offering the opportunity to literate Romans to read a range of works in Latin and Greek, and to discuss and debate these works as well as general questions of history, literature, and taste, and to listen to readings by contemporary authors from among their own number. By the second century AD, Rome contained seven such public libraries, providing an alternative to private collections (Cavallo and Chartier 1999). The existence of multiple copies of works in private and public libraries aided their survival beyond the end of Roman hegemony in the West. Empire itself spread reading, both through its need for administrators and in its creation of local nobilities desirous to out-Roman the Romans through acquisition of an education in Latin – if not for themselves, then at least for their children. Booksellers existed to cater for the demand for reading material not only in the imperial capital, but also in the provinces of Gaul and Britain. Pliny the Younger purrs with self-satisfaction: 'That there are booksellers in Lugdunum [modern Lyons], I had no idea, and so learn all the more pleasingly from your letter that my books are finding buyers there' (Fischer 2003: 72).

Learning to read, for Romans and their subjects, began with recognition of the capital letters of the Roman alphabet. Such learning might take place, depending upon individual circumstances, within the family, at the feet of a tutor, or in a public school. The pattern was similar to the template sketched above: the shapes and names of individual letters were followed by syllables and then whole words. The pupil learned to read aloud with increasing fluency, and as much attention was expended, according to Quintilian, on developing the appropriate voice and manner as on complex text recognition (Cavallo and Chartier 1999). It is not surprising, therefore, that some forms of writing were privileged over others in this rhetorical approach to reading: epic poetry was followed by other verse genres and then speeches and histories. Learning to read also meant learning to take the undifferentiated blocks of *scripta continua*, or unbroken writing, and picking out the meaningful phrases and sentences without the aid of systematic punctuation. The later adoption of the codex also brought the use of layout and punctuation that eased this difficulty for the learner. This education was successful in creating a reading public scattered throughout the Roman Empire, small but capable of sustaining a diversity of book-making production.

The Middle Ages

The Middle Ages could be seen as a decline from this Classical achievement, but also as a more substantive move away from reading as performance to reading as an introspective pursuit. Until the thirteenth century in Western Europe, the Christian Church taught reading and writing as part of its training program for the clergy, and transmitted these skills, as well as knowledge of the language of written communication, Latin, to only a small minority of the lay population. The church enjoyed a near monopoly in book production for this time, and its buildings, cathedrals, and monasteries contained the only libraries, themselves accessible only to the ordained. Not that this necessarily created a relationship of trust, as the existence of 'chained libraries,' where the books were fettered to the reading desks, attests (Saenger 1999). In these ecclesiastical libraries, from the beginning of the thirteenth century, silent reading became compulsory to enable individual reading and meditation; reading aloud continued in the refectory and in some work areas. The church began to publish books for the devoted laity, particularly Books of Hours, providing information about the church calendar and the liturgy. However, many of these were so sumptuously produced that they had the status of art object as well as almanac. Where other functions demanded literacy – for example, government and other aspects of civil administration, such as courts – the clergy were employed to supply secretarial and scribal services. This is important to note in the light of Roger Chartier's discussion of resistance to literacy (Chartier 1989b). The Socratic suspicion of literacy, and the clear sense of loss that writing specifically entailed, has already been noted in Chapter 2 (Ong 1982). What Chartier is highlighting is a medieval peasant fear of literacy based on its links to authority, often a seeming arbitrary and arrogant authority, to the law, not often on the side of the peasant, and to the sacred, often ill-distinguished from magic, curses, and witchcraft.

The beginning of the thirteenth century also marked the foundation and growth of the first universities in Europe. Teaching took the form of the lecturer (and the root of the word lecture is the Latin *lectura*, 'reading') reading aloud from a particular text and encouraging students to transcribe or own their own copy of it. So each student would begin to build up his own meager but personal collection of books, often, as noted in Chapter 3, through copying and/or purchase of installments, the *pecia* system (Hamesse 1999). These books, or part-books, would be read silently within the communal student lodgings, as would any manuscripts consulted within the institution's library. Libraries necessitated catalogs to ensure the more efficient discovery of the relevant holding. By the end of the fourteenth century, according to Chartier, 'silent reading was the norm, at least for readers who also knew how to write and who belonged to segments of society that had long been literate' (Chartier 1989b: 125). The 'Quiet Please' signs associated with libraries have a long pedigree.

Many of the students graduating from the early universities were to become lawyers. Together with a growing merchant class within cities and large towns, they were the most prominent example of the growing spread and secularization of reading within urban, but not rural, society. The nobility, once freed from martial duties and a Darwinian selection based on martial skills, also began to develop an interest in the collection of books and the pursuit of reading, while the wives and daughters of the nobility started to move beyond Books of Hours and other works of piety to more clearly secular texts, such as manuals of household management. However, the total number of readers would have been relatively and proportionately small. It may have risen from 0.1 per cent of the population of the Roman Empire in the first two centuries AD to less than 5 per cent of the population of France in the mid-fifteenth century, then arguably the most advanced state in Western Europe (Chartier 1995). Books retained a high monetary value, often being featured items in wills; students were even able to use them as collateral for loans.

The teaching of reading remained substantially unchanged from the Classical era, albeit focused on Christian texts and, beyond the family, directed by the church: letters were followed by syllables and then whole words; phrases and sentences had to be disentangled from the text and read aloud with due pronunciation, accentuation, and rhythm. Given that Latin was no longer – if ever, in its literary form – a mother tongue, grammar books introduced systematic analysis or parsing as a means of working out semantic relationships through grammatical relationships. Latin is still largely taught today through the learning of grammatical relationships such as noun declensions and verb conjugations as a preliminary to learning the sense of the text. Mothers who were literate began the process of teaching literacy in the home. Books of Hours often contained illustrations of the Virgin Mary herself learning to read from her mother, St. Anne. Public schools – in towns – began to supplement church institutions in the fifteenth century as the developing merchant class began to assert its civic independence. Both followed the common curriculum of the *trivium* (rhetoric, grammar, and logic), and both sexes attended. However, only boys generally went on, as early as age fourteen, to university to pursue the *quadrivium* (arithmetic, geometry, astronomy, and music). Texts contained commentaries and glosses, and new readers were not reluctant to add their own remarks in the manuscript margins, creating a form of interaction not only with the text (and its putative author and known commentators), but also with subsequent readers of that particular copy. *Scripta continua* remained the norm for texts, even into the period of printing. However, the use of red ink to indicate starting points, or rubrics, and of decorated initial letters, together with the gradual introduction into manuscripts of some punctuation marks, indicated a clear transition from marking up for oral performance to clarifying for silent internal interpretation (Saenger 1999).

The printed book

The invention of printing, discussed in Chapter 3, drew on and accelerated the spread of reading. Yet, it was not the only factor. Increased economic prosperity, partly based on the discovery of new lands for exploitation and colonization; the rediscovery of classical texts and the growth of Humanism labeled as the Renaissance; the schisms in the church created by the Reformation and the reaction of the Counter-Reformation; the consolidation of nation-states and the desire to create new distinctive senses of nationhood; a beginning to scientific exploration of the everyday world to parallel physical exploration of the Americas, Asia, and Africa: all contributed to the spread of reading. Initially, printing produced more of the same more quickly and more cheaply; but over time it permitted changes to the nature of the book to facilitate the reader. New fonts grew out of existing manuscript hands. Aldus Manutius in Venice developed smaller, more portable sizes of book that did not require a lectern or reading stand, or cause the reader's arms to ache from holding them (Lowry 1979). The range of subject matter, while still dominated by the needs of religion and law, began to expand more rapidly.

The corresponding expansion in the number and nature of readers fueled suspicion in existing authorities, the state and the church. Dissent could more easily flourish and spread if printed in multiply copied books. Forms of regulation were introduced not only in order to control what was being printed, but also to restrict those who could buy and read it to those sections of society with least to gain from subversion of state and church. Licensing presses was the most direct method of controlling output, coupled with severe sanctions for those found in breach of the law. Restriction of readership could be maintained through a ban upon material in vernacular languages, limiting publications, in other words, to the languages (principally Latin) of the educated and the clergy, and through taxation of paper, printing, and the finished product to ensure that only the well-off could afford to buy books. These forms of indirect censorship persisted well into the twentieth century in many countries. The authorities were undoubtedly correct in their suspicions. Lay readers began to question dogma and to rediscover pre-Christian writings, leading to the adoption of a Humanist perspective that emancipated the reader from authority and clarified a new sense of individuality.

The growth of Humanism, discussed in Chapter 3, incorporated not only new ideas in philosophy, religion, jurisprudence, and history, but also poetry both old – Ovid and Catullus – and contemporary – Dante and Petrarch (Grafton 1999). Readers sought stimulation of the imagination and emotions as well as of the intellect. These were the books that shrank in size from the original large folios to ease carrying and lending. However, one of the advantages of the larger printed books was that they gave themselves more readily to marginal and inter-columnar glosses. Surviving examples of these, often in the writing of more than one reader, illustrate again an interactive form of reading in which the reader enters into an ongoing dialog with the author (and sometimes with other readers) in the form of added commentary, questions, and refutations. Reading can be more clearly seen not as the reception (and acceptance) of authority, but as an interpretation that admits ambiguity and difference. Meaning could be the creation of the reader from the text rather than solely framed by the text itself. Yet, paradoxically perhaps, this view is accompanied by increasing insistence upon the accuracy of texts and the need for some form of authorization of that accuracy. Printing seemed to promise this. As texts, and texts about texts, multiplied, so too did the need for catalogs that attempted to keep track of all that was being published. Readers needed assistance from these early 'search engines' to find their way around the proliferation of publications.

Latin began slowly to give way to vernacular languages, as the examples of Dante and Petrarch show. The former argued that the vernacular was to be prized above Latin, as Adam must have spoken a vernacular language in Eden since vernacular languages are learned organically, unlike the systematic analysis of Latin noted above, and since vernacular languages are universal, whereas Latin had a limited number of users. William Caxton printed

74 books in English from an approximate total of 90 issued before his death in 1491 (Feather 1988). That movement in favor of the vernacular accelerated during the Reformation, often characterized as a battle of the books. One of the tenets of the Reformation was the unmediated relationship between the laity and God, on the one hand, and the laity and the revealed Word of God – that is, the Bible – on the other. The Reformers sought to ensure that direct relationship by increasing literacy and the availability of the Bible, and other religious writings, in the vernacular. Luther himself understood the importance of printing as a means of achieving this, where earlier Reformers such as Wycliffe and Hus had failed, while Calvin in Geneva and Knox in Scotland created schools to teach the necessary reading skills (Gilmont 1999).

Once learned, those skills could not be confined to religious subjects alone, and possession of books by individual households became a marked feature of those Northern European countries where the Reformation took hold. Moreover, all books acquired something of the reverence with which the Book, the Bible itself, was regarded; in an almost platonic relationship, the reading of books, in general, derived a high status from the reading of the Word of God. The Counter-Reformation, in its response to the religious and social changes now set in motion, had to tread a narrow line between exploiting the possibilities for mass communication in the printed book and following the reformers in subverting the gap between clergy and laity. That line resulted in the publication of many *Lives of the Saints*, simple commentaries on the nature of Christianity, and catechisms to reinforce the distinct dogma of the Roman Catholic Church in its unbroken descent from Peter. These were also produced in the vernacular, and in themselves demanded the acquisition of sufficient skill to read them. The battle of the books may have been joined; but its more peaceful dividends included increases in the number of readers, in the number of printed publications available, including secular works, in the reading of material written in vernacular languages, and in the status of reading as a practice (Manguel 1996).

To assert this is to run the risk of exaggeration in some respects: this was still largely an urban phenomenon, and it was primarily confined to the middle and upper classes: the bourgeoisie and the nobility. However, one of the case studies often quoted for this period is that of Menocchio, a relatively well-off miller who lived in the mountains to the north of Venice from 1532 to 1600 (Ginzburg 1980). The record of his reading survives because he was the subject of trials for heresy in 1583 and again in 1599, when he was condemned to the stake. The accounts of the trial reveal that he had a lively and inquisitive mind that drew him into disputation and debate with his neighbors, particularly on the topic of the Bible. He himself owned an illegal translation of the Bible in the vernacular, as well as at least 11 other books, both sacred and secular, including the *Decameron*, although he may have borrowed some of them. He was very proud of being able to read (and to know these books), the credit for which he assigned to the clergy. He blended book-learning and his rural experience to construct his own views of religion and its beliefs. The example of St. Theresa of Avila is also worth quoting: although she came from a bourgeois background in which books were present, her limited education as a girl restricted her to *Lives of the Saints* or tales of chivalry, both written in the Castilian vernacular. At later points in her life, she found herself handicapped by her lack of Latin. In particular, the Bible was a closed book to her as the church had forbidden its translation into Castilian. Any quotations she did know from the Bible were memorized from the sermons of others or learned by heart from the permitted publications of the Counter-Reformation. Others even more limited in their reading abilities than St. Theresa relied upon a combination of simple text with explanatory images (Manguel 1996).

Some were more concerned at the increasing scale and expanding nature of reading: concerns ranged, on the one hand, from asserting that reading itself, rather than the lighting conditions for reading, led to blindness, to believing that too much reading of fiction, such as tales of chivalry, would result in madness, much as Don Quixote experienced. Figures for the ability to read are more difficult to verify than details of the titles and distribution of books (Chartier 1989b). In Shakespeare's *Henry VI, Part Two*, rebellious Jack Cade anachronistically represents the view of the classes excluded from reading in seeking to turn back the tide initiated by Gutenberg: 'Thou hast most traitorously corrupted the youth of the realm in erecting a grammar school: and whereas, before, our forefathers had no other books but the score and the tally, thou hast caused printing to be used.' However, Aldus Manutius customarily produced 1000 copies of his editions in Greek of Aristotle, Plato, and Thucydides, and in Latin of Virgil, Horace, and Ovid (Lowry 1979). He published, in addition, the dictionaries and grammar books that would facilitate the training of new readers for his titles. New editions in his portable format were issued from April 1501 every two months for the following five years. The profitability of his enterprise indicates that his books were finding buyers across Western Europe. These buyers regarded books as precious commodities, not for their economic value – now dropping as a result of print – but as the source of individual enlightenment and communal advancement through knowledge.

The limits of reading

Books were clearly still objects of economic value, particularly for the sixteenth-century equivalent of Jack Cade. An unbound copy of *Hamlet* could cost sixpence. Yet, an artisan, cobbler, joiner, or shopkeeper would earn, on average, about sixteen pence per day. So, to buy a copy would have cost him about three-eighths of his day's salary (Altick 1957). At the prices of the day, he could for the same sum have bought two dinners, or gone to the Globe Theatre and watched the play in the standing area for six performances. Books would therefore have been restricted to the wealthy or those with a passion for

Table 6.1 Comparative prices and incomes for the late seventeenth century

Books	General goods	Average income, 1688
Folios: 7 to 10 shillings	Butter: 6 pence a pound	Clergyman: approximately 1 pound per week
Octavo: 1 to 4 shillings unbound	Coffee: 3 shillings a pound	Farmer: 16 shillings, 4 pence per week
Unbound plays: 1 shilling	Sugar: 6 pence a pound	Shopkeeper: 17 shillings, 4 pence per week
Sermons, pamphlets: 6 pence	Canary wine: 7 shillings a gallon	Artisans or handicraftsmen: 14 shillings, 7 pence per week
Admission to theater gallery: 12 or 18 pence		

Note: 1 shilling = 12 pence.
Source: derived from Altick (1957)

learning. Table 6.1, derived from Altick, indicates some comparative prices for goods in the late seventeenth century.

In other words, price remained a limiting factor on the wider circulation of books and, therefore, the most effective instrument of censorship. Statutory devices, such as the necessity in France from 1563 to apply for royal privilege or in England from 1538 to seek the permission of the Privy Council, became obstacles for ingenious printers and publishers to circumvent. The Roman Catholic Church published its first *Index Librorum Prohibitorum*, the official list of banned books, in 1559; its ban was generally effective initially in the Catholic countries of Southern Europe, but had the unanticipated effect of stimulating the production of these titles in Protestant Northern Europe, from where copies crept back into France, Spain, and Italy. Language became, as we have seen, a declining restrictive factor as more titles were issued in vernacular languages. The Stationers' Company in London, for example, gave up its stock of Latin books in 1625. Only scientists such as Newton, who wanted to communicate to an international readership of their peers, continued to write in Latin (Feather 1988). The price of books, on the other hand, continued to restrict access to knowledge and ideas, despite widespread piracy, until the nineteenth century and the twin factors of the industrialization of printing and the development of collective purchasing through commercial and public libraries. Until then, reading and what was read reflected the growth in status and wealth of the bourgeoisie. Moreover, publishers were quick to realize the spending power and influence of the female members of that class and to reflect their tastes and preferences in their publications (Flint 1993).

The rise of the popular

The late seventeenth and eighteenth centuries saw further expansion in the number of readers and the development of new forms of publication to suit their needs and tastes. Popular reading was encouraged in France through the creation of the *Bibliothèque bleue* by consecutive dynasties of printers and booksellers in Troyes (Chartier 1987). This series, named for its blue paper covers, was specifically designed for a wide readership. The books were printed on cheap paper; they were short and small; they often consisted of extracts from much longer works; the texts were abridged or edited to simplify or censor; the content comprised tales of chivalry (such as had affected Don Quixote), tales of romance, fairy stories, practical guides, guides to etiquette, religious works, and almanacs; they were distributed by peddlers and sold through numerous outlets; and they were relatively inexpensive. The series was a great success and sold in the tens of thousands. It prefigured the success of the novel in the eighteenth century.

The novel, a genre that owed its existence arguably to the rise of the bourgeoisie, grew in popularity from *Don Quixote* to *Robinson Crusoe* (1719) throughout Europe and North America. One index of that popularity is the number of complaints about either the corrupting effect of so much fiction, in an echo of Plato that can be heard even today, or the waste of time involved in such a trivial pursuit. Reading in bed, with the improved illumination from an oil lamp, was now more common but drew greatest criticism. Reading had become definitively individual and introspective. Samuel Richardson's *Pamela* (1740) attracted chiefly a female readership both because its details of domestic life chimed with their own experience and because it seemed to offer an intimate insight into its eponymous heroine. It combined the narrative suspense of a contemporary soap opera with the moral lessons of a Sunday sermon. In other words, it was both daring and safe. Readers were enthralled. The craze for novel reading persisted: 276 new novels were issued in Germany in 1803 (Wittmann 1999). The genre's predominance continues to this day.

If the novel increasingly filled leisure time and contributed to the impetus toward self-improvement through refinement of feelings, then the growth of encyclopedias, and other compendia of expertise, fueled the impetus toward self-improvement through the acquisition of knowledge. Chambers's *Cyclopedia* of 1728 led directly to the more famous *Encyclopédie* of Diderot appearing from 1751 to 1772 (Darnton 1982a). People read to educate themselves about the world around them; reading could slake a thirst for knowledge unsatisfied by more formal institutions of education. The implicit challenge to established orthodoxies in the spread of a rational approach to knowledge, the Enlightenment, as well as more explicit criticisms, helped to create a climate of questioning of authority leading to the American and French Revolutions, as remarked in Chapter 3. However, the researches of Robert Darnton in the archives of the Swiss Société Typographique de Neuchatel (STN) have highlighted the importance of another genre – pornography. Twenty-one per cent of a sample of 457 titles ordered by booksellers was pornographic (Darnton 1982b). This can partly be seen as a challenge to moral authority analogous and linked to those other challenges to political and ecclesiastical authority;

and partly as the readiness of the STN to satisfy the needs of readers. It is, more importantly, the sign of the development of a popular and underground trade in reading material. Collectors, among whom lawyers and doctors were prominent, established private libraries on quite large scales, and booksellers proliferated to meet their demands as well as those of a much larger group of steady readers drawn from the rest of the bourgeoisie. Darnton draws attention to the French businessman Jean Ranson, who bought books both from the STN and from his local bookseller in La Rochelle. Ranson ordered 59 works from Switzerland between 1775 and 1785. He purchased the *Encyclopédie*, the works of Rousseau, and religious and educational titles. His contemporary, Imbert-Colomès, a silk manufacturer from Lyons, accumulated 10,000 books.

The nature of reading changed throughout the eighteenth century from 'intensive' to 'extensive' (Engelsing 1974). This is not a 'reading revolution,' but the steady shift in general dominance from one norm to the other (Wittmann 1999). Prior to the last decades of the seventeenth century, readers would have typically read and re-read, memorized in whole or in parts, pondered and discussed a small number of books such as the Bible or John Bunyan's *The Pilgrim's Progress* (1678–1684). After this period, readers devoured as much as they could, promiscuously and voraciously, and publishers, such as the Oudot family in Troyes, produced a flood of relatively cheap printed material to satisfy their appetites (Chartier 1987). Not only were people reading more, but more people were reading. Literacy rates, as evidenced by the ability to sign one's name, were increasing in rural areas as well as in towns and cities (Chartier 1989b). The demand for educational materials, particularly primers, increased, in turn, and such books began to replace religious works as the bedrock of publishers' lists. The Lutheran Church in Sweden from 1686 had taken a carrot and stick approach to increasing literacy rates: women living in the countryside were encouraged to teach their children to read and write; and illiterates were banned from the Eucharist and from marriage. The strategy was successful in raising the percentage of those who could read to 80 per cent, although the numbers able to write were much lower.

Reading industrialized

The radical changes of the nineteenth century, particularly the urbanization of a population serving the needs of complex manufacturing, brought in their train a requirement for a more literate workforce that could only be created if the state invested in compulsory publicly managed education for the lower classes. The industrialization of book production – more cheaper copies – established a virtuous circle between producers and consumers – more poorer people.

Reading may have been a survival skill for industrialized societies, but its uses moved well beyond the need to read instruction manuals or order sheets.

Restrictions, especially fiscal burdens, were lifted from print at this time in most countries and a boom in reading material of all kinds ensued as prices fell. If an outright purchase was still not possible or desired, then subscription libraries or clubs allowed borrowing for smaller fees. As railway networks expanded, reading became a preferred method of passing the journey, and station bookshops were established to meet this new demand. W. H. Smith opened its first bookstall at Euston Station in London in 1848 (the example of Hachette in France has already been discussed in Chapter 5). The introduction of gas lighting improved illumination. Leisure time, even if only at first a Sunday afternoon, slowly but surely increased. Reading aloud revived in terms of family readings and of literary salons to complement readings, by now predominantly solipsistic in nature. Dickens's public readings of his own work attracted mass audiences in Britain and the USA as his publications attracted a mass readership.

By the end of the century, the nations of Western Europe and North America had achieved literacy rates of approximately 90 per cent of their populations (Monaghan 1989; Fischer 2003). Inequities between town and country were less pronounced, as were differences between men and women. The existence of the latter as a distinctive reading market was more clearly recognized in the variety of publications geared to presumed female tastes and needs. Novels of all kinds were the preferred form of book – from the literary to the disposable, from Walter Scott to the adventures of Buffalo Bill. Some novelists, such as Scott or Jules Verne, were able to transcend language barriers, and the many translations of their works gave them an international readership and fame. Books were a mass medium. However, they competed for readers with other products of print culture, newspapers and magazines. Collusion replaced competition when serials in magazines were reprinted in book form, as in the case of Dickens or Victor Hugo; but newspapers and magazines offered a rival range of informative and, from the end of the nineteenth century, entertaining material. Their diversity allowed the targeting of particular groups of readers in a very effective manner and the increasingly sophisticated use of illustration offered them an advantage in the mass marketplace (West 1985).

Publishers during the nineteenth century began to see children as a distinct market in acknowledgment, again, of growing parental disposable income, as well as the niche provided by school and Sunday-school prizes. From the 1870s onward, compulsory primary education became the norm in Western Europe. The demand for educational texts rose, as did the opportunities for the production of other forms of publication designed for children in the home. Book publishers were able to compete successfully in this market because of parental prejudices in favor of books – more worthy, more substantial – and against magazines – more frivolous, more transient (Hunt 2001). Whether the children preferred the more didactic material commonly found in books remains in doubt as the memoirs of worthy and substantial adults can be unreliable in the invention of their own childhoods. Only a few writers such as Verne had the imaginative strength to escape the chains of pedagogy.

Public lending libraries were particularly clear that their children's sections should be the home only of edifying and moral literature. In Britain, most of these had been founded after 1850 when a specific rate (local tax) could be levied to pay for their direct costs. In Edinburgh, where we are writing this book, this led to the creation of a strong central library, with an impressive reference and non-fiction collection, and six community libraries in the relatively compact city. Public support was enhanced by private sponsorship: in the case of Edinburgh by Nelsons the publishing company and by Carnegie the steel magnate (who endowed libraries in both Britain and the USA). The emphasis on non-fiction in these libraries was primarily a desire not to use public money on trivial and potentially corrupting matter such as fiction, but also because novels were the staple of the subscription or private library (Rose 2001). Not that they waived the right not to stock a book that might cause offence and, indeed, to engage in pre-emptive censorship in their relationship with publishers eager to please a key volume purchaser. However, a strong tradition of autodidacticism among the working class in Britain and Germany enabled a match between its needs and what the public libraries were willing to provide. Autobiographies and other extant testimony, such as diaries, reveal the power of the drive to learn, to acquire knowledge and understanding. Maxim Gorky ironically entitled a volume of his autobiography *My Universities* (1923) as they included long shifts on a variety of jobs in the course of which he attempted to maintain his self-directed program of reading. The central character in A. J. Cronin's *The Stars Look Down* (1935) reads avidly while working as a miner until he can escape the pit by obtaining a scholarship to college. He does so under conditions – fatigue, poor light, lack of privacy – that strike an authentic note in the novel.

The nature of reading

The advent of new media such as the cinema, radio, and then television at the beginning of the twentieth century to join existing print rivals marked not only increasing competition, but a confirmation that the book had lost its status as the mass medium while reading continued to be as important as ever. Even the early silent films relied on the audience's ability to read to fill in the gaps in the narrative or to explain complex elements of it. Contemporary television is characterized, in its news broadcasts, at least, by the use of sometimes two or three static or rolling banners of text in addition to the pictures and sound. In other words, literacy has not changed, but the nature of what we read has changed in the course of the twentieth century. The growth of paperback series such as Reclam or Penguin and the success of particular bestsellers such as the Harry Potter series do not efface the general decline in reading books as an activity if measured by the numbers participating (McCleery 2002). On the other hand, there is anecdotal evidence that the use of tablets, iPads, and other electronic devices to access textual material is increasing demand for reading material in forms other than print. Across the developed world, fewer people may be reading fewer printed works but more electronic texts. Perhaps a question to ask is whether this is a trend that will continue, demonstrating a similar crossover of social interaction with texts that was witnessed during the long transition from written and manuscript works to print.

The act of reading can seem more anarchic in terms of the loss of textual authority. The extremist wing of the reader-as-interpreter perspective would argue that the reader can create anything he or she likes from a text without boundaries or restriction. A more moderate view would agree that reading is not a passive activity in which the reader decodes a text with a single meaning. This may have been true of the first records, and may continue to be true of today's equivalent of Jack Cade's score and tally, but it is not characteristic of most of what we read. In the past, church and state (and authors) may have tried to impose a particular meaning upon a text, but texts and readers resist such conformity. Wolfgang Iser argues that meaning emerges from the inter-action of text and reader (Iser 1980). To the creation of meaning the text brings its words, a set of linguistic units, while the reader brings an individual set of experiences that color the semantic value given to those units separately and jointly. There is, therefore, no particular 'correct' meaning, although the range of possible meanings is constrained by the fixed nature of the text, of its component words. Jerome McGann would add at this juncture that the reader interprets not a text, but a material object – the book; that the words of the text are in a particular font and size, on a particular paper, in a particular book, between particular covers; and that these particularities of the physical book also influence and constrain the range of possible meanings (McGann 1991).

Stanley Fish might then, in our imaginary roundtable on reading, stress that the range is constrained by the individual reader's values, experiences, and cultural references (Fish 1976). He would go on to argue that these are less unique than we sometimes care to think. The fact that there are many readers of one text does not necessarily result in a wide range of meanings, as our shared values, experiences, and cultural references limit that range. Common meaning, as in the case of Schlink's novel at the beginning of this chapter, signals our membership of 'interpretive communities,' broad groups of other individuals with whom we share values, experiences, and cultural references. One of the positive elements of belonging to a book group, whether virtual like Oprah's or one that meets in homes, bookshops, or libraries, is the sense of solidarity derived not just from a common activity, reading the same book, but from membership of an 'interpretive community' expressed through common or close views on that book (Hartley 2001). It is clear from Janice Radway's interviews with readers of romance fiction that a similar sense of solidarity is felt there (Radway 1984). This is the point where reading, as it has developed as an individual interpretive act, and reading as a distinct social activity intersect and merge.

Conclusion

You have completed the reading of this chapter, and on doing so you should now be familiar with some of the concepts of reading studies and the history of society's engagement with this most democratic and important of communication skills. With a greater or lesser degree of facility, then, you have used a skill that is seen as essential in terms both of your nature as an individual and of your ability to function effectively within society. This is a skill that is inextricably linked to the technology of writing but tends to outpace it, so that 'literacy' implies primarily reading and only secondarily writing. However, as written or printed texts are what survive, the reconstruction of reading history presents difficulties in the amount and nature of evidence available. Book history attempts to integrate understanding of the individual act of reading – how you are creating meaning at this moment from these symbols in ink that we have written and the publisher has chosen to present in this format – and of the social history of reception – why you bought or borrowed this book, who you are, where and when you are reading this – often aggregated with details of other readers to create a social profile of readership. Book history can exploit both individual accounts of reading and wider statistical sources, as well as books, to create a history of reading itself that ranges from the earliest decoding of commercial and administrative data to the extensive and often eclectic nature of contemporary reading. Such a history provides a necessary corrective to the emphasis upon the production of books typical of much previous book history; it assists the humanization of the field, not least by asking us to reflect on our own experience as readers.

Points to ponder

We leave you with some points to ponder as you read about the hows, whats and whys of reading. Throughout history, certain types of reading material and ways of reading were promoted by groups (churches, schools, libraries, political groups) intent on directing reading patterns: how do and did readers respond to such directions and recommendations? In an age of new media, what is the purpose of reading? Are we witnessing a significant shift in the way we access and read books and texts? And, finally, what is the value of reading, how do you do it, and what do you gain the most from in doing it?

7

THE FUTURE OF THE BOOK

Introduction

The history of science fiction is marked by the failed prophecies of respected writers of their time. It is impossible to predict the future; only trends can be extrapolated and these pay no regard to possible maverick changes (this view lies at the heart of Isaac Asimov's *Foundation* series). At the time of writing the first edition of this chapter, we could not predict the success of the Amazon Kindle or the Apple iPad; and, of course, as you read this, both may well have been superseded by other types of technology or their business models made redundant by new forms of distribution and ownership. We are conscious that a local band has called itself 'We Were Promised Jetpacks' in an ironic reference to a vision of the future made popular in television series such as *The Jetsons*. Perhaps the methodology employed in considering 'the future of the book' possesses greater importance than any actual predictions made as a result of it.

However, the continuing inclusion of a chapter on this topic derives from at least two factors: the persistent rumors of the death of the book since the beginning of the twentieth century, and our equally obdurate but perhaps naive view of history that the past prefigures the future. For the former, speculative writers, such as Wells in *When The Sleeper Awakes* (1899), envisaged a future in which the book had been superseded by other forms of audio-visual information storage and entertainment. For the latter, the two previous revolutions in communications technology – in the shifts from orality to the technology of writing and from manuscript to print, discussed in Chapters 2 and 3 – heighten the sense that we are living through a third revolution in the shift from print to digital media that combine textual, graphical, and oral materials. Yet, books retain for the moment a power to communicate and influence: every major political election stimulates the publication of books to promote the interests of candidates or the ideas upon which they have based their platform, as well as television commercials, blogs, and tweets; minority groups such as the plethora of conspiracy obsessives, from believers in a lost Atlantis to adherents of the Holy Grail, still produce minutely argued books to support their views, as well as websites and YouTube videos; and those with fundamentalist religious beliefs constantly monitor school textbooks for infringements, moral or scientific, of those beliefs, as they also do cinema releases and music downloads. The latter concern with textbooks should also remind us that books are still the basic tools of education in developing as well as developed countries, perhaps more so.

The evidence supports the case, contrary to intimations of their mortality, that books are being published in increasing numbers, both in terms of titles and print run, but that, in developed countries at least, many consumers are exercising the choice to settle on alternatives, including e-books, whether for information or for leisure. In these countries, fewer readers are reading, and buying, more books, both print and electronic, and particular groups such as children or women may account for most of this extensive reading. Yet, there is also a concern that the nature of that reading may consolidate the development of a homogenization of global culture. We can analyze both the production and the distribution of books at a global level and the reception of such global goods within specific cultures. There are strong precedents for examination of both within book history as, indeed, there are also examples confirming that uniformity of production does not imply uniformity of reception. This chapter will examine four related aspects of the immediate past and present of the book – technology, industry organization, readership, and the role of the state – to identify the drivers and direction of the changes that will create the future of the book.

Technological determinism

The notion that the book is an obsolete medium originates in a fixation with the pace of technological change and the concomitant rapid introduction of new and newer forms of information storage, retrieval, and communication. In particular, the printed word has been challenged across a range of instrumental as opposed to cultural functions by a succession of digital media, from laser discs to CD-ROMs to e-books. It retains an edge in that its enabling technology, literacy, is universal, or widespread in the developing countries that cannot afford the new media, while each of the latter demands access to technologies that are not universally available, or, as in the case of laser discs, are obsolescent and raise issues of 'future-proofing.' The printed word loses out to the ability to search rapidly and retrieve a diversity of information and to the abilities of digital media to integrate text, sound, and images, still and moving. The storage capacity of a device such as the Kindle saves on the weight and volume of an equivalent number of printed books. The printed word gains in the variety of languages (and alphabets) in which it is found, while online information and access is primarily in English (and the Roman alphabet) and demands a reading knowledge of English from all users. It may even, as in the case of text messaging, increasingly call for understanding of a particular subset of English.

Paul Duguid introduces two concepts relevant to this discussion: super-session and liberation (Duguid 1996). The first embodies the notion that new technologies replace and erase the old. In the case of the book, it is that digital media have killed it or are slowly smothering it. The history of the book helps to put such a scenario into perspective. At the beginning of the twentieth century, the then new analog media of radio, cinema, and, later, television also challenged and eventually overturned the supremacy of the book, and print generally, as a virtually monopolistic medium of communication and information. The book, however, did not die out: publishers developed, as we have noted, new popular forms such as the paperback; they extended the range of retail outlets; and they enjoyed a symbiotic relationship with the producers of the analog media by both offering a source of material for radio, cinema, and television, and exploiting the popularity of the new media by creating the book of the radio serial, of the film, or linked to the television program. Indeed, this relationship, and the general trade in intellectual property rights, described in Chapter 4, brought renewed prosperity, at best, or the means of survival, at worst, for many publishers.

Duguid emphasizes that the appeal of supersession lies to a great extent in its clear rejection of the past as a principle in itself and as a means of characterizing or branding the new media as just that – 'new' and therefore innovative, exciting, revolutionary, and necessary. The book becomes, in other words, last century's model or fashion, and in a consumerist society we are impelled to reject it in favor of the 'new.' The opposite tendency should be noted (for example, in the writings of Sven Birkerts) – that is, to idealize the past through an idyllic representation of print culture, reading, and education (Birkerts 1996). The defense of the book has often been in the hands of cultural conservatives such as Harold Bloom who are concerned with preserving certain books and certain forms of reading that seem to them to embody a past culture and its clear values to be set against the muddled nature of the contemporary (Bloom 1996, 2001). The use of the term 'culture' here is key: that concern is not for encyclopedias, recipe books, help manuals, or generally anything that has a purely informative value. It derives from a privileged status given to literature, biography, scholarship – particularly in the humanities – and generally anything that has a potential cultural value. Partly this is a concern to preserve material of lasting significance as opposed to that of immediate usefulness; partly it is also a form of reactionary nostalgia. As such, it becomes clear that the 'revolutionaries,' the advocates of the all-conquering nature of the new media, and these defenders of the book are offering absolutist and simplistic views from the two ends of what is, in fact, a spectrum.

The idea of 'revolution' in the new media often stems from the sense that they have somehow liberated information as opposed to the book's control and restriction of it. Duguid's second concept, of liberation, is based on this view that digital technologies, particularly the World Wide Web, empower all by providing all with the ability to become authors whose work can be read and widely appreciated. The computer has replaced not only the typewriter but also the publisher and the bookseller. Liberation does not create the 'death of the author,' but the making of the author into his or her own publisher. Liberation can also imply the loosening of the bonds of intellectual property law and not only the availability of material, but also the seeming license to make different versions of it. Jay David Bolter, himself an advocate of the predestined marginality of the book, writes: 'The computer is restructuring our current economy of writing. It is changing the cultural status of writing as well as the method of producing books. It is changing the relationship of the author to the text and of both author and text to the reader' (Bolter 1991: 3). Digital technologies, in the view of the liberationist revolutionaries, act as the Robin Hoods of contemporary culture, allowing theft from the information- and power-rich to empower democratic communities. All information becomes available to all consumers.

A version of this argument lies behind the view that the fax machine and the photocopier brought about the end of the Cold War, while the internet and e-mail have the capacity to change controlled societies such as China (Wirtén 2003). It is an argument that, however plausible, underestimates the need for some sort of validation of information, in the past literally provided by the book's imprimatur. It may also deny the importance of the book in creating and supporting social communities, from Benedict Anderson's 'imagined communities' of nationhood to Janice Radway's 'interpretive community' of romance readers (Anderson 1983; Radway 1984). Online access may conversely stress the isolation of the individual, disintegrating rather than forming 'virtual communities.' This is contrary to McLuhan's vision of the 'global village,' based admittedly more on the effects of television during the mid-1960s than on digital technologies and the internet (McLuhan 1962, 1964). McLuhan, clearly an influence on Ong's characterization of orality, argued that where literacy and, in particular, its adaptation in print promoted linear, sequential thought and individual reading, the post-print technologies recreated Socratic dialog and brought the world into the village of oral culture (Ong 1982). Manuel Castells, our contemporary McLuhan, further sees the convergence of digital media that gives rise to the network society leading to a commonality of cultural experience (Castells 1996). Members of the anti-globalization movement certainly fear a homogenization of culture and the uniform creation of an American global village, usually seen in shorthand as the 'coca-colonization' of the world, and they view a US-based media, and the linguistic domination of the internet by English, as the engine for the process (Tunstall 1994). This is a point to which we will return in the following section.

However, there is an additional valuable lesson to be drawn from book history in its stress upon publication as an act of socialization. Communication circuits, similar to Darnton's familiar model, do exist and are being developed for digital technologies (Darnton 1982b). These may not be merely the empowerment of the individual as author and publisher, whether singly or as part of a collective and collaborative effort, such as Wikipedia. New entrepreneurs and website facilities have appeared such as Smashwords or Scribd who perform similar roles as the agents within the Adams and Barker version of Darnton's model (Adams and Barker 1993). Retail outlets such as the Amazon Kindle Store or Apple's iBooks (iTunes) have gained a predominant gatekeeping role within a very short period. However, liberationists propound a decentralized vision, somewhere between the empowered individual and a cottage industry such as is characterized by fanzines, that underestimates the power of professionalism of presentation (and imprimatur) as well as the survival instincts of existing industries. The contemporary institutional context of the new media, in terms of production and distribution, remains frequently that of the transnational corporation, itself containing a book publishing division (p-books and e-books) within its overall media operations.

The growth of e-books parallels that of the early period of print, particularly during the Reformation; and as the early printed books reflected manuscripts in their appearance and organization, so, too, contemporary e-books provide merely a digital analog to the printed book. Indeed, many of them represent the digitization of the publisher's backlist with the distinct advantage to the consumer of everything remaining available and nothing going 'out of print.' However, if the parallel with the development of the printed book is valid, then current experiments in creating enhanced content will result in new forms of e-book that bear only a superficial resemblance to their ancestor. Such developments will make new demands of readers (users) and technological potential will need to keep pace with market acceptance. At times, readers will need to learn new ways of making meaning from the e-book; at other times, new forms of e-book will fail initially in the marketplace because of consumer resistance. This resistance for the moment derives from a sense of the insecurity and instability of e-books (compared to print) that includes concern over ownership, transferability, and resale. Ironically, these anxieties do not seem to be shared by publishers and retailers; yet both these groups are themselves anxious about the threat to their own ownership and control that comes from digital piracy.

Authors, publishers, retailers, and readers cannot ignore e-books, however ignorant they may be of their future development. For authors, the lack of investment by the publisher in paper, printing, binding, and carriage should see a higher proportion of the e-book price coming to them as a reward for their creativity. Efforts to self-publish or through a technological facilitator will, of course, increase the author's revenue even further; but, as we have argued above, this may be to sacrifice additional sales, including rights, resulting from the quality assurance in editing and the professionalism in marketing offered by the publisher. Publishers themselves must make clear the value of those services while at the same time investing, as they have always done, in the enhancement of content – in the context of e-books, through exploitation of the technical platform to add value to the reader's experience. Those publishers who are content simply to create a 'long tail' of e-books by digitizing their print backlist will not survive long without innovation. The domination of a small number of retailers, particularly Amazon and Apple, who have also built the devices upon which the e-books are read, cannot endure within an entrepreneurial, competitive marketplace. The lack of interoperability, the attempt to fix prices, the limitation of potential content by the specifications of their devices: all militate against their twin oligopoly (selling to readers) and oligopsony (buying from publishers) persisting for very long.

Media globalization

Globalization in this heading refers specifically to three areas in the recent history of the book that might again affect its future: the predominantly transnational ownership of the book publishing sector of the media; the increased transnational flow of books, not as material objects or even as e-books, but as the source of texts that can be translated both into other languages and into other media; and the alleged commonality of transnational culture. These three areas are not discrete elements but aspects of a cyclical, reinforcing process for which the term 'globalization' applies (Giddens 1990).

As noted at the close of Chapter 3, during the latter half of the twentieth century, publishing houses came together through merger and acquisition to form large, often transnational conglomerates. It might seem from this that the book publishing industry has become one of the engines for the globalization of culture as much as it had been perceived to provide the motive power for the Reformation, Renaissance, and the Enlightenment. However, it was also noted that two types of conglomerate had emerged: one which was primarily print based and operating in a number of different countries (the example given was the German-based Bertelsmann); and the other operating in different media, of which book publishing was only one and not necessarily the most important (the example given was News Corporation, which owned HarperCollins). The distinction here has become less clear cut than implied earlier, as companies that had grown as a result of horizontal integration began also to expand through vertical integration of activities up and downstream from the core publishing business. The ongoing transition, driven partly by digital technologies, from publishers producing only books and, for example, studios producing only films and television programs to conglomerates doing both (and more), has blurred the distinction between the two types of conglomerate from the 1990s onwards. The ability to exploit digital material, whether text, sound, or image, across a number of media has added value to the often debased term 'synergy.' The original publishing conglomerates share the characteristics of other contemporary media industries: large capital investment, mass production for mass markets, and the creation of marketable products that may also form a cultural asset.

Greco recorded a general rising trend in merger and acquisition activity in the USA between 1960 and 1989, although fiscal reforms introduced by the US Congress in 1987 did lead to a subsequent slowing down in activity (Greco 1995). In a further study published in 1996, he tracked a dramatic resumption of mergers and acquisitions from 1990: he tallies a total of 557 media acquisitions between 1990 and 1995 that comes close to the entire number during the period covered by his earlier analysis (Greco 1996). This second phase during the 1990s created large transnational media conglomerates covering a range of products and activities. The year 2000 marked not only the end of the century but the merger of AOL, chiefly an internet service provider, with Time-Warner, itself a media conglomerate containing book publishing among its interests, to build the largest such corporation in the world. During the same year, the French conglomerate Vivendi, comprising both an environmental services division and a media division, within which book publishing was a key constituent, acquired Universal with its extensive interests in music, film, and television. Many other media conglomerates were fired by the 'dotcom mania' of the 1990s to acquire interests in the new digital technologies and products with which to complement, and cross-promote, existing interests in analog services and products, again including book publishing. The synergy sought by these companies was based on a clear model of integration, itself dependent upon the ability to translate the value of intellectual property from medium to medium. The avatar of that model was the Disney Corporation, whose keen awareness of the value of its brands such as Mickey Mouse even led to a change in US intellectual property law. The exploitation of those brands included not only films, television, theme parks, CDs, and merchandizing, but the direct publication or licensing of children's books based on them, both as spin-offs of new products and as the continuing development of long-established ones.

The consolidation of publishing within media groups, through these processes of take-over, merger, and integration, has led to a concentration of the book market (in turn, exaggerated through examples of horizontal integration such as the acquisition in the UK of Hodder Headline by W. H. Smith, a deal itself following the Smith purchase of the retailing arm of John Menzies). Meier and Trappel collated statistics from the European Union to provide a country-by-country index of the market share of its top five publishing companies (Meier and Trappel 1998). The percentages ranged from 95 in The Netherlands and the UK to 42 in Finland. Bagdikian has compiled a measure of market concentration across the analog media in the USA from 1983 onward (Bagdikian 2000). He calculated for the predominant companies within book publishing, newspapers and magazines, television, and cinema how many of them it took to total 50 per cent of the market share. On this basis, he produced figures year on year for market concentration within the media: 50 firms in 1983 had fallen to 29 in 1987, 10 in 1997 and only 6 by 2000. The significance of such concentration lies in the conclusions that critics have drawn from it about choice, quality, and 'coca-colonization.' Such a concentration results, it is argued, in a decrease in consumer choice and an increase in the commonality of transnational culture (in turn, exaggerated by the integrated marketing of a range of media products within the one group). This seemed contrary to evidence such as that provided by Greco indicating in the USA alone an increase in new titles from 15,012 in 1960 to 53,446 in 1989 (Greco 1996).

An explanation of the seeming contradiction may lie in the lack of diversity and a sense of unchallenging homogeneity within such an increase in titles. There is a particular mechanism which creates and constantly reinforces the failure to take risks within conglomerates and which distinguishes them from independent houses. When a company is taken over by a conglomerate, the emphasis changes from cross-subsidy of titles to each title being expected to make a prescribed contribution to both overheads and profit. When the Bertelsmann conglomerate took over the Random House conglomerate in 1998, the new owners expected Random House to make a 15 per cent profit and to increase turnover by 10 per cent annually. This would have entailed a leap in profits from $1 million to $150 million on annual sales of roughly $1 billion; it would also have involved a concurrent growth in those sales of $100 million (Schiffrin 2001). As a corollary, the emphasis was placed on a frontlist with an immediate impact rather than the building up of a backlist that would add significantly to profits, including now as e-books. André Schiffrin sums up the conclusion to this: 'The logic of the profit center began to be counterproductive. The need for each entity [within the conglomerate] to achieve an annual increase in sales and profit forced every part of the publishing house to duplicate the other's efforts and to compete for the most lucrative titles' (Schiffrin 2001: 76).

Commissioning editors have profit and loss accounts kept for their specific titles, and each editor will be expected to generate a prescribed amount of revenue and profit each year, more often than not the basis for performance-related pay. The need to find the 'sure thing' leads, in turn, to the offering of huge advances to celebrities of all kinds whose fame might be expected to deliver the necessary sales and margins (in 1998, HarperCollins announced that it had written off $270 million of unearned advances). Or large advances are offered to authors whose work produced by an independent publisher has demonstrated the 'surety' of its sales. Or, again, books are produced as part of, and derivative from, a media package centered on a film or even a computer game. And in order to make the sure thing more secure, the conglomerates expend large advertising budgets, employ huge sales forces, and exploit strong media connections (often within a sister company). Even if the conglomerate product does not sell – and the public is, on occasion, perverse enough to assert its own tastes, both negatively by rejecting the 'sure thing' and positively as in the word-of-mouth acclamation of *Captain Corelli's Mandolin* – it is not without want of promotion and publicity (Gardiner 2000).

The cultural pessimism that is the legacy of the early twentieth-century Frankfurt School of social critics, specifically their stigmatization of the mass production of culture and its incorporation within a modern capitalist, industrial process, has resulted in concerns not just about choice and diversity, but about the quality of what is on offer (Adorno and Horkheimer 1944). In this, there is an obvious link to the cultural conservatives defending the survival of the printed book on the basis of a limited definition of the culturally significant. The most full-blooded attack on the quality of conglomerate publishing appears in a 1997 study by Mark Crispin Miller. Like Schiffrin, Miller looks back to an era of publishing that was text rather than profit centered. Random House (pre-Bertelsmann) is one of three American publishing houses he accuses of shifting from great novels and other works of cultural significance to market-oriented '*dreck*.' He catalogs the latter as including celebrity-derived books, either about, by, or linked to the famous, and leisure or hobby books, whether decoration, cooking, or gardening. He excoriates a commissioning policy that leads to the 'empty and self-serving' memoirs of the Duchess of York (Miller 1997: 116). He also condemns the poor editing and proof-reading that result in a book as 'half-baked, ill-informed, and crudely written as Newt Gingrich's *To Renew America*' (Miller 1997: 116). While there is much that as individuals we might agree with in this partisan diatribe as far as the merits of particular titles are concerned, there are problems in its selectivity and lack of analytical rigor. It begins with its conclusion and then fails satisfactorily to provide the evidence that would lead to it. Janice Radway's study of the Book-of-the-Month Club presents a much better account of the relationships between publishers and their markets (Radway 1997). In its subject, it antedates the age of conglomerates, yet it supplies a convincing, objective, and detailed analysis that might with benefit be applied to contemporary commissioning and selection processes.

The book products of the media conglomerates do find an international market that was in previous centuries the achievement only of sacred books, particularly the Christian Bible. The example of J. K. Rowling's series of books about the young wizard Harry Potter is instructive in this instance. These books have achieved an immense international success, initially in the English-speaking world and then, as the series progressed, in over 40 translations (the time lag between English-language publication and French translation of *Harry Potter and the Order of the Phoenix* led to the English version becoming the number one children's bestseller in France in the interval – a phenomenon repeated in Germany in 2007 with the publication of *Harry Potter and the Deathly Hallows*). That success has been enhanced by the making of the novels into movies, and the consequent re-promotion of the titles; it has been strengthened by crossover sales between the children's and adult markets encouraged by the book's publishers, for example, in the provision of separate jackets or covers for each; and it has been optimized by the manipulation of hardback and paperback publishing schedules to ensure maximum purchase of the more expensive format before the cheaper is issued on a fresh wave of publicity and expectation. The success has been sufficient, and the reputation of the books so widespread, that Rowling has undertaken herself the sale of the e-books (with additional content) without the involvement of her UK or US publishers.

Such an international outreach, particularly from the making of the movies onward, might constitute evidence for 'coca-colonization' or the homogenization of international culture – albeit in the British tradition of boarding school adventure that has a long, indigenous narrative pedigree (yet, there have been few studies of the reception of the Harry Potter novels beyond accounts of the reaction of fundamentalist Christians in the USA). This criticism of globalization, and the activities of transnational media conglomerates, as found, for example, in Herman and McChesney's important 1997 work, has echoes of earlier charges of cultural imperialism (Herman and McChesney 1997). This essentially referred to the imposition of the values and norms of the developed world upon the cultures of the developing world through export of cheap media products with higher production values (relative to those that were being produced locally, if any were). One of the present authors remembers looking forward to the weekly highlight, and incongruity, in Accra, Ghana, in 1972 of watching the US series *Mission Impossible* on television. Such programs (and the Western series *Bonanza* was another weekly favorite contrasting with the studio-based, didactic local programs that bookended it during the few limited hours of broadcasting each evening) provided points of reference and role models, in language and behavior, that seemed more glamorous than indigenous norms and traditions. Reading Shakespeare and the rest of the canon of English literature in African schools, because those were the (imported) books available, at best exposed students to different values and stressed positive links with the former colonial power; at worst, it created a sense of dissonance with the environment of the reader and challenged a secure sense of local identity. (The other author contributes a memory of watching a 1976 Latin American broadcast of a dubbed BBC TV production of *The Golden Bowl*, the classic novel by American-born but British-based author Henry James. This experience also highlights the continuing exploitation of texts through different media and different languages.) Thirty years on, the cultural imperialism charge in both cases seems weak in its failure to comprehend both the dynamic, as opposed to static, nature of cultures and the reader's active creation of meaning from texts, as discussed in the previous chapter, rather than its passive absorption.

However, books have been less complicit anyway in 'coca-colonization' than other media products: linguistic differences continue to be respected through catering for different language communities; books are often customized for different cultures, as the example of Harlequin demonstrates; and smaller, local, or niche publishers can continue to thrive based on higher levels of creativity and lower inputs of capital (particularly compared to cinema or television) (Wirtén 1998). The conglomerates monitor these smaller companies and will often take them over for the high value they place upon the creativity and innovation to be found there. Greco noted in his study of merger and acquisition activity that the number of publishing companies in the USA had increased from 993 in 1960 to 2,298 in 1987 (Greco 1996: 234). The existence of these smaller companies catering to the diverse needs of a range of readers also gives the lie to the cultural pessimism of Miller and others. As independent companies or local imprints of the conglomerates, they represent a source of growth and vitality for the future of the book within niche markets and developing countries.

Death of the reader

When Roland Barthes wrote about the 'death of the author,' he was celebrating the triumph of the reader in the sense of the acknowledgment of the latter as the key agent in the creation of meaning (Barthes 1977). As again discussed in the previous chapter, theorists such as Barthes and Iser privileged the role of the reader in his or her interaction with the text over that of the author (Iser 1980). Yet, at the moment of triumph, the reader may also seem to be in danger of death or gradual disappearance, where 'reader' signifies the reader of books. Reports from the UK and the USA over the last decade and more emphasize the decline in the number of such readers. The report from the US National Endowment for the Arts in 2004 quantified the decline as a fall from 56.9 per cent of American adults reading fiction for pleasure in 1982 to a figure of 46.7 per cent in 2002 (NEA 2004). The chief factor involved in that decrease was competition from other activities for disposable time: television may no longer be the major rival and, indeed, may promote reading books in a number of ways; and the period surveyed has seen growth in the use of the internet as a leisure activity, as well as the proliferation of games consoles and computer games. The report also noted with some incredulity that the decline comes during a period in which book clubs (including the dramatic success of the televised Oprah's Book Club), bookshops, online book retailers, and sales of bestsellers are booming. One explanation of this came in the 2000 UK report *Reading the Situation*, sponsored by the Library and Information Commission: fewer people were reading more books. In the UK, 15 per cent of adults claimed to read for pleasure for at least 11 hours a week (BML 2000). One of the questions for which we now need evidence is whether this declining group has also been buying e-book devices and e-books or whether promotion of the Kindle, iPad and Nook has increased the number of active readers (and book purchasers across both print and electronic).

Reading as a general activity, on the other hand, continues to thrive whether on paper or on screen: by the beginning of the twenty-first century, the high literacy rates that had been achieved in Western Europe and the USA 100 years earlier as a result of concerted emphasis on compulsory elementary schooling are within sight across the world as a result of the acknowledgment of reading's key role in economic development. The primary vehicle for literacy education is still the book, particularly, as noted above, in the developing world, where books are the most cost-effective, and sometimes the only, medium available. In the developed world, the growth of the 'information society' has also placed a greater premium on the ability to read as a technical ability. Although the importance of print media may be declining in these cultures relative to other forms of information, texts coming through other communication channels continue to compete for the reader's attention. Any café in a Western European city today will contain a young person tapping in a text message on a mobile phone or reading messages received. If it is an internet café, then there will be others writing and reading e-mail messages. Seen in this light, Don McKenzie's relabeling of bibliography or the history of the book as the 'sociology of texts,' and the inclusiveness that that implies, represents an extension of the perspectives gained from the book and print into all forms of communication (McKenzie 1986). For the future of the book, nevertheless, the crucial issue is no longer illiteracy but aliteracy: those who can read but will not read books.

The profile of the representative reader in Western Europe or the USA today would acknowledge his or her extensive, indeed eclectic, reading, influenced by publicity and promotion but also by word-of-mouth recommendations (*Captain Corelli's Mandolin* has already been cited as a beneficiary of word-of-mouth praise and so, too, was *Harry Potter and the Philosopher's Stone* when first published in a small hardback print run). Newspaper editors know that book review sections are popular with their readers and those readers use the reviewers' judgments as guides to potential purchases or borrowings. Reading habits change in the course of the individual's lifecycle. Most men give up reading for pleasure after they leave formal education; if they resume reading books, it is in middle age when activities such as sport and socializing take up less of their leisure time. Women read more consistently from school onward and if reading books tails off, it does so when they have young children, before picking up again as their offspring grow older. Women read more fiction than men and, indeed, constitute the major market for novels with the exception of some genre fiction. Women are more likely to be members of book groups than men, to recommend books to their peers, and, indeed, to be more adventurous in their choices of book (Hartley 2001). The UK report indicated that 'those who enjoy reading from an early age tend never to give up the habit, and though during some stages in life they may be forced by their circumstances to read less than they would like, they usually become "heavy" readers again once they get the chance' (BML 2000: 10). 'Heavy' readers are created in childhood: if children are encouraged to read in the home environment and have at least one parent who is also an enthusiastic reader, then they will tend to grow up to read extensively.

Some readers use printed, particularly paperback, books as disposable objects, both literally and in terms of the reading experience. Through the respondents in the UK survey, the uses and gratifications of book reading for pleasure were clarified to some extent: 52 per cent saw it as a means of relaxing or relieving stress, 27 per cent as escapism, and 24 per cent as an opportunity to exercise their imagination (BML 2000: 12). The ability simultaneously to stimulate and to relax may be a strong survival characteristic, perhaps, of the book. The environment in which book reading takes place varies: from in bed, typically just before going to sleep; in a train carriage or on a plane; to a busy and noisy station or airport surrounded by ebbing and flowing crowds. There is also no single practice of reading: it varies from the scanning of the limited text within heavily illustrated 'coffee-table' books, to deciphering a complex description within an unfamiliar field, to being fully engrossed in the strong narratives of genre fiction.

The reader has importantly triumphed in the guise of the 'market' to which the publishing and retailing of books, particularly as directed by the media conglomerates, must be subordinate. Retailing of printed books has split into two different paths to accommodate the needs and nature of the reader: online ordering of books from companies such as Amazon enables the searching of databases, often served by 'intelligent agents' predicting the reader's preferences based on previous purchases, a choice from a wider stock than any physical retailer could offer, and some element of discounting on the price; contemporary bookshops provide welcoming and comfortable environments, including reading areas and coffee shops, to recreate book-buying as a leisure activity in which specific selections are more likely to be made on impulse rather than pre-planned. The reading of books becomes, in turn, either a necessary function of education or employment, where it is most under threat from online forms of information retrieval, or a lifestyle leisure choice, where it is competing with other forms of activity and may be the preference of identifiable and distinct sub-groups. The latter become the targets of publishers eager to establish dominance within these sub-groups for particular authors or series. The international success of Harlequin, its dominance of the publication of romantic fiction, stems from its knowledge of its markets in different countries and its ability to adapt basic formulae for them – as well as the economies of scale it achieves through such global exploitation of its intellectual property (Wirtén 1998). E-books, in turn, as we have argued, assist the publisher in servicing these sub-groups or market segments by supporting the ability to increase the number of titles available while reducing the financially viable print run of each. The publisher of this textbook, for example, can exploit these technologies to reprint, on demand, relatively small numbers of its backlist in addition to making them available as e-books, thereby extending consumer choice.

The role of the state

However, if technological advances in production are not sufficient to create books that match both the expectations and the budget of these small groups of readers, or offer sufficient choice, then a new actor can enter the stage to intervene in what otherwise would be a market-led process. The state, or agencies empowered by the state, can ensure that what for cultural, educational, linguistic, or national reasons are seen as a positive benefit – that is, books – should continue to be available to readers even if they are not financially viable to produce and sell. The state has traditionally been seen in an antagonistic role to publishing and, until the late twentieth century, often intervened, as noted in Chapters 3 and 6, to suppress, as opposed to supporting, publications for moral or political motives. D. H. Lawrence's *Lady Chatterley's Lover* was not widely available in its unexpurgated version until the 1959 trial of Grove Press in the USA and the 1960 trial of Penguin Books in the UK (McCleery 2002). The Nazis staged book-burning ceremonies to dramatize their loathing of books by those who, by religion, ethnic origin, or thought, were deemed to oppose them. However, moral censorship of books has been largely abdicated by states in Western Europe and North America; the cudgel has been taken up by lobby groups such as religious fundamentalists who have sought in differing ways to ban books, from the Harry Potter novels to Salman Rushdie's *Satanic Verses* (1989). For the former, those who object to witchcraft and wizards operate within democracies to persuade libraries and schools not to stock the novels; for the latter, a sentence of death was pronounced on the author and anyone involved in the book's publication, translation, or sale. Despite the views of conspiracy theorists, states in the developed world undertake little overt political censorship except in cases of national security, and even there, as in the UK prosecution of *Spycatcher* (1987), the results are, at best, fresh publicity and increased demand for the publication.

Today, the relationship between the state and publishing in the developed world is generally a positive one. By defining books as a cultural good, an educational necessity, a defense against the erosion of national language or identity, the state can support both proactively and passively their publication and reading. For the latter, the support of a strong library system might seem to be an infrastructural necessity. However, state support for public library services has been in general decline for many years – partly as a result of the decrease in readers, the transformation of bookshops and bookselling, and an increase in the range of provision that libraries are expected to offer – and this has created a vicious circle of further decline as readers reject poor book stock and dowdy environments. States can also use fiscal or statutory means to support reading (and readers): in the UK, books are zero-rated for purchase tax (VAT), and in France *la loi Lang* of 1981 established retail price maintenance, the UK version of which, the voluntary, rather than statutory, Net Book Agreement, had been allowed to lapse by book publishers in 1995.

More proactive models of support are available from countries concerned to protect local languages from the hegemony of English and/or from those concerned to safeguard national interests and values from the market dominance of the transnational publishing industry. Throughout the 1990s and beyond, for example, the Government of Canada developed a wide range of programs to support the growth and development of the publishing industry throughout Canada, with an emphasis on equal development of material in the two state languages, English and French. Some of these programs were common to the development of the cultural industries as a whole, while others were targeted directly at specific sectors of the industry (Lorimer 1996; Lorimer with Gasher 2000). Support ranged from direct grants to support the writing and publishing of books, to discount financing to support the growth and development of small businesses. In 2001, the federal government in Ottawa paid out US$1.1 million in emergency advances to 22 Canadian publishers who were in difficulty following high returns (in some cases 50–70 per cent) from the Chapters chain of booksellers. The impact of these programs and a wide range of marketing and promotional initiatives saw the volume of books of indigenous origin sold in Canada rise from between 3 and 5 per cent in 1970 to almost 30 per cent in 2000. Sales of books in Canada reached almost US$1.35 billion.

By contrast, the Irish publishing industry has been largely independent of the major international players. Major overseas publishing groups, primarily those with a strong UK presence, do compete in the Irish market, usually from a base in the UK but often using a dedicated sales team on the ground in Ireland. Imports represent approximately 70 per cent of the market, but there are substantial variations between the type of material. In the educational sector, it is estimated that 90 per cent of the market demand is held by Irish publishers, whereas in the general sector, foreign publishers dominate, comprising over 85 per cent of the market. Irish publishers have increased the level of business undertaken on the home market and now hold approximately 14 per cent of the market. Book publishing in the Irish language is a small niche area with approximately 100 new titles being published each year. The majority of Irish literary titles receive financial assistance from either Bord na Leabhar Gaeilge (Gaelic Books Board) or the Irish Arts Council. The total income of Irish language publishers is estimated to be less than US$2 million, with approximately one-third of this income received by way of grants. Due to limitations in the demand for publications in the Irish language, it is difficult for the sector to achieve economic self-sufficiency, and a certain level of continuing dependency upon public agencies for funding would seem to be inevitable (PWC 1995).

Non-English-speaking countries seem protected by a language barrier from international penetration, although some markets, particularly academic and professional, are more vulnerable to English-language imports than others. The problem in these countries is how to reconcile a small language-based market with prices low enough to encourage consumption. The continuation of Government funding is seen to be a critical factor in ensuring the development of minority-language publishing, whether an internal minority, as in the case of Canada and Ireland, or a minority in international terms. Over 80 per cent of the material available online is in English, a further factor reinforcing the hegemony of the English language. Generally, as the decrease in the number of readers continues and print runs for many books also fall, there will be increased pressure in many states for the introduction of support measures to ensure that consumer choice does not extend only to the products of the transnational conglomerates.

Conversely, few foreign-language titles were or are published in the UK and USA, even in English translation; there has never been much traffic in the other direction as the English language, and its texts, established their current global hegemony (including China, as evidenced by the sheer number of learners of English and of pirated English texts). The motive power behind the globalization of English is not, as it was for Latin, the hard power of Roman military might and conquest; nor may it, anymore, be economic power, certainly not of the UK and perhaps decreasingly of the USA. It is the impact of the cultural industries of the USA and the UK and (given its intimate relationship with the written language), in particular, publishing. Yet, and there is, of course, a peculiar irony here, the Anglo-American publishing industry is – in terms of its major players, its globalized conglomerates – no longer dominated by an indigenous ownership. Random House is currently owned by Bertelsmann, and other European companies, such as Hachette, have large stakes in English-language publishing and other media. The USA exercises a great deal of cultural influence, of 'soft power'; but due to that loss of economic power, it no longer necessarily owns the vehicles through which that soft power is mediated.

States also intervene at the international level to protect reciprocal national interests. They have participated in a number of international bodies – including, significantly, the International Copyright Act (Berne Convention) of 1886 – to regulate increasingly globalized commerce and communication in a manner that would protect, in the case of copyright, the interests of its creators, owners, and licensees. Yet, this also represented a gradual secession of national legal sovereignty to organizations such as the General Agreement on Tariffs and Trade (GATT), the World Trade Organization (WTO) and the World Intellectual Property Organization (WIPO) that perhaps prefigured the loss of national cultural sovereignty, seen itself as an outcome of globalization.

Conclusion

This chapter has not been about predicting in detail the future of the book. It has examined the factors that play a part in shaping and influencing that future. Books will co-exist alongside new developments in technology, the nature and effect of which are notoriously difficult to prophesy. The uses of mobile phones are a case in point: no-one anticipated their use for text (SMS) messaging and no-one can predict how the next generation of smartphones and their uses will evolve. Books will continue to fulfill needs, although their functions will be more severely circumscribed to leisure or retrogressed as expensive objects of beauty to admire but not necessarily read. Their production will be chiefly in the control of transnational media conglomerates that view them as just another product, albeit one that has a consistent record of supplying the intellectual property from which other media products can be fashioned. However, small publishers will exercise creativity and innovation while remaining prey to their larger competitors. E-books will continue to develop beyond their simple imitation of printed books in appearance and functionality. Their legal availability and transferability will become more flexible, and the link to specific reading devices will be lost. Readers of books have decreased in number; but, as a lifestyle choice, reading encourages a passionate and extensive reading habit. The state may need to intervene increasingly to promote and protect the reading of books, particularly in languages other than English, as it does for other activities considered as positive assets within civil society. If you are reading this a few years after we have written it, then there is no refund available if none of these statements, made to seem more dogmatic by being a summary, ever come true.

Points to ponder

Before you move onto the Conclusion of this book, consider the following main points raised in this chapter. What do you believe lies ahead for the future of the printed book, of the e-book, and of readership of books as an activity? It might also be useful to review at this stage whether any development in the history of the book can be seen, with hindsight, to have grown consistently out of prior trends.

CONCLUSION

The preceding chapters have traced the historical arc of manuscript and book production from the pre-Christian age through the Industrial Revolution to contemporary times. Along the way we have examined:

- issues relating to authorship;
- the transfer of print 'authority' from religious to individual contexts;
- the establishment of printing centers and the accompanying development of a national and international trade in printed texts;
- the role of the book in shaping reading communities and challenging authority; and
- the theoretical concepts increasingly utilized to investigate the place of texts and print culture in cultural communication.

Chapter 1 outlined some of those theoretical concepts. It surveyed the work of major theorists who have shaped the discipline of print culture and book history studies over the past century. It showed how book history has moved from past traditions in bibliographic and textual studies to current preoccupations with cultural and social contexts. It also discussed how current book history interests are increasingly integrating studies of authorship and readership within studies of textual production, points that were then picked up in later chapters.

Chapter 2 explored the challenges marking the shift in Western European culture from oral to written, a shift that adopted and overlaid oral communication methods and processes upon new cultural templates. The chapter also examined how a similar process of adoption, adaptation, and reshaping marked the move from written to print culture, how critics of the integration of oral culture into written culture had to deal with the notion that the spreading of knowledge equaled 'profanation,' and how they had to face changes in their chosen methods of processing information. Finally, this chapter discussed the use of writing in the service of state, institutional, and political interests.

Chapter 3 continued discussion of the shift from a manuscript-based culture to a print-based one. It considered the role of the printing press as an agent of change during the Reformation and Renaissance, and outlined the development of industry structures for the selection, production, and distribution of printed books. The chapter covered the attempts by established power structures, state, and church to control the spread of printing and its products through licensing, statutory restrictions and fiscal measures. The industrialization of the book was detailed, as was the retrenchment in the industry at the end of the twentieth century as competition from other media intensified.

Chapter 4 examined authorship as a concept and activity in Western European traditions. It discussed medieval concepts of authorship, charted the shifts in the authorship function with the advent of print in the fifteenth century, and offered insight into the changing economic and social structures supporting authorial activity in modern times. The section also briefly covered twentieth-century interpretations of the functions of authors for an insight into current debates on the subject, and noted how new paradigms of authorial activity and redefinitions of what constitutes 'authorship' are predicted with the onset of digital technology in the twenty-first century.

Chapter 5 looked at the various players and agents involved in the circulation of print culture, and surveyed the manner in which industrial and technological advances in producing, disseminating, and consuming print and texts in Western Europe were exported, adopted, and adapted in other countries. It also drew attention to the history and insertion of various cultural agents into the business of promoting books and print in contemporary society.

Chapter 6 defined reading as both an individual act of interpretation in which the reader creates meaning from a text, and a distinct social activity. It traced the history of reading from the earliest decipherment of data, through the movement from intensive to extensive reading during the eighteenth century, to the key role of reading in education and self-development over the following 200 years. The nature of reading was examined in the light of Iser's (1980) model of the individual's creation of meaning and Fish's (1976) stress on the 'interpretive community.'

Chapter 7 considered the future of the book from four perspectives drawing on book history: the effect on the book of the development of new existing and newer undiscovered technologies; the creation of new industry structures within which book publishing sits, and the effects of these structures upon diversity, choice and culture; the decline in the number of readers and the concomitant 'heavy' reading by that reduced number; and, finally, the movement in the role of the state from the regulation of the book to the support of publishing and reading.

A significant theme to be drawn from our study is the increasing importance in book history studies of 'mediation.' Contemporary book and print culture historians are increasingly focused on answering questions raised by the med-iating role of print. Questions asked include:

- Who and what mediates activity in the complex path taken by books and texts from producer to consumer?
- What is the place of strategic cultural alliances and 'literary fields' in shaping the promotion and reception of particular texts?
- Who plays a part in aiding some books and authors to become cultural touchstones, while others during the same era fail to make a mark in cul-tural and economic terms?
- How do technological advances become an 'invisible' part of social com-munication structures?
- What role does mass print media play in shaping social discourse?

Contemporary print culture studies must also (as noted in Chapter 7) take into consideration transnational and comparative matters – the effects that globa-lization of the book trade has had both in economic, cultural, and social terms; the opportunities posed by digitization and new electronic technologies; and the homogenizing effect of transnational publishing and bookselling consortia practices changing the face of the industry.

The future of the history of the book is surely bound up in uncovering answers to such questions. At the same time, it is important to acknowledge that there are gaps in our knowledge and coverage of print culture history. Most obvious for those who work in European and North American contexts is that much remains to be said and researched in non-Eurocentric print cul-ture arenas. For example, the history of the development of paper and print in the Islamic world, and its influence on Western culture, remains to be explored in great depth. Similarly, non-textual materials are currently underutilized as potential resources in print culture research; oral histories and interviews, film and visual materials, and ephemeral documentation are likely to offer powerful sources supplementing and enhancing our understanding of the social, cultural, and historical contexts of print culture and book production and reception. Other issues that book historians are training their focus on include gender, class, race, migration, and the place of print in maintaining and constructing social, cultural, and national identities. As we have noted, reading and reading habits are research areas from which much new work is emanating, with new studies covering issues such as reading revolutions and the place of reading in forming individual and communal identities.

This is an exciting time to be involved in studying book history. New con-nections have been made in such award-winning books as Jonathan Rose's *The Intellectual Life of the British Working Classes* (2001) and Elizabeth McHenry's *Forgotten Readers: Recovering the Lost History of African American Literary Societies* (2002). Others have followed over the past decade with their own insights into print culture. What we are seeing is a move to chart both

general and specific aspects of book history – from the initial projects uncovering national histories of the book in Australia, Canada, France, Ireland,
New Zealand, the UK, and the USA, through collaborative examination of
post-colonial and globalized/globalizing publishing, to case studies published
about specific publishers, reading communities, and print culture phenomena.
The number of courses that have developed to study book history in an interdisciplinary context is evidence of the strength of interest in the subject. What
is on offer is an intellectual world without frontiers – new, still in the process
of definition, and infinitely exciting in its possibilities. Engaging with book
history is to engage with our humanity and with the social communication
processes that have underpinned the gathering and spreading of knowledge
throughout society.

GLOSSARY

Analog author: A term used by Mark Poster in *What's the Matter with the Internet?* to define traditional authorship – that is, authors as individuals producing work published through the physical confines of print technology.

***Annales* school:** French-influenced social historical movement developed during the 1950s, led by Robert Escarpit, Henri-Jean Martin, Lucien Febvre, and others, emphasizing the application of quantitative social history methods to the study of the production, transmission, and reception of texts.

Backlist: The titles that a publisher continues to issue and sell over a number of years, as opposed to the 'frontlist,' which consists of the new titles issued in any given year. A strong backlist bringing in steady revenue represents the goal of most publishers.

Bibliography: A term generally used to describe the study of the material transmission of literary and other documents – that is, the study of the material means by which texts have been created and reproduced. Traditionally, such work has been subdivided into such thematic areas as the study of printing methods (analytical or critical bibliography); descriptions and arrangements of primary documents (descriptive bibliography); and the study of the physical form of textual transmission, such as paper, ink, calligraphy, and the printed forms of texts (textual bibliography).

Bio-bibliography: Terminology used by Thomas Adams and Nicolas Barker in their influential 1993 article 'A new model for the history of the book,' arguing in favor of a book history studies model focusing on processes centered on texts, rather than on processes centered on a communication circuit as proposed a decade before by Robert Darnton.

Book of Hours: A devotional book of prayers for personal use by the laity, often by noblewomen. Books of Hours were popular between the eleventh and sixteenth centuries, making the transition between manuscript and print.

Codex: Originally referring to flat, wooden, or ivory writing tablets bound together to form individual leaves or pages like those in a book, but later used to refer to a similarly hinged or bound manuscript volume of vellum pages.

Communication Circuit: A book history studies model proposed during the early 1980s by Robert Darnton, stressing a social history approach to studying books and print, and centered on investigating the place of books within social communication processes.

Composing stick: Before mechanical composition, the compositor would select the pieces of type, each a single letter, in the correct order with one hand and place them in a wooden stick the length of one line that he held in the other hand. As the lines were completed, they were assembled one at a time in a galley tray before the next stage of dividing the galley into pages and locking each, perhaps also containing blocks for illustrations, into a frame ready for printing. See **forme** below.

Cuneiform script: A system of writing using pictographic, wedge-shaped symbols created with a stylus, or sharp writing implement, and impressed onto clay tablets. In use between ca. 3500 BC and 100 BC throughout Mesopotamia and the Near East. The term derives from the Latin word for wedge (*cuneus*).

Digital author: A term used by Mark Poster in *What's the Matter with the Internet?* to define authorship in contexts of emerging digital technology – that is, authors as individuals producing work published in a more fluid, unstable digital environment, where meaning is not fixed and reproduced through a printed page, but may be copied, developed, rewritten, and retransmitted in various digital formats.

Distribution: The actual type used in printing represented a considerable investment by the printer, most of whom held only a limited amount. After each **forme** (see below) was printed, it was the task of the apprentice to dismantle it and distribute the pieces of type back into the appropriate sections of the case of type from where they came, and from where the compositor could reuse them for another setting.

Exemplar: The original official manuscript text provided by university authorities in pre-print periods, from which multiple copies, or *peciae*, were made for use by students.

Forme: The composed type and any blocks for illustrations were transferred into a frame known as a 'chase' and secured ready to be printed. The 'locked-up' chase with type was known as a 'forme.'

Gutenberg gap: A term used by information scientists to describe the period between an initial scientific or other discovery and its dissemination through publication in print.

Hieroglyphic script: An early form of written communication based on pictograms and pictographic symbols in common use in Egypt from ca. 3000 BC.

Histoire du Livre: A social history movement dating from the 1980s, building on the pioneering work of the ***annales school*** of book history study, and emphasizing the value of linking the study of the material text to social history and empirically informed studies of readers, readership, and textual reception. Chief exponents of such work include Roger Chartier and Robert Darnton.

Imprimatur: The permission for a particular title to be printed, granted by the monarch or the church, was indicated by a sign or mark within the book.

Incunabula: The earliest books printed, specifically those printed before 1501.

Intellectual property: The concept of ownership in a text that views the latter as a form of intangible property from which revenue can be gained for any use or representation. Copyright is a license to copy – to reproduce – a text. The protection of such rights, and the corresponding assignment of responsibilities, is the function of intellectual property law.

Literary field: A term popularized by the French social theorist Pierre Bourdieu, used to indicate common social, intellectual, and ideological arenas interlinking producers (publishers, editors, and authors) and products (books, periodical publications, literary works). Such fields have been presented as existing to perpetuate particular literary hierarchies, strengthen dominant cultural groups, or create networks for the support of particular types of cultural production.

New Bibliography: A school of bibliographic study that emerged during the early twentieth century, led by Anglo-American scholars such as W. W. Greg, Fredson Bowers, and R. McKerrow, proposing a scientifically informed study of texts and books as physical objects (such as determining differences in type, paper, ink, printing methods, and so on).

Paratext: The liminal devices that control how a reader perceives the text, such as front and back covers, jacket blurbs, indexes, footnotes, tables of contents, forewords, and prefaces.

Parchment: The skin of an animal, usually a sheep or a goat, prepared to provide a surface for writing, illustration, or printing. 'Vellum' is a finer-quality version of the same, but made from calfskin or the hide of some other young animal.

Peciae: A section of exemplar manuscript texts copied out by scribes for use in universities from the thirteenth century onward. Made from treated and trimmed sheepskin, individual section sizes would be either four pages if folded in folio size, or eight pages if folded in quarto size.

Print capitalism: A term utilized in Benedict Anderson's influential book *Imagined Communities* to denote the interaction between a system of economic production (capitalism) and a technology of communication (print) that grew increasingly interlinked in the years that followed the introduction of printing during the 1450s – 'a stage on the road to our present society of mass consumption and standardization' (Febvre and Martin 1976, 259–260).

Print culture: An alternative way of describing book history studies, emphasizing the production, distribution, reception, and social relationships of print to culture, framed particularly within the context of social communication structures and studies.

Punch: The tool used to impress the shape of the letter into the mold, or matrix, into which molten metal, an alloy of tin, antimony, and lead, was poured to cast the piece of type. The latter carried a relief image, in reverse, to produce the required printed image.

Scriptorium: The room or space in a monastery where manuscripts were produced and copied.

Socialization of the text: Phrase coined by Jerome McGann to describe the manner in which books and print make their way from private to public spaces via the production process, part of his emphasis on the importance of studying the impact of books as social artifacts.

Sociology of the text: Phrase coined by Don McKenzie during the early 1980s as part of his attempts to extend the remit of contemporary bibliographic study to integrate textual analysis with *annales* and *Histoire du Livre* book history interests in order to encompass the economic, social, aesthetic, and literary meanings of texts.

Stereotyping: A method of overcoming the costs involved in owning, storing, or distributing large quantities of type that was developed during the eighteenth century. A plaster cast was made of the page of composed type and acted as a mold from which whole printing plates could be made. It was popular with publishers who had otherwise to pay the printer for keeping type set up or for resetting if reprints were required.

Typographic fixity: Phrase coined by Elizabeth Eisenstein to indicate the manner in which the print technology that developed in Western Europe during the fifteenth century, capable of rapidly reproducing the same text in identical formats and large numbers, subsequently shaped reception of the written word, allowing it to be fixed and transmitted in a printed durable fashion.

NOTES

INTRODUCTION

1 The bookseller Rick Gekoski, responsible for the sale, notes that he passed up the offer of several pairs of Tolkien's old shoes and tweed jackets, which no doubt would now be worth a great deal to the dedicated Tolkien fan. For more on Rick Gekoski's passing connection with Tolkien, see Gekoski (2004: 13–24).

1 THEORIZING THE HISTORY OF THE BOOK

1 A. W. Pollard's distinction between 'good' and 'bad' versions of Shakespeare's quartos (articulated in Pollard 1909), and his methods at arriving at such conclusions, would influence McKerrow, Greg, and Bowers's subsequent development of general principles governing New Bibliography.

2 FROM ORALITY TO LITERACY

1 Roger Chartier offers a useful analysis of Foucault's insights into the author function in Chartier (1994: 25–60).
2 In this piece, Chartier is particularly insightful and informative on the impact of cultural influences upon shifting literacy rates in early modern Western European social history.

4 AUTHORS, AUTHORSHIP, AND AUTHORITY

1 Wogan-Browne et al. The translation is adapted from Alistair Minnis (1988: 94). A slightly different translation of the same text is utilized by Elizabeth Eisenstein (1979, vol 1: 122), adapted from John Burrow (1976: 615).
2

Adam Scribe, if ever it thee befall Boethius or Troilus to write anew, Under thy long locks thou must have the scale, [scaly condition of the scalp] So often daily I must thy work renew, It to correct and also to rub and scrape And all is through thy negligence and haste. [translation]

(Benson 1988: 650)

BIBLIOGRAPHY

Adams, T. and N. Barker (1993) 'A new model for the study of the book', in N. Barker (ed) *A Potencie of Life: Books in Society*. London: British Library: 5–43.

Adorno, T. and M. Horkheimer (1944; repr. 1977) 'The culture industry: Enlightenment as mass deception', in J. Curran, M. Gurevitch and J. Wollacott (eds) *Mass Communication and Society*. London: Edward Arnold: 349–383.

Altick, R. (1957) *The English Common Reader: A Social History of the Mass Reading Public, 1800–1900*. Chicago, IL: University of Chicago Press.

Amory, H. and D. D. Hall (eds) (2007) *A History of the Book in America, Vol 1: The Colonial Book in the Atlantic World*. Chapel Hill, NC: University of North Carolina Press.

Anderson, B. (1982) *Imagined Communities*. London and New York: Verso.

Ascher, M. and R. Ascher (1981) 'El quipu como lenguaje visible', in H. Lechtman and A.-M. Soldi (eds) *La Tecnología en el Mundo Andino*. Mexico: Universidad Nacional Autónoma: 407–431.

Assmann, J. (1994) 'Ancient Egypt and the materiality of the sign', in H. U. Gumbrecht and K. L. Pfeiffer (eds) *Materialities of Communication*. Stanford, CT: Stanford University Press: 15–30.

Bagdikian, B. H. (2000) *The Media Monopoly* (sixth edition). Boston, MA: Beacon Press.

Barnard, J. and D. F. McKenzie (eds) (2002). *The Cambridge History of the Book in Britain: Volume 4, 1557–1695*. Cambridge: Cambridge University Press.

Barnes, J. J. and P. B. Barnes (1984) 'Thomas Aspinwall: First transatlantic literary agent', *The Papers of the Bibliographical Society of America*, vol 78, no: 321–332.

Baron, D. (2009) *A Better Pencil: Readers, Writers and the Digital Revolution*. Oxford: Oxford University Press.

Barthes, R. (1977) *Image, Music, Text*. London: Fontana Press.

Bayly, C. A. (1996) *Empire and Information: Intelligence Gathering and Social Communication in India 1780–1870*. Cambridge: Cambridge University Press.

Belich, J. (1996) *Making Peoples: A History of the New Zealanders*. London: Allen Lane, Penguin.

Bell, B. (ed) (2007) *The Edinburgh History of the Book in Scotland, Vol 3: Ambition and Industry 1800–1880*. Edinburgh: Edinburgh University Press.

Benson, L. D. (ed) (1988) *The Riverside Chaucer*. Oxford: Oxford University Press.

Biriotti, M. and N. Miller (eds) (1993) *What Is an Author?* Manchester, UK: Manchester University Press.

Birkerts, S. (1996) *The Gutenberg Elegies: The State of Reading in an Electronic Age*. London: Faber and Faber.

Bland, M. (2010) *A Guide to Early Printed Books and Manuscripts*. Oxford: Wiley-Blackwell.

Bloom, H. (1996) *The Western Canon*. London: Macmillan.

——(2001) *How to Read and Why*. London: Fourth Estate.

BML (Book Marketing Ltd.) (2000) *Reading the Situation: Book Reading, Buying and Borrowing Habits in Britain*. London: BML.

Bolter, J. D. (1991) *Writing Space: The Computer, Hypertext, and the History of Writing*. Hillsdale, IN: Erlbaum Associates.

Bonham-Carter, V. (1978) *Authors by Profession, Vol 1*. London: Society of Authors.

——(1982) *Authors by Profession, Vol 2*. London: Society of Authors.

Bourdieu, P. (1993) 'Field of power, literary field and habitus', in R. Johnson (ed) *The Field of Cultural Production: Essays on Art and Literature*. New York: Columbia University Press: 27–73.

Bowers, F. (1950a) 'Current theories of copy-text, with an illustration from Dryden', *Modern Philology*, vol LXVIII: 19–36; repr. in O. M. Brack, Jr. and W. Barnes (eds) (1969) *Bibliography and Textual Criticism: English and American Literature, 1700 to the Present*. Chicago and London: Chicago University Press: 59–72.

——(1950b) *Principles of Bibliographical Description*. Princeton, NJ: Princeton University Press.

Brack, O. M., Jr. and W. Barnes (eds) (1969) *Bibliography and Textual Criticism: English and American Literature, 1700 to the Present*. Chicago and London: Chicago University Press.

Brake, L., B. Bell and D. Finkelstein (eds) (2000) *Nineteenth-Century Media and the Construction of Identities*. Basingstoke, UK: Palgrave Macmillan.

Brands, H. W. (2000) *The First American: The Life and Times of Benjamin Franklin*. New York: Bantam Dell Publishing Group.

Brewer, J. (1997) *The Pleasures of the Imagination: English Culture in the Eighteenth Century*. London: HarperCollins.

Brewer, J. and I. McCalman (1999) 'Publishing', in I. McCalman (ed) *An Oxford Companion to the Romantic Age: British Culture 1776–1832*. Oxford: Oxford University Press: 197–206.

Briggs, A. and P. Burke (2002) *A Social History of the Media, from Gutenberg to the Internet*. London: Polity Press.

Brooks, D. (2000) *From Playhouse to Printing House: Drama and Authorship in Early Modern England*. Cambridge Studies in Renaissance Literature and Culture, 36. Cambridge: Cambridge University Press.

Brouillette, S. (2007) *Postcolonial Writers in the Global Literary Marketplace*. Basingstoke, UK: Palgrave Macmillan.

Brown, C. J. (1995) *Poets, Patrons, and Printers: Crisis of Authority in Late Medieval France*. Ithaca, NY: Cornell University Press.

Brown, S. and W. McDougall, (eds) (2011) *The Edinburgh History of the Book in Scotland, Vol 2: Enlightenment and Expansion, 1707–1800*. Edinburgh: Edinburgh University Press.

Burrow, J. (1976) 'The Medieval Compendium', *Times Literary Supplement*, 21 May: 615.

Canfora, L. (1989) *The Vanished Library* (translated M. Ryle). London: Hutchinson.

Casper, S. E., J. D. Groves, S. W. Nissenbaum and M. Winship (eds) (2007) *A History of the Book in America, Vol 3: The Industrial Book, 1840–1880*. Chapel Hill, NC: University of North Carolina Press.

Castells, M. (1996) *The Rise of the Network Society*. Oxford: Blackwell.

Cavallo, G. (1999) 'Between Volumen and Codex: Reading in the Roman world', in G. Cavallo and R. Chartier (eds) *A History of Reading in the West* (translated L. G. Cochrane). Cambridge: Polity Press: 64–89.

——(2003) 'Lire, écrire et mémoriser les Saintes Écritures', in C. Jacob (ed) *Des Alexandries II: Les métamorphoses du lecteur*. Paris: Bibliothèque Nationale de France: 87–102.

Cavallo, G. and R. Chartier (eds) (1999) *A History of Reading in the West* (translated L. G. Cochrane). Cambridge: Polity Press.

Cave, R. (1986) *Printing and the Book Trade in the West Indies*. London: Pindar.

Cave, R. and K. Coleridge (1985) 'For Gospel and wool trade: Early printing in New Zealand', *Printing History*, vol 7, no 1: 15–27.

Chakava, H. (2001) 'The origins and development of publishing systems in English-speaking Africa: In search of an independent model', in J. Michon and J.-Y. Mollier (eds) (2001) *Les Mutations du Livre et de L'édition dans le Monde du XVIIIe Siècle à L'an 2000*. L'Harmattan: Les Presses de L'Université Laval: 339–349.

Chartier, R. (1981) 'L'ancien régime typographique: réflexions sur quelques travaux récents', *Annales E.S.C.*, vol 36: 191–209.

——(1987) *The Cultural Uses of Print in Early Modern Europe* (translated L. G. Cochrane). Princeton, NJ: Princeton University Press.

——(ed) (1989a) *The Culture of Print*. Oxford: Polity Press.

——(1989b) 'The practical impact of writing', in R. Chartier (ed) *A History of Private Life III: Passions of the Renaissance*. Cambridge, MA, and London: Harvard University Press; repr. in D. Finkelstein and A. McCleery (eds) (2001) *The Book History Reader*. London: Routledge: 118–142.

——(1994) *The Order of Books: Readers, Authors, and Libraries in Europe between the Fourteenth and Eighteenth Centuries* (translated L. G. Cochrane). Stanford, CT: Stanford University Press.

——(ed) (1995) *Histoires de la Lecture: Un bilan des recherches*. Paris: IMEC.

——(1997a) 'The end of the reign of the book', *SubStance*, vol 82: 9–11.

——(1997b) *On the Edge of the Cliff: History, Language, and Practices* (translated L. G. Cochrane). Baltimore, MD: Johns Hopkins University Press.

Charvat, W. (1993) *Literary Publishing in America, 1790–1850*. University Park, PA: Pennsylvania State University Press.

Christin, A.-M. (ed) (2001) *A History of Writing: From Hieroglyph to Multimedia*. Paris: Flammarion.

Copeland, R., D. Lawton and W. Scase (eds) (1999) *New Medieval Literatures 3*. Oxford: Clarendon Press.

Crone, R. and S. Towheed (eds) (2011) *The History of Reading, Vol 3: Methods, Strategies, Tactics*. Basingstoke, UK: Palgrave Macmillan.

Darnton, R. (1982a) *The Literary Underground of the Old Regime*. Cambridge, MA: Harvard University Press.

——(1982b) 'What is the history of books?', *Daedalus*: 65–83; repr. in D. Finkelstein and A. McCleery (eds) (2001) *The Book History Reader*. London: Routledge: 9–26.

——(1986) 'First steps towards a history of reading', *Australian Journal of French Studies*, vol 23: 5–30; repr. in R. Darnton (1990) *The Kiss of Lamourette*. London: Faber and Faber: 154–190.

——(1996) *The Forbidden Best-Sellers of Pre-Revolutionary France*. New York: Norton.

——(2001) 'Literary surveillance in the British Raj: The contradictions of liberal imperialism', *Book History*, vol 4: 133–176.

——(2003) 'The heresies of bibliography', *New York Review of Books*, vol 50, no 9: 43–45.

Davidson, C. (ed) (1989) *Reading in America: Literature and Social History*. Baltimore, MD: Johns Hopkins University Press.

Davis, N. Z. (1983) 'Beyond the market: Books as gifts in sixteenth-century France', *Transactions of the Royal Historical Society*, vol 33: 69–88.

Docherty, T. (2003) 'On reading', *Critical Quarterly*, vol 45, no 3: 6–19.

Duguid, P. (1996) 'Material matters: The past and futurology of the book', in G. Nunberg (ed) *The Future of the Book*. Berkeley, CA: University of California Press: 63–101.

Eggert, P. (2003) 'Robbery under arms: The colonial market, imperial publishers, and the demise of the three-decker novel', *Book History*, vol 6: 127–147.

Eisenstein, E. (1979) *The Printing Press as an Agent of Change: Communications and Cultural Transformations in Early-Modern Europe, Vols I and II*. Cambridge: Cambridge University Press.

——(1983) *The Printing Revolution in Early Modern Europe*. Cambridge: Cambridge University Press.

——(2002a) 'AHR Forum: An unacknowledged revolution revisited', *American Historical Review*, vol 107, no 1 (February): 87–105.

——(2002b) 'AHR Forum: Reply', *American Historical Review*, vol 107, no 1 (February): 126–128.

Eliot, S. and J. Rose (eds) (2009) *A Companion to the History of the Book*. Oxford: Wiley-Blackwell.

Engelsing, R. (1974) *Der Bürger als Leser: Lesergeschichte in Deutschland, 1500–1800*. Stuttgart: Metzler.

Escarpit, R. (1966) *The Book Revolution*. London and Paris: George G. Harrap & Co. Ltd. and UNESCO.

——(1971) *The Sociology of Literature* (translated E. Pick). London: Cass.

Ezell, M. J. M. (1999) *Social Authorship and the Advent of Print*. Baltimore, MD: Johns Hopkins University Press.

Feather, J. (1988) *A History of British Publishing*. London: Croom Helm.

Febvre, L. and H.-J. Martin (1958) *L'Apparition du Livre*. Paris: Albin Michel.

——(1976) *The Coming of the Book: The Impact of Printing, 1450–1800* (translated D. Gerard, from *L'Apparition du Livre*). London: NLB; repr. 1997, London: Verso.

Feltes, N. N. (1986) *Modes of Production of Victorian Novels*. Chicago, IL: University of Chicago Press.

——(1993) *Literary Capital and the Late Victorian Novel*. Madison, WI: University of Wisconsin Press.

Finkelstein, D. (2002) *The House of Blackwood: Author–Publisher Relations in the Victorian Era*. University Park, PA: Pennsylvania State University Press.

Finkelstein, D. and A. McCleery (eds) (2006) *The Book History Reader*, 2nd edition. London: Routledge.

Finkelstein, D. and A. McCleery (eds) (2007) *The Edinburgh History of the Book in Scotland, Vol 4: Professionalism and Diversity, 1880–2000*. Edinburgh: Edinburgh University Press.

Finkelstein, D. and D. Peers (2000a) '"A great system of circulation": Introducing India into the nineteenth-century media', in D. Finkelstein and D. Peers (eds) *Negotiating India in the Nineteenth-Century Media*. Basingstoke, UK: Macmillan: 1–23.

——(eds) (2000b) *Negotiating India in the Nineteenth-Century Media*. Basingstoke, UK: Macmillan.

Fischer, S. R. (2003) *A History of Reading*. London: Reaktion Books.

Fish, S. (1976) 'Is there a text in this class?', *Critical Enquiry*, vol 2, no 3: 465–486; repr. in D. Finkelstein and A. McCleery (eds) (2001) *The Book History Reader*. London: Routledge: 350–358.

Fleming, P. L., G. Gallichan and Y. Lamonde (eds) (2004) *History of the Book in Canada, Vol 1: Beginnings to 1840*. Toronto: University of Toronto Press.

Flint, K. (1993) *The Woman Reader, 1837–1914*. Oxford: Oxford University Press.

Foucault, M. (1969) 'Qu'est-ce qu'un auteur?', *Bulletin de la Société française de Philosophie*, vol 63, no 3: 73–104; repr. as 'What is an author?' in D. F. Bouchard (ed) (1977) *Language, Counter-memory, Practice*. Ithaca, NY: Cornell University Press: 113–138.

——(1984) *The Foucault Reader*. Ithaca, NY: Cornell University Press.

Fox, A. (2000) *Oral and Literature Culture in England, 1500–1700*. Oxford: Oxford University Press.

Fraser, R. (2008) *Book History through Postcolonial Eyes: Rewriting the Script*. London: Routledge.

Fraser, R. and M. Hammond (eds) (2008) *Books Without Borders, Vol 1: The Cross-National Dimension in Print Culture*. Basingstoke, UK: Palgrave Macmillan.

Fritschner, L. M. (1980) 'Publishers' readers, publishers, and their authors', *Publishing History*, vol 7: 45–100.

Fyfe, A. (2012) *Steam-Powered Knowledge: William Chambers and the Business of Publishing 1820–1860*. Chicago, IL: University of Chicago Press.

Gameson, R. (ed) (2011) *The Cambridge History of the Book in Britain: Vol 1, c.400–1100*. Cambridge: Cambridge University Press.

Gardiner, J. (2000) 'Recuperating the author: Consuming fictions in the 1990s', *Papers of the Bibliographical Society of America*, vol 94, no 2: 255–274.

Gedin, P. (1982) *Literature in the Marketplace* (translated G. Bisset). London: Faber and Faber.

Gekoski, R. (2004) *Tolkien's Gown and Other Stories of Great Authors and Rare Books*. London: Constable.

Genette, G. (1997) *Paratexts: Thesholds of Interpretation* (translated J. E. Lewin). Cambridge: Cambridge University Press.

Gerson, C. and J. Michon (eds) (2007) *History of the Book in Canada, Vol 3: 1918–1980*. Toronto: University of Toronto Press.

Ghosh, A. (2003) 'An uncertain "coming of the book": Early print culture in colonial India', *Book History*, vol 6: 23–56.

Giddens, A. (1990) *The Consequences of Modernity*. Stanford, CT: Stanford University Press.

Gillespie, R. and A. Hadfield (eds) (2006) *The Oxford History of the Irish Book, V 3: The Irish Book in English, 1550–1800*. Oxford: Oxford University Press.

Gillies, M. A. (1993) 'A. P. Watt, literary agent', *Publishing Research Quarterly*, vol 9 (spring): 20–34.

Gilmont, J.-F. (1999) 'Protestant Reformations and reading', in G. Cavallo and R. Chartier (eds) *A History of Reading in the West* (translated L. G. Cochrane). Cambridge: Polity Press: 213–237.

Ginzburg, C. (1980) *The Cheese and the Worms: The Cosmos of a Sixteenth-Century Miller* (translated J. Tedeschi and A. Tedeschi). Baltimore, MD: Johns Hopkins University Press.

Gómez, A. C. (ed) (2001) *Historia de la cultura escrita*. Gijon: Ediciónes Trea.

Gomme, R. (1998) 'Edward Thomas and the literary agency of London', *The Book Collector*, vol 47, no 1 (spring): 67–78.

Goody, J. (1987) *The Interface between the Oral and the Written*. Cambridge: Cambridge University Press.

Grafton, A. (1997) *The Footnote: A Curious History*. Cambridge, MA: Harvard University Press.

——(1999) 'The humanist as reader', in G. Cavallo and R. Chartier (eds) *A History of Reading in the West* (translated L. G. Cochrane). Cambridge: Polity Press: 179–212.

Greco, A. (1995) 'Mergers and acquisitions in the US book industry, 1960–89', in P. G. Altbach and E. S. Hoshino (eds) *International Book Publishing: An Encyclopedia*. New York and London: Garland Publishing: 229–242.

——(1996) 'Shaping the future: Mergers, acquisitions, and the U.S. publishing, communications, and mass media industries, 1990–95', *Publishing Research Quarterly*, vol 12, no 3: 5–16.

Greenspan, E. and J. Rose (1998) 'Introduction', *Book History*, vol 1: ix–xi.

Greg, W. W. (1914) 'What is bibliography?', *Transactions of the Bibliographic Society*, vol 12 (1914): 39–53.

——(1950) 'The rationale of copy-text', *Studies in Bibliography*, vol III: 19–36.

Griest, G. (1970) *Mudie's Circulating Library and the Victorian Novel*. Bloomington, IN and London: Indiana University Press.

Griffith, P., R. Harvey and K. Maslen (eds) (1997) *Book and Print in New Zealand: A Guide to Print Culture in Aotearoa*. Wellington: Victoria University Press.

Gross, R. and M. Kelley (eds) (2010) *A History of the Book in America: Vol 2: An Extensive Republic: Print, Culture, and Society in the New Nation, 1790–1840*. Chapel Hill, NC: University of North Carolina Press.

Gumbrecht, H. U. and K. L. Pfeiffer (eds) (1994) *Materialities of Communication*. Stanford, CT: Stanford University Press.

Hall, D. D. (1996) *Cultures of Print: Essays in the History of the Book*. Amherst, MA: University of Massachusetts Press.

Halsey, K. and W. R. Owens (eds) (2011) *The History of Reading, Vol 2: Evidence from the British Isles, 1750–1950*. Basingstoke, UK: Palgrave Macmillan.

Hamesse, J. (1999) 'The scholastic model of reading', in G. Cavallo and R. Chartier (eds) *A History of Reading in the West* (translated L. G. Cochrane). Cambridge: Polity Press: 103–119.

Harris, W. V. (1989) *Ancient Literacy*. Cambridge, MA: Harvard University Press.

Hartley, J. (2001) *The Reading Groups Book*. Oxford: Oxford University Press.

Havelock, E. (1988) *The Muse Learns to Write: Reflections on Orality and Literacy from Antiquity to the Present*. New Haven, CT: Yale University Press.

Helgesson, S. (2008) *Transnationalism in Southern African Literature: Modernists, Realists, and the Inequality of Print Culture*. London: Routledge.

Hellinga, L. and J. B. Trapp (eds) (1999) *The Cambridge History of the Book in Britain: Volume 3, 1400–1557*. Cambridge: Cambridge University Press.

Hepburn, J. (1968) *The Author's Empty Purse and the Rise of the Literary Agent*. London, New York and Toronto: Oxford University Press.

Herman, E. S. and R. W. McChesney (1997) *The Global Media*. London: Cassell.

Hobbes, R. G. (1851) 'Calcutta', *Bentley's Miscellany*, vol 30: 361–368.

Howsam, L. (1991) *Cheap Bibles: Nineteenth-century Publishing and the British and Foreign Bible Society*. Cambridge: Cambridge University Press.

——(2006) *Old Books and New Histories: An Orientation to Studies in Book and Print Culture*. Toronto: University of Toronto Press.

Hunt, P. (2001) *Children's Literature*. Oxford: Blackwell.

Innis, H. and A. John Watson (2007) *Empire and Communications*. Toronto: Dundurn Press.

Isaacson, W. (2003) *Benjamin Franklin: An American Life*. New York: Simon and Schuster.

Iser, W. (1980) 'Interaction between text and reader', in S. K. Suleiman and I. Crosman (eds) *The Reader in the Text: Essays on Audience and Interpretation*. Princeton, NJ: Princeton University Press: 106–119.

Jackson, H. J. (2001) *Marginalia: Readers Writing in Books*. New Haven, CT: Yale University Press.

Jacob, C. (ed) (2003) *Des Alexandries II: Les métamorphoses du lecteur*. Paris: Bibliothèque Nationale de France.

Johanson, G. (2000) *Colonial Editions in Australia, 1842–1972*. Wellington, New Zealand: Elibank Press.

Johns, A. (1998) *The Nature of the Book: Print and Knowledge in the Making*. Chicago, IL: University of Chicago Press.

——(2002) 'AHR Forum: An unacknowledged revolution revisited', *American Historical Review*, vol 107, no 1 (February): 106–125.

Johnson-Woods, T. (2000) 'The virtual reading communities of the *London Journal*, the *New York Ledger* and the *Australian Journal*', in L. Brake, B. Bell and D. Finkelstein (eds) *Nineteenth-Century Media and the Construction of Identities*. Basingstoke, UK: Palgrave Macmillan: 350–362.

Jordan, J. O. and R. L. Patten (eds) (1995) *Literature in the Marketplace: Nineteenth-Century British Publishing and Reading Practices*. Cambridge: Cambridge University Press.

Joseph, M. (1925) *The Commercial Side of Literature*. London: Hutchinson & Co.

Joshi, P. (2002) *In another Country: Colonialism, Culture, and the Development of the English Novel in India*. New York: Columbia University Press.

Justice, G. L. and N. Tinker (eds) (2002) *Women's Writing and the Circulation of Ideas: Manuscript Publication in England, 1550–1800*. Cambridge: Cambridge University Press.

Kaestle, C. F. and J. Radway (eds) (2009) *A History of the Book in America, Vol 4: Print in Motion: The Expansion of Publishing and Reading in the United States, 1880–1940*. Chapel Hill, NC: University of North Carolina Press.

Keating, P. (1991) *The Haunted Study: A Social History of the English Novel 1875–1914*. London: Fontana Press.

Ker, N. R. (1960) *English Manuscripts in the Century after the Norman Conquest*. Oxford: Clarendon Press.

Kernan, A. (1987) *Printing Technology, Letters and Samuel Johnson*. Princeton, NJ: Princeton University Press.

Kirsop, W. (2001) 'From colonialism to the multinationals: The fragile growth of Australian publishing and its contribution to the global Anglophone reading community', in J. Michon and J.-Y. Mollier (eds) (2001) *Les Mutations du Livre et de L'édition dans le Monde du XVIIIe Siècle à L'an 2000*. L'Harmattan: Les Presses de L'Université Laval: 324–329.

Knowles, D. (1950) *The Religious Orders in England, Vols I and II*. Cambridge: Cambridge University Press.

Kuskin, W. (1999) 'Reading Caxton: Transformations in capital, print, and persona in the late fifteenth century', in R. Copeland, D. Lawton and W. Scase (eds) *New Medieval Literatures 3*. Oxford: Clarendon Press: 149–183.

Lamonde, Y., P. Lockhart Fleming and F. A. Black (eds) (2005) *History of the Book in Canada, Volume 2: 1840–1918*. Toronto: University of Toronto Press.

Laurenson, D. T. and A. Swingewood (1972) *The Sociology of Literature*. London: MacGibbon and Kee.

Lavallée, D. (2001) 'The Peruvian *Quipus*', in A.-M. Christin (ed) *A History of Writing: From Hieroglyph to Multimedia*. Paris: Flammarion: 190–191.

Lechtman, H. and A.-M. Soldi (eds) (1981) *La Tecnología en el Mundo Andino*. Mexico: Universidad Nacional Autónoma.

Lee, A. J. (1976) *The Origins of the Popular Press in England 1855–1914*. London: Croom Helm.

Lemaire, A. (2001) 'The origin of the Western Semitic alphabet and scripts', in A.-M. Christin (ed) *A History of Writing: From Hieroglyph to Multimedia*. Paris: Flammarion.

Littau, K. (2006) *Theories of Reading: Books, Bodies and Bibliomania*. London: Polity Press.

Livingstone, A. (1986) *Mystical and Mythological Explanatory Works of Assyrian and Babylonian Scholars*. Oxford: Clarendon Press.

Lorimer, R. (1996) 'Book publishing in Canada', in M. Dorland (ed) *Canada's Cultural Industries: Problems, Prospects and Issues*. Toronto: James Lorimer.

Lorimer, R. with M. Gasher (2000) *Mass Communications in Canada* (fourth edition). Toronto: Oxford University Press.

Love, H. (1998) *The Culture and Commerce of Texts: Scribal Publication in Seventeenth-Century England*. Amherst, MA: University of Massachusetts Press.

——(2003) 'Early modern print culture: Assessing the models', *Parergon*, vol 20, no 1: 45–64.

Lowry, M. (1979) *The World of Aldus Manutius*. Oxford: Blackwell.

Lyons, M. (2010) *A History of Reading and Writing in the Western World*. Basingstoke, UK: Palgrave Macmillan.

Lyons, M. and J. Arnold (eds) (2001) *A History of the Book in Australia, 1891–1945: A National Culture in a Colonised Market*. St. Lucia, Queensland: University of Queensland Press.

McCleery, A. (2002) 'The return of the individual to book history: The case of Allen Lane', *Book History*, vol 5: 85–114.

MacDonald, M. L. (2001) 'The modification of European models: English Canada before 1890', in J. Michon and J.-Y. Mollier (eds) (2001) *Les Mutations du Livre et de L'édition dans le Monde du XVIIIe Siècle à L'an 2000*. L'Harmattan: Les Presses de L'Université Laval: 84–93.

McDonald, P. (1997) *British Literary Culture and Publishing Practice 1880–1914*. Cambridge: Cambridge University Press.

McDonald, P. D. (2009) *The Literature Police: Apartheid Censorship and its Cultural Consequences*. Oxford: Oxford University Press.

McDonald, P. and M. F. Suarez (eds) (2002) *Making Meaning: 'Printers of the Mind' and Other Essays*. Amherst, MA: University of Massachusetts Press.

McGann, J. (1991) *The Textual Condition*. Princeton, NJ: Princeton University Press.

McHenry, E. (2002) *Forgotten Readers: Recovering the Lost History of African American Literary Societies*. Durham, NC: Duke University Press.

McKenzie, D. F. (1969) 'Printers of the mind: Some notes on bibliographical theories and printing-house practices', *Studies in Bibliography: Papers of the Bibliographical Society of the University of Virginia*, vol 22: 1–75.

——(1981) 'Typography and meaning: The case of William Congreve'; repr. in P. McDonald and M. F. Suarez (eds) (2002) *Making Meaning: 'Printers of the Mind' and Other Essays*. Amherst, MA: University of Massachusetts Press: 198–236.

——(1984) 'The sociology of a text: Orality, literacy and print in early New Zealand', *The Library*, vol 6, no 4: 333–365.

——(1986) *The Panizzi Lectures, 1985: Bibliography and the Sociology of Texts*. London: British Library.

——(2002) 'What's past is prologue'; repr. in P. McDonald and M. F. Suarez (eds) *Making Meaning: 'Printers of the Mind' and Other Essays*. Amherst, MA: University of Massachusetts Press: 259–275.

McKerrow, R. B. (1927) *An Introduction to Bibliography for Literary Students*. Oxford: Clarendon Press.

McKitterick, D. (2003) *Print, Manuscript and the Search for Order, 1450–1830*. Cambridge: Cambridge University Press.

McKitterick, D. (ed) (2009) *The Cambridge History of the Book in Britain: Vol 6, 1830–1914*. Cambridge: Cambridge University Press.

McLuhan, M. (1962) *The Gutenberg Galaxy: The Making of Typographic Man*. Toronto: University of Toronto Press; repr. New York: New American Library, 1969.

——(1964) *Understanding Media: The Extensions of Man*. New York: McGraw-Hill; repr. Cambridge, MA: MIT Press, 1994.

Macherel, C. (1983) 'Don et réciprocité en Europe', *Archives Européennes de Sociologie*, vol 24, no 1: 151–166.

Manguel, A. (1996) *A History of Reading*. Bath, UK: Flamingo.

Marek, J. E. (1995) *Women Editing Modernism*. Lexington, KY: The University Press of Kentucky.

Martin, H.-J. (1995) *The History and Power of Writing* (translated L. G. Cochrane). Chicago, IL: University of Chicago Press.

Mauss, M. (1954) *The Gift: Forms and Functions of Exchange in Archaic Societies* (translated I. Cunnison). London: Cohen and West.

Meier, W. A. and J. Trappel (1998) 'Media concentration and the public interest', in D. McQuail and K. Siune (eds) *Media Policy*. London: Sage: 38–59.

Michon, J. and J.-Y. Mollier (eds) (2001) *Les Mutations du Livre et de L'édition dans le Monde du XVIIIe Siècle à L'an 2000*. L'Harmattan: Les Presses de L'Université Laval.

Miller, M. C. (1997) 'The publishing industry', in P. Aufderheide et al (eds) *Conglomerates and the Media*. New York: The New Press: 107–134.

Milner, A. (1996) *Literature, Culture and Society*. London: UCL Press.

Minelli, L. (ed) (1992) *I regni preincaici e il mondo inca*. Milan: Jaca Books.

Minnis, A. (1988) *Medieval Theory of Authorship: Scholastic Literary Attitudes in the Later Middle Ages*. Aldershot, UK: The Scolar Press.

Mitchell, W. (1995) *City of Bits: Space, Place, and the Infobahn*. Cambridge, MA: MIT Press.

Modiano, R., L. F. Searle and P. Shillingsburg (eds) (2004) *Voice, Text, Hypertext: Emerging Practices in Textual Studies*. Seattle, WA and London: University of Washington Press.

Mole, T. (2003) 'Byron's "Ode to the Framers of the Frame Bill": The embarrassment of industrial culture', *Keats–Shelley Journal*, vol 52: 111–129.

Monaghan, E. J. (1989) 'Literacy instruction and gender in Colonial New England', in C. Davidson (ed) *Reading in America: Literature and Social History*. Baltimore, MD: Johns Hopkins University Press: 53–80.

Morgan, E. S. (2002) *Benjamin Franklin*. New Haven, CT: Yale University Press.

Morgan, N. and R. M. Thompson, (eds) (2008). *The Cambridge History of the Book in Britain: Vol 2, 1100–1400*. Cambridge: Cambridge University Press.

Motte, D. de la and J. M. Przyblyski (eds) (1999) *Making the News: Modernity and the Mass Press in Nineteenth-Century France*. Amherst, MA: University of Massachusetts Press.

Mueller-Vollmer, K. (ed) (1985) *The Hermeneutics Reader: Texts of the German Tradition from the Enlightenment to the Present*. New York: Continuum.

Müller, J.-D. (1994) 'The body of the book: The media transition from manuscript to print', in H. U. Gumbrecht and K. L. Pfeiffer (eds) *Materialities of Communication*. Stanford, CT: Stanford University Press; repr. in D. Finkelstein and A. McCleery (eds) (2001) *The Book History Reader*. London: Routledge: 143–150.

Munns, J. (ed) (1993) *A Cultural Studies Reader*. London: Longman.

Murphy, J. (ed) (2011) *The Oxford History of the Irish Book, Vol 4: The Irish Book in English, 1800–1891*. Oxford: Oxford University Press.

Nagy, G. (2003) 'Lire la poésie grecque à haute voix', in C. Jacob (ed) *Des Alexandries II: Les métamorphoses du lecteur*. Paris: Bibliothèque Nationale de France: 131–144.

NEA (National Endowment for the Arts) (2004) *Reading at Risk: A Survey of Literary Reading in America*. Washington, DC: NEA.

Nile, R. and D. Walker (2001) 'The "paternoster row machine" and the Australian book trade, 1890–1945', in M. Lyons and J. Arnold (eds) *A History of the Book in Australia, 1891–1945: A National Culture in a Colonised Market*. St. Lucia, Queensland: University of Queensland Press: 3–18.

Noegel, S. B. (2004) 'Text, script and media: New observations on scribal activity in the Ancient Near East', in R. Modiano, L. F. Searle and P. Shillingsburg (eds) *Voice, Text, Hypertext: Emerging Practices in Textual Studies*. Seattle, WA and London: University of Washington Press: 133–143.

Nord, D. P., J. S. Rubin and M. Schudson (eds) (2009) *A History of the Book in America, Vol 5: The Enduring Book: Print Culture in Postwar America*. Chapel Hill, NC: University of North Carolina Press.

Norton, D. F. and M. J. Norton (1996) *David Hume Library*. Edinburgh: National Library of Scotland.

Olivier, J.-P. (2001) 'Aegean scripts of the second millennium BCE', in A.-M. Christin (ed) *A History of Writing: From Hieroglyph to Multimedia*. Paris: Flammarion: 197–202.

Ong, W. J. (1982; repr. 2002) *Orality and Literacy: The Technologizing of the Word*. London: Methuen.

Parkes, M. B. (1999) 'Reading, copying and interpreting a text in the Early Middle Ages', in G. Cavallo and R. Chartier (eds) *A History of Reading in the West* (translated L. G. Cochrane). Cambridge: Polity Press: 90–102.

Pollard, A. W. (1909) *Shakespeare's Folios and Quartos*. London: Methuen.

Poster, M. (2001) *What's the Matter with the Internet?* London and Minneapolis, MN: University of Minneapolis Press.

Price, L. (2000) *The Anthology and the Rise of the Novel: From Richardson to George Eliot*. Cambridge: Cambridge University Press.

——(2002) 'The tangible page', *London Review of Books*, 31 October: 36–39.

——(2004) 'Reading: The state of the discipline', *Book History*, vol 7: 303–320.

PWC (PriceWaterhouseCoopers) (1995) *The Strategic Future of the Irish Publishing Industry*. Dublin: Coopers and Lybrand.

Radicati de Primeglio, C. (1992) 'L'interpretazione del quipu', in L. Minelli (ed) *I regni preincaici e il mondo inca*. Milan: Jaca Books: 190–192.

Radway, J. (1984) *Reading the Romance: Women, Patriarchy, and Popular Literature*. Chapel Hill, NC: University of North Carolina Press.

——(1996) 'Books and reading in the age of mass production', in *The Adams Helms Lecture 1996*. Stockholm: The Swedish Publishers' Association and the Stockholm University Library.

——(1997) *A Feeling for Books: The Book-of-the-Month Club, Literary Taste, and Middle Class Desire*. Chapel Hill, NC: University of North Carolina Press.

Reed, D. (1997) *The Rise of the Popular Magazine in Britain and the United States, 1880–1960*. Toronto: University of Toronto Press.

Rose, J. (1992) 'Re-reading the English Common Reader: A preface to a history of audiences', *Journal of the History of Ideas*, vol 53: 47–70; repr. in D. Finkelstein and A. McCleery (eds) *The Book History Reader*. London: Routledge, 2001: 324–339.

——(2001) *The Intellectual Life of the British Working Classes*. New Haven, CT: Yale University Press.

Rose, M. (1993) *Authors and Owners: The Invention of Copyright*. Cambridge, MA: Harvard University Press.

Ross, T. (1992) 'Copyright and the invention of tradition', *Eighteenth-Century Studies*, vol 26: 1–27.

Rubin, J. S. (2003) 'What is the history of the history of books?', *The Journal of American History*, vol 90, no 2: 555–575.

Saenger, P. (1999) 'Reading in the Later Middle Ages', in G. Cavallo and R. Chartier (eds) *A History of Reading in the West* (translated L. G. Cochrane). Cambridge: Polity Press: 120–148.

Schiffrin, A. (2001) *The Business of Books: How the International Conglomerates Took Over Publishing and Changed the Way We Read*. London: Verso.

Schleiermacher, F. D. E. (1985) 'General hermeneutics', in K. Mueller-Vollmer (ed) *The Hermeneutics Reader: Texts of the German Tradition from the Enlightenment to the Present*. New York: Continuum: 72–97.

Schlink, B. (1997) *The Reader* (translated Carol Brown Janeway). London: Phoenix House.

Schmandt-Besserat, D. (1982a) 'The emergence of recording', *American Anthropologist*, vol 84: 871–878.

——(1982b) 'How writing came about', *Zeitschrift für Papyrologie und Epigraphik*, vol 47: 1–5.

Schneirov, M. (1994) *The Dream of a New Social Order: Popular Magazines in America, 1893–1914*. New York: Columbia University Press.

Secord, J. A. (2000) *Victorian Sensation: The Extraordinary Publication, Reception, and Secret Authorship of Vestiges of the Natural History of Creation*. Chicago, IL: University of Chicago Press.

Sheahan-Bright, R. and C. Munro, (eds) (2006) *A History of the Book in Australia, Vol 3: Paper Empires*. Queensland: University of Queensland Press.

Sheehan, D. (1952) *This Was Publishing*. Bloomington, IN: Indiana University Press.

St Clair, W. (2004) *The Reading Nation in the Romantic Period*. Cambridge: Cambridge University Press.

Suarez, M. F. and M. L. Turner, (eds) (2009). *The Cambridge History of the Book in Britain: Vol 5, 1695–1830*. Cambridge: Cambridge University Press.

Suarez, M. F. and H. R. Woudhuysen, (eds) (2010) *The Oxford Companion to the Book, 2 Volumes*. Oxford: Oxford University Press.

Sutherland, J. (1976) *Victorian Novelists and Publishers*. London: Athlone Press.

——(1988) 'Publishing history: A hole at the centre of literary sociology', *Critical Enquiry*, vol 13, no 3: 574–589.

Tanselle, G. T. (1979) *Selected Studies in Bibliography*. Charlottesville, VA: University Press of Virginia.

——(1991) 'Textual criticism and literary sociology', *Studies in Bibliography*, vol 44: 83–143.

Taylor, A. (1999) 'Authors, scribes, patrons and books', in J. Wogan-Browne, N. Watson, A. Taylor and R. Evans (eds) *The Idea of the Vernacular: An Anthology of Middle English Literary Theory 1280–1520*. Exeter, UK: University of Exeter Press.

Thomas, M. (1976) 'Manuscripts', in L. Febvre and H.-J. Martin (eds) (1997) *The Coming of the Book: The Impact of Printing, 1450–1800* (translated D. Gerard, from *L'Apparition du Livre*). London: Verso.

Thompson, J. B. (2010) *Merchants of Culture: The Publishing Business in the Twenty-First Century*. Cambridge: Polity Press.

Tompkins, J. (2001) '*Masterpiece Theater*: The politics of Hawthorne's literary reputation', in D. Finkelstein and A. McCleery (eds) *The Book History Reader*. London: Routledge: 250–258.

Towheed, S. and W. R. Owens (eds) (2011) *The History of Reading, Vol 1: International Perspectives, c. 1500–1990*. Basingstoke, UK: Palgrave Macmillan.

Towheed, S., R. Crone and K. Halsey (eds) (2010) *The History of Reading*. London: Routledge.

Traue, J. E. (1997) 'But why Mulgan, Marris and Schroder? The mutation of the local newspaper in New Zealand's colonial print culture', *Bibliographical Society of Australia and New Zealand Bulletin*, vol 21, no 2: 107–115.

——(2001) 'The two histories of the book in New Zealand', *Bibliographical Society of Australia and New Zealand Bulletin*, vol 25, no 1: 8–16.

Tunstall, J. (1994) *The Media Are American* (2nd edition). London: Constable.

Van der Vlies, A. (2007) *South African Textual Cultures: White, Black, Read all Over*. Manchester, UK: Manchester University Press.

Walsh, P. and C. Hutton, (eds) (2011) *The Oxford History of the Irish Book, Vol 5: The Irish Book in English, 1891–2000*. Oxford: Oxford University Press.

Waugh, A. (1930) *A Hundred Years of Publishing*. London: Chapman and Hall.

Wernick, A. (1993) 'Authorship and the supplement of promotion', in M. Biriotti and N. Miller (eds) *What Is an Author?* Manchester, UK: Manchester University Press: 85–103.

West, J. L. W., III (1985) *American Authors and the Literary Marketplace since 1900*. University Park, PA: Pennsylvania State University Press.

Whyte, F. (1928) *William Heinemann, a Memoir*. London: Jonathan Cape.

Williams, R. (1965) *The Long Revolution*. Harmondsworth, UK: Penguin.

——(1966) *Culture and Society 1780–1950* (first reprint). London: Pelican Books.

Winship, M. (1993) 'Afterword', in W. Charvat (1993) *Literary Publishing in America, 1790–1850*. University Park, PA: Pennsylvania State University Press: 91–102.

Wirtén, E. H. (1998) *Global Infatuation: Explorations in Transnational Publishing and Texts*. Uppsala: Literature Department, University of Uppsala.

——(2003) *No Trespassing: Authorship, Intellectual Property Rights, and the Boundaries of Globalisation*. Toronto: University of Toronto Press.

Wittmann, R. (1999) 'Was there a reading revolution at the end of the eighteenth century?', in G. Cavallo and R. Chartier (eds) *A History of Reading in the West* (translated L. G. Cochrane). Cambridge: Polity Press: 284–312.

Wogan-Browne, J., N. Watson, A. Taylor and R. Evans (eds) (1999) *The Idea of the Vernacular: An Anthology of Middle English Literary Theory 1280–1520*. Exeter, UK: University of Exeter Press.

Woudhuysen, H. (1996) *Sir Philip Sydney and the Circulation of Manuscripts, 1558–1640*. Oxford: Oxford University Press.

INDEX

Note: page numbers in **bold** refer to tables.